Michael W. Apple

Class, Codes and Control

Primary Socialization, Language and Education
Edited by Basil Bernstein
University of London Institute of Education
Sociological Research Unit

I   *Social Class, Language and Communication*
Walter Brandis & Dorothy Henderson

II   *A Linguistic Description and Computer Program for Children's Speech*
Geoffrey J. Turner & Bernard A. Mohan

III   *Talk Reform*
D. M. & G. A. Gahagan

IV   *Class, Codes and Control*
Volume 1 *Theoretical Studies towards a Sociology of Language*
Volume 2 *Applied Studies towards a Sociology of Language*
Basil Bernstein

V   *A Question of Answers (2 vols)*
Peter Robinson & Susan Rackstraw

VI   *Social Control and Socialization*
Jenny Cook-Gumperz

Class, Codes and Control

Volume 1
Theoretical Studies towards a Sociology of Language

Basil Bernstein
Professor in the Sociology of Education
Head of the Sociological Research Unit,
University of London Institute of Education

LONDON   ROUTLEDGE & KEGAN PAUL

First published in 1971
by Routledge & Kegan Paul Ltd
Broadway House,
68–74 Carter Lane,
London EC4V 5EL
Second revised edition 1974
Printed in Great Britain by
Unwin Brothers Limited
The Gresham Press,
Old Woking, Surrey
and set in 10 on 11 pt Times Roman
© Basil Bernstein 1971
ISBN 0 7100 7060 8

For Marion

Contents

		Acknowledgments	ix
		Foreword by Donald MacRae	xi
		Introduction	1
Part	I	**Beginnings**	*Page*
	1	Some sociological determinants of perception	23
	2	A public language: some sociological implications of a linguistic form	42
	3	Language and social class	61
Part	II	**Developments**	
	4	A review of *The Lore and Language of Schoolchildren*	71
	5	Linguistic codes, hesitation phenomena and intelligence	76
	6	Social class, linguistic codes and grammatical elements	95
	7	A socio-linguistic approach to social learning	118
Part	III	**Explorations**	
	8	A socio-linguistic approach to socialization: with some reference to educability	143
	9	Social class, language and socialization	170
	10	A critique of the concept of compensatory education	190
	11	On the classification and framing of educational knowledge	202
		Addendum: a note on the coding of objects and modalities of control	231
		Postscript	237
		Index	259

Acknowledgments

My greatest debt is to the members of the Sociological Research Unit, Department of the Sociology of Education, University of London Institute of Education. I would also like to thank Miss Patricia Dyehouse, administrative secretary to the Department of the Sociology of Education, for her guidance in resolving the many difficulties in the preparation of this and the accompanying volume.

The papers in this book have been reprinted from the following journals and books. I am very grateful to the editors for their permission to reprint.

1 'Some sociological determinants of perception', *British Journal of Sociology* IX, 159–74, 1958.

2 'A public language: some sociological implications of a linguistic form', *British Journal of Sociology* X, 311–26, 1959.

3 'Language and social class', *British Journal of Sociology* XI, 271–6, 1960.

4 'A review of *The Lore and Language of Children* by Opie, I. and Opie, P.', *British Journal of Sociology* XI, 178–81, 1960.

5 'Linguistic codes, hesitation phenomena and intelligence', *Language and Speech* 5, 31–46, 1962.

6 'Social class, linguistic codes and grammatical elements', *Language and Speech* 5, 221–40, 1962.

7 'A socio-linguistic approach to social learning', *Penguin Survey of the Social Sciences*, ed. Gould, J., Penguin, 1965.

8 'A socio-linguistic approach to socialization: with some reference to educability', in *Directions in Socio-linguistics*, eds. Hymes, D. and Gumperz, J. J., Holt, Rinehart & Winston, New York, 1971.

9 'Social class, language and socialization,' *Current Trends in Linguistics*, Vol. 12, Associate Editors: Abramson, A. S. *et al.*, Mouton Press, 1971.

10 'A critique of the concept of Compensatory Education', paper given at the Work Conference of the Teachers College, Columbia University, New York, 1969; appeared in *Improving Opportunities for the Disadvantaged*, ed. Passow, A. H., Teachers College Press, Columbia University. (In press.)

11 'On the classification and framing of educational knowledge', in *Knowledge and Control*, ed. Young, M.F.D., Collier-Macmillan, 1971.

12 Addendum: 'A note on the coding of objects and modalities of social control', appendix to 'Class and pedagogies: visible and invisible', O.E.C.D. (C.E.R.I.) Paris, 1973.

13 Postscript: 'A brief account of the theory of codes', in *Social Relationships and Language*, Block 3 of the Educational Studies Second level course, Language and Learning, The Open University, 1973.

I should like to thank the DSIR, the Nuffield Foundation, the Department of Education and Science, the Ford Foundation and the Social Science Research Council for their grants to the Sociological Research Unit, which made the empirical research possible.

Foreword

Donald G. MacRae

Professor of Sociology, London School of Economics and Political Science

At the heart of all actual proceedings which we call scientific or
scholarly lie unresolved inconsistencies and incompatibilities.
Around, constricting yet supporting, all such activities is a structure
of expectations about the nature of knowledge, of science, of particular disciplines, of what is culturally appropriate. And in its turn
this structure is made possible by institutional elements embedded
in it like the stressed metal bars in ferro-concrete beams. Very often,
therefore, it is extremely difficult for novel work to get done in the
world of science and learning, and even more difficult for it to be
recognized. Novelty can always be condemned because attention can
be drawn to its inherent incoherencies—incoherencies which, as I
said, exist everywhere but which are unreflectingly accepted where
nothing is unexpected and all is orthodox. In the increasingly in-
stitutionalized, centralized and costly world of the foundations,
councils, learned societies and so on, working under the stresses of
limited resources and a genuine responsibility, novelty is perturbing.
Only the established can innovate: only non-innovators are established.

There are several consequences of this. There are today more,
better-trained scientists and more science than ever before, but I do
not think that at the ultimate level of creativity this investment of life
and means has produced a great age of innovation comparable to
the late seventeenth century, or the late nineteenth and early twentieth centuries. Our institutions and expectations are concerned with
discovery, the finding of what is, in some sense, *out there*. By accredited navigational techniques more islets are found and accurately
placed on the map. But that metaphor will not do what it does very
well for discovery, at all well for scientific creativity. Creation, great
or small, involves novelty of a different order, and it raises, of its
nature what we would like to neglect, the inconsistencies and incompatibilities at the heart of the enterprise of knowledge.

Now this is not to condemn discovery or to regard all of it as easy

xi

—far from that. Yet discovery has two modes which are genuine, but not very hard, at its core. The first of these is mimicry: the continuation or replication in another place or time of what has previously been done. This involves industry and technical competence and nothing more. The other mode, not quite unrelated, I privately call the mymecine. It is the exercise of an ant-like, scurrying energetic, part random, part purposeful industry which moves small particles of matter in great number. Both of these might meet the definition of genius as the infinite capacity to take pains. It is a very bad definition. Not all discovery is reducible to the mimetic or mymecine, but much is. There is always serendipity, the discovery and recognition—not always easy—of the unexpected. There is room for talent and art as well as for skill and strength. Nor should craftsmanship be despised.

Another consequence is that creativity is often forced into disguise, to wear the masks and play the roles of discovery, while really devoted to quite different ends. Sometimes this results in mere misconception: the novelty and force of creation is not recognized. Or it may result in fury, when the mask is penetrated and the passionate life beneath is glimpsed. Or, with rare luck, the role may be transformed and the new life be accepted, the original part be forgotten, and the creator acclaimed. Once this happens is a new time for discovery, even for the formation of a school, for a worth-while exercise of imitation and industry.

In fact, and now I come to sociology and the work which Basil Bernstein has honoured me by asking me to introduce, there is in science and scholarship a cycle or circulation of the kind which Pareto discerned in politics. Bernstein's work is creation, creation in my judgment sometimes disguised by the necessary masks of scientific procedure so that its true nature does not always at first appear. It is now, though the Beckmessers may grumble, involved in a school and with that flattery which ought to be genuinely gratifying, the flattery of fruitful imitation and the rewards of discovery. This, however, is not to say that the creation is over: the implications of Basil Bernstein's work are not, even perhaps in his own head, fully developed, nor their implications fully understood, and what is more important, his work is open: to me the most important of these papers are chronologically the first and the last, in particular chapter 11.

If I am right this introduces us to certain paradoxes about what he has done. He has asked me to write this foreword, but I am, in the whole of sociology, probably least concerned with what is usually described as the sociology of education. Yet all this work is apparently about the sociology of education and I find it fascinating.

My relative lack of concern does not of course, involve an unfavourable judgment *a priori*. It is the consequence of two things. One is the simple fact that one cannot, try as one will, pay attention to everything. The other is that until recently this field has been one, on the whole, given over to styles of research which seemed to me unlikely to produce results of much general interest even if they were of particular utility. But with Basil Bernstein's work (and also some developments during the last decade in France) this last point has not been true. The point is simple: with these papers we are concerned with aspects of the enormous, single but many-faceted issue at the heart of sociology: how is society possible? One aspect of the answer is through the institutionalization of communication both in its boundaries and its openings.

For nearly twenty-five years I told students this when intoducing them to the elementary analysis of social structure. I told them this both as a fact about the sustaining and changing of society—as giving the choreography, in one of my favourite metaphors, of society as dance—and as a clue to socialization, the fact that we transmit and receive and internalize a culture and a place, however loosely defined, within it. I pointed out, as well as I could, the relevance of this to all things we can call social, including animal society. I sketched certain major codings, largely non-verbal, and then I passed on. I had other things to do, and in this area I could do no more. It was into this limited and cursory recognition and formulation that Basil Bernstein's work burst with an ever-increasing and continuing illumination. Nothing in more than a decade had done more to force a recasting or so extended the competence of the theory of social structure, or shown so much promise for the clearing up of the messy problems which beset our understanding of the relationship between culture and structure in society.

That all this bore in ways that some people found very specific on the functioning of stratification and the parameters of social mobility, on the social arrangements of the school and of curricula, on the early socialization of the child and on the real differences—i.e. differences of content, not only formal, of institutions—between university systems in different countries, is true and exciting. Even if the versions of 'early Bernstein' that have got into textbooks and manuals are simplified, vulgarized and reified and consequently over-specific, yet these are not trivial points. But unfortunately, while it was right to see them, elaborate or reduce them, it has concealed something at a rather deeper level. The carapace is perhaps the most glittering part of a biological specimen, but the underlying tissue and nerve and total physiology is even more interesting. In Basil Bernstein's work this living tissue is full of anatomical and physiological complexities and is concerned with the nature of knowledge, the sociology of epistemology, of knowing as a social and personal process, with questions of philosophical anthropology and the enterprise of being human.

In this sense and in others its concerns, but not its procedures, are Durkheimian and the relation of Bernstein to Durkheim—and not the Durkheim of the textbooks—would be worth serious exploration. For Durkheim raises questions that the other great sociological theorists from Ferguson to the present have either not seen or have avoided. In a way what Bernstein does is to attack the questions of *The Elementary Forms of the Religious Life* but in terms of categories forged not out of Kantian categories but out of categories derived from the half-century of sociology since Durkheim's death, from the author's own thought and feeling, from his researches, and, by a circuitous route, from the neo-Kantianism of Ernest Cassirer. One sometimes says in critical writing that a book is suggestive: it is praise, but a praise tinged with disappointment. Basil Bernstein is suggestive certainly, but one says this in gratitude and without regret. And this work goes on.

As he himself says in his Introduction his work was thought at first radical and now is condemned as conservative in its practical consequences. There is a sense, which has nothing to do with political parties or movements, in which all sociology must be conservative if it is genuine. Reality is not consoling. Knowledge is knowledge of of constriction and limitation—of Durkheim's *constraint*. This conservatism can be combined with generous personal, social and political intent in the sociologist operating as citizen. But those who condemn its existence in sociology as a discipline are merely people who see their science as the continuation of politics, often with a public subsidy, by other means. They are I judge guilty of bad faith. Their objections are worthless.

But this matters very little. We have here the collected work in progress of a creator in sociology. I have tried to put it in a context, not explain what it is, for the Introduction and the papers which follow do that with an unusual honesty. The rhetoric of presentation in science is not 'to tell it as it is' but to disguise *ex post* what has been done and put it into an inhuman form of methodological orthodoxy and logical entailment. This series of papers reveals rather the process of creation with all the travails of reality. For that I am grateful, too. If in what I have said I have concentrated too little on the directly educational and linguistic aspects of the papers, that results from a desire to correct the balance of opinion and vested interest. But both education and linguistics are so justly central to public and learned concern that no harm can result from this neglect.

Introduction

In this volume I have put together a series of papers which form a continuous record of the ideas I have been trying to master over the past twelve years. I have done this with a distinct feeling of unease. Writing a paper is one thing: offering a book which has this form is quite another thing. Each paper is an attempt to come to terms with an obstinate idea in me which I could neither give up nor properly understand. I always felt that the only paper worth reading was the next one to be written. The preceding papers became a source of embarrassment rather like paintings which did not come off, and because of the very nature of the activity never would. I have been asked repeatedly to bring the papers together in book form and for many years I could not see that this was justified. As many of the papers are in journals or books not readily available, and as there has been a very close relationship between the theory and the research, I believe now that the time is right to bring them together.* It is also the case that many people appear to have had access only to early papers which appeared between 1958 and 1961, and as the reader will find, these papers represent only an attempt to find the problem. I have always been deeply aware that the ideas were about people, about communities and their symbolic realizations and regulation. Since the very beginning I was conscious of the danger of premature and misleading inferences although I had, then, no idea of the temporary disturbance that the ideas would cause on the ideological educational scene. As a result, only once in twelve years have I publicized the ideas through the media of the public press or television. My reticence also had its origins in the knowledge that the guiding ideas were constantly developing. On a less elevated level, I have never been able to contain the thesis in the kernel required for mass consumption.

* The papers are offered as they were originally published with the exception of minor changes in format. This has given rise to some unavoidable repetition of argument. If I attempted to alter a paper now it could only be done with hindsight.

1

It is also the case that for various reasons I worked somewhat isolated from the academic community of sociologists. This was an advantage. I doubt in the early years that I would have survived the criticism for which my colleagues are justly famed, for the simple reason that I could not even grasp the problem. Indeed, initially, I used very insensitive indices: anything to create some structure. The reader will find some distinctions like those between form and content [sic] which appear in the first paper, never appear again. On the other hand, the distinction between universalistic and particularistic (derived from Talcott Parsons), which is first used in 1962 ('Social class, hesitation phenomena and intelligence'—*Language and Speech*), plays a central role in paper ten in this volume, written in 1969. Occasionally, a concept is useful and can take endless exploration: more often, it carries little potential. The list of attributes of a public or formal language are a rag-bag, possessing no linguistic respectability, as so many critics have so rightly pointed out, yet for me they were critical focusing points in order to explore an intuition. The intuition is not original and can be found in linguistics, sociology, anthropology and psychology; indeed, it is realized in numerous novels and plays. As Professor Douglas has written, the most important exploration is that of the obvious. The reader will undoubtedly find much inconsistency across the papers, but I do not regard this as a fault, but rather as a sign of growth. However, what is a sign of growth for the writer may well be disconcerting for the reader and perplexing for the researcher. There is an important distinction between inconsistency and adhocery. An *ad hoc* a day may keep a theory in play but in the end destroys it, because it prevents any rethinking of the basic structure.

Before I turn to a discussion of the conceptual development of the ideas, it may be helpful to give some account of my personal history which bears upon the development of the guiding ideas.

After the 1939–45 war, I was fortunate to be accepted as a resident worker at the Bernhard Baron Settlement in Stepney. I was there for three years, both prior to going up to the London School of Economics, and for my first undergraduate year. During my stay at the Settlement, I took part in the running of boys' clubs spanning the ages of nine to eighteen years, for which the Bernhard Baron was rightly famed. I was also introduced to family casework. This experience in more ways than one had a deep influence upon my life. It focused and made explicit an interest I always seemed to have had in the structure and process of cultural transmission. In the Settlement, the discontinuity and sometimes conflict between the values held by the senior members of staff and those held by club members often became transparent. The discontinuity was not simply related to secular values. The Settlement was religious in spirit and purpose and drew its strength from Reform Judaism; whereas the traditional Judaism of the community the Settlement served was Orthodox. A significant percentage of the parents and the children were members of the Reform Synagogue of the Settlement. Thus the Settlement introduced me to the inter-relationships between social class and religious belief within the context of an apparently distinct and homogeneous cultural group. I was both fascinated and disturbed by the *process* of transmission of the Settlement's values and standards of conduct. I do not want to give the erroneous impression that the Settlement community was rife with class and religious tension, because that certainly was not the case. For several decades the Settlement, under the leadership of Sir Basil Henriques and eventually his nephew Lionel Henriques, played a vital role in the life of the various communities which made up Stepney.

In 1947 I was accepted by the LSE to read for the Diploma in Social Science, but after the first month my tutor Miss Slack recommended that I transfer to the course leading to the BSc. Econ. degree, special subject sociology. I can't say I enjoyed my years at LSE. I seemed for ever to be catching up with reading I should have done before I came. I waited eagerly for the second year when the courses in sociology would begin. It took some time before I began to see the nature of sociological explorations. I initially could not understand how a subject which offered such a range of ideas could be obscured through endless discussions of the logic of enquiry (with the emphasis upon the logic) and fierce debates on conflict and functionalist approaches to the analysis of society. I became aware that my interest in socialization (even when I tarted it up to become cultural transmission) stood very low in the status hierarchy of legitimate sociological problems. I read very widely in the borderland between sociology and psychology. I read Durkheim and although I did not understand him it all seemed to happen. I did not care that he was a naughty functionalist with an over-socialized concept of man, that he neglected the institutional structure and the sub-strata of conflicting interests, that his model of man contained only two terms, beliefs and sentiments. In a curious way I did not care too much about the success of his various analysis. It was about the social bond and the structuring of experience. I listened to Donald MacRae during tutorials with something like awe as ideas were sympathetically explored, historically placed and used as jumping-off points. Here was substance, not talk about talk. Ideas became alive and so did his students. I did not obtain what is called a 'good' degree: my work was too undisciplined and I had agonizing difficulties in expressing what I was trying to grasp. I wrote, and still write, very slowly.

I registered for a higher degree and my area of enquiry was into the nature of primary groups. I decided to compare two extreme types of non-institutionalized (i.e. informal) primary groups—one I called 'withdrawn' and the other 'predatory'. Both sets of groups I studied through the method of participant observation, for about a year. I did not have a grant and it became difficult to survive on the curious jobs which gave me the time I required for the study. In a way I felt that it was not, at bottom, my problem. I decided to become a teacher.

In 1954 I passed the post-graduate certificate in education, which I obtained from the Westminster College of Education. I spent much of my year as a student teacher at the Kingsway Day College, then—as it is today—a leading centre of innovation in further education. In 1954 I was appointed to the City Day College as a grade 'A' teacher, and I stayed at the College until 1960.

The majority of students at the College then were on one-day-a-week release from the GPO, where they were employed as messenger boys. There were other groups of students from various industries, and a small but lively group from the London Docks. The GPO students were split into two groups. One group prepared for a minor Civil Service examination (Postal and Telegraphic Officers) and the larger group prepared for nothing. I officially taught English, arithmetic and civics to the larger group, and occasionally physical education when the professional PE man was away. The principal of the College at that time was Mr Edwards, who encouraged me—as he did other members of his staff—in a number of teaching ventures. Mr Edwards also allowed me to carry out some research enquiries.

I was to begin with baffled and quite desperate. The level of formal attainment of the students was one of the best indictments of the educational system. There was no good reason for them to be interested. School had given them up many years earlier. Teaching was often an uneasy truce based upon an output norm and interest level set by the students. This is not the place to go into how the students taught me to teach myself, and then perhaps them. I started in 1956 to take a group for nearly the whole day, much of it spent outside the College, concerned with the study of elementary vehicle maintenance. The course involved visits to ROSPA House, Piccadilly, where the students received lectures (involving demonstrations) on the internal combustion engine, the general mechanics and electrics of the car, and the advanced study of road safety. The same boys who appeared to have a short attention span in the classroom listened avidly to fifty-minute lectures at ROSPA House, and took notes to write up later. I had one major difficulty. I could not drive and knew little about the inside of a car or motor-cycle. My difficulty was in ensuring that this lacuna in my knowledge did not become public. We used the playground to demonstrate problems of stopping distance and curve taking. I performed a number of remarkable arabesques around the theme 'The course is for you to demonstrate your skill, not mine'. English, arithmetic, general science, even civics were built around the core course. At the end of the course, the students received a certificate in elementary vehicle maintenance, which was especially printed and embossed. The certificate was formally handed to the students by the principal. One student, after he had received the certificate, said to me, 'What do I do with this, guv?' I felt the whole course was in the balance. With my heart in my mouth I replied, 'Send it to your insurance firm. They might do something about your premium.' About a month later the same student came up to me with a broad grin and said, 'It worked. They've reduced it!' We were in business, both metaphorically and materially. The course was developed by Mr Palmer, a colleague who was an experienced driver and mechanic, to include a workshop, courses in first aid which led into, I believe, biology and the general study of transport. I perfectly well realize that such a course does not topple the class system, but it successfully demonstrated to each boy that the educational experience was an experience to which he could both contribute, explore and, in part, control. I tried a number of approaches to English, each based upon unsentimental validation of the extra-school experience of the students. I do not want to give the impression that I was the only teacher at the College who was experimenting with fresh approaches. Indeed, many members of staff were so engaged. They had to be if they were to survive unembittered and alive.

During the first two years I realized that the problem was, in Forster's phrase, 'Only connect'. Not being a born teacher, I had to learn by sensing that structure of meanings which were latent in the speech and writing. All this may seem to be an exaggeration. One day I took a piece of a student's continuous writing and broke it up into its constituent sentences and arranged the sentences hierarchically on the page, so that it looked like a poem. The piece took on a new and vital life. The gaps between the lines were full of meaning. I took a Bob Dylan ballad and produced a second version in which the lines were arranged continuously as in prose. I invited the students to read both versions. I then asked whether they felt there was any difference between the two versions. Yes, there was a difference. Poetry *among* other things has something to do with the hierarchical, and so spatial, ordering of lines. The space between the lines, the interval, allowed the symbols to reverberate against each other. The space between the lines was the listener or reader's space out of which he created a unique, unspoken, personal meaning. This may be bad aesthetics, but we experimented, putting together often weird or bizarre, sometimes unexpectedly beautiful series of lines, and exploring the symbolic nature of the space. I became fascinated by condensation; by the implicit. In my teaching I covered a range of contents and contexts, and yet, despite the variations, I felt that here was a speech form predicated upon the implicit. I wrote up an account which eventually became the first and second papers in this volume. The only evidence I could offer was the very large, expected, discrepancy between verbal and performance test scores of the GPO boys.

At this time (1956) I began to read Sapir, who said it all so beautifully, Whorf and especially Cassirer's *Philosophy of Symbolic Forms:* and back to Whorf, chasing the linguistic relativity literature. During the preparation of the second paper ('A public language: some sociological implications of a linguistic form') for publication, I discovered Strauss and Schatzman's paper on Social class and forms of communication, and here I read a most insightful and sensitive description of the speech used by working-class men and women to describe their experience of a tornado in Arkansas. I was very excited, because this was the only reference I had found which gave such detailed description. Vygotsky's book *Thought and Language* had not been translated in 1958, but I found an article of his translated by Luria, which appeared in *Psychiatry*, II, 1939.

I had not come across this particular view of language in my reading of psychology, and Luria's approach was as great a surprise. From Vygotsky and Luria, I absorbed the notion of speech as an orientating and regulative system. I spent the whole summer vacation of 1958 reading, and wrote a fairly detailed review of the field, entitled 'Some sub-cultural determinants of learning; with special reference to language', which appeared in the *Kölner Zeitschrift fur Soziologie und Sozialpsychologie* in 1959. The bibliography ran to some 140 references.*

I felt that some kind of limited enquiry was needed in order to obtain speech under relatively controlled conditions. The enquiry had to be limited, as I had no external support and, apart from Donald MacRae, very little encouragement among sociologists. Indeed, LSE turned down an application to re-register for a higher degree. I decided to hold a series of discussion groups with boys matched for age, variously matched for ability on two tests, but who differed in

---

* I write this because it has been said that the papers offer very inadequate references.

terms of their inferred social class background. I am very indebted to Mrs Cunliffe and the then Betty Brownstein (Now Mrs E. Wolperz); to the former for introducing me to the head of a major public school, and to the latter for helping me carry out the testing of the public school boys. I wrote up the comparison of ability test scores of the two groups of pupils. This was published as a research note entitled 'Language and social class' in the *British Journal of Sociology* in 1960, and is included in this volume. Then I was stuck, for I had neither the time nor the skill to work on the speech. My teaching commitment at the City Day College, as with all staff at the College, was heavy, although during the year of 1960 the then LCC allowed me half a day a week free of teaching to use for research.

As the professional sociologists were not very interested (and at that time, let me add, there were few) and, more importantly, because I felt I needed further training, I applied to University College London in order to read for a higher degree in linguistics. I was directed to the Department of Phonetics, where I was interviewed by Dr Frieda Goldman-Eisler,* who was sympathetic and encouraging. Dr Goldman-Eisler advised me not to read for a higher degree, but instead to concentrate upon the research. That interview was marvellous. I had not talked to anyone before who knew about speech in the way I wanted to know. It was the most critical encounter of my academic life. Dr Goldman-Eisler invited me to bring the tape-recordings of the various discussion groups to our next meeting, and gave me a number of her papers. I read them and immediately recognized that her theoretical and experimental work on the relationship between hesitation phenomena and types of verbal planning offered an exciting approach to the analysis of speech I had collected. Dr Goldman-Eisler introduced me to Professor D. Fry, Head of the Department of Phonetics, who offered to sponsor a grant application to the Department of Scientific and Industrial Research for the analysis of the speech. The application was successful and in January 1961 I went to the Department of Phonetics as an honorary research assistant, under Dr Goldman-Eisler.

During my two-year stay at the Department of Phonetics, the ideas underwent a major transformation. I finished a paper not included in this volume, entitled 'Social class and linguistic development: a theory of social learning', which was published in *Education, Economy and Society*, edited by A. H. Halsey, J. Floud and A. Anderson. This paper I regard, despite the possible pretentiousness, as the end of the beginning stage. In the Department of Phonetics I was able to talk to members of staff, and learned avidly, in particular from Professor Fry. My debt to Dr Goldman-Eisler was immense.

* Now Professor Goldman-Eisler.

Not only did I see in her fundamental researches into the nature and function of hesitation phenomena an opportunity to test in some way my ideas, but she opened up to me a new literature and she spent many hours both discussing with me and teaching me. Dr Goldman-Eisler showed me the importance of Hughlings Jackson and Bartlett, developed my understanding of Luria, introduced me to information theory and to the philosophy of language. I do not know how to express my gratitude to Professor Fry and to Dr Freda Goldman-Eisler, for giving me a unique opportunity, for their patience, and for the time they freely gave to a peripheral research member of the Department.

In my first year in the Department of Phonetics, Donald MacRae sent me the Opies' book, *The Lore and Language of Children*, to review for the *British Journal of Sociology*. I tried to apply Hughlings Jackson's ideas of the different strengths of the coding of speech in that review and to relate such coding to a particular social structure. I have included the review in this volume, because it shows in embryo, in early 1960, the interpretative system I was trying to develop. The review was important for another reason. Donald MacRae sent the review to Professor Dell Hymes, who was at that time in the Department of Social Anthropology at Berkeley. Through Dell Hymes I met John Gumperz, and a friendship and deep intellectual co-operation began with both and which has continued since. My stay at the Department of Phonetics culminated in two papers which embodied a new conceptualization and were published in *Language and Speech* in 1962 ('Linguistic codes, hesitation phenomena and intelligence' and 'Social class, linguistic codes and grammatical elements'). The notion of codes was first introduced in these papers, and they were defined in terms of the ease or difficulty of predicting the syntactic alternatives taken up to organize meaning. In an elaborated code, relative to a restricted code, the speakers explore more fully the resources of the grammar and therefore I considered there were more possibilities of combination. The concept code represented an attempt to go behind the list of attributes given as indices of public and formal language, and to suggest the underlying regulative principle. This definition, since Dr Lawton's criticism in his book *Language and Social Class*, has been subject to continuous criticism for basically two reasons. The first is that it disregards the contextual constraints upon speech, and secondly because the notion of predictability can be given little statistical meaning. More of this later. The period which I have called Development culminated in the paper 'A socio-linguistic approach to social learning', published in the *Penguin Survey of the Social Sciences*, edited by Julius Gould in 1965. Essentially, the section called

Development reflects the two years spent in the Department of Phonetics.

It has been said that the papers show no sign of any movement away from a descriptive use of social class as a crude correlational device and as a consequence the basic conception was essentially static. More than this, that there was little indication of how social class position gave differential access to what many years later Miss J. Cook, research officer in the Sociological Research Unit, in her Ph.D. thesis, called different interpretative principles. However, in late 1962 I wrote a piece which was to be the concluding section of my Ph.D. thesis, entitled 'Family role systems, communication and socialisation'. In this piece I distinguished between different types of family structures, positional and personal, and examined the forms of communication and control which I considered would arise. I also examined the conditions I thought would give rise to a change of coding orientation. Within the same piece I distinguished between codes which would orientate and facilitate the realization of relationships between objects, and codes which would orientate and facilitate the realization of relationships between persons. There was also a highly speculative linkage of object and person codes to the family types. Mrs J. Floud, who was my supervisor, suggested that, to her mind, this was a new departure and therefore should not be included in the thesis. A summary of the chapter was given as a paper to an international conference on Cross-Cultural Research into Childhood and Adolescence, held in Chicago in 1963. At that period, Professor R. Hess was carrying out some highly original research into maternal teaching styles and communication. Professor Hess used the family role and communication analysis developed in the chapter as the interpretative framework for his enquiries (Hess, R. D. and Shipman, V. (1965), 'Early experience and the socialisation of cognitive modes in children', *Child Development*, 36). Although the analysis in that chapter, for some reason, was never published until 1970, when it appeared as the second section of a long paper entitled 'A socio-linguistic approach to socialisation; with some reference to educability', it provided the basic framework for the family structure, communication and control studies later undertaken by the Sociological Research Unit in 1964. I have included the above paper in this volume.

The grant which I had been given by the DSIR was for only a period of two years (1960–2). Early in 1962 I submitted an ambitious research proposal to the then Department of Education. The original proposal outlined a cross-sectional study of children of different measured ability, and of varying social class backgrounds, through the nursery age until fifteen years of age. The research also included a study of the families of the children. The study also explicitly referred to the study of children's use of speech in different contexts. I had hoped to study the code realization of different speech contexts and also to examine the conditions for change of code.

From the spring of 1962 until almost the end of the year, continuous discussions took place at the Department of Education which eventually resulted in a very different research proposal. The Department considered the original proposal to be too academic, and pressed me towards an applied study which would involve an attempt to design a programme for infant school children which would enhance their contextual use of speech. I felt very unhappy about this proposal. I knew nothing about infant school children, and even less about the infant school. My only contact with little children (apart from my own) was three months spent observing and collecting speech from four-year-old middle-class and working-class children in nursery schools. I also felt that it was premature to apply a theory which was conceptually weak, and for which hardly any data existed. For various reasons, I was not in a strong position to bargain. It was continuously pointed out to me (and the future to some extent confirmed this) that I could develop the theory through the research, and even more by its application. In the end I accepted the focus of the research required by the Department of Education. From that point until the conclusion of the research, I was haunted by the problems of the language programme, its implications and possible deleterious outcomes. For the programme was no academic puzzle; it involved children. I also saw that the sampling procedure for the whole research necessarily would be dictated by an experimental design required to evaluate the effects, if any, of the language programme. The tail would wag—and indeed, did wag not very comfortably—the research dog.

There was also the small problem of deciding upon an area to do the study and obtaining the permission and the support from the Local Educational Authority. I have written of this in the introduction to the first SRU Monograph. Here I would like to repeat my gratitude to the Deputy Education Officer, and in particular to the educational psychologist of a large borough in East London, both of whom played a major part in the preliminary discussions with the Department of Education and in the early planning stages of the research.

On 1 January 1963 the research began, and at the same time I was appointed as Senior Lecturer in the Sociology of Education to the University of London Institute of Education. This is not the place to enter into the history of the research, suffice to say that during the next seven years I found myself with a dual and often conflicting responsibility; one to the SRU and the other to the Department of the Sociology of Education. The SRU at one period had a staff of over twelve members, drawn from the disciplines of sociology, psychology and linguistics. I learned a great deal of the nature of interdisciplinary research. Irrespective of its potential, the theory then was conceptually weak and therefore horrifyingly coarse at the level of specificity; I am of the opinion that our major research errors can be traced to the under-developed nature of the theory. However, I would also maintain that the interpretative framework it provided was probably stronger than that used in other British sociological studies at that period.

Conceptual development

From 1964 onwards there was a continuous interaction between the theory and the research. Looking back always involves some reconstruction of the past and one imposes upon the past a rationality it did not originally possess. It is not easy to be accurate. It is also the case that much of the interaction between theory and research is built initially into the research design and research procedures and secondly into the methods used to create and selectively pattern the data which are realizations of the theory. In the accompanying volume to this one, the reader will get a glimpse of this. Here I will briefly comment upon more conceptual matters. What seemed to happen was that ideas written about 1962—that is, in the section of this volume called 'Developments'—were given, I hope, a greater generality and specificity. The distinction between universalistic and particularistic orders of meaning, which initially appeared in 1962 in the paper 'Linguistic codes, hesitation phenomena and intelligence', did not reappear in major conceptual work until 1968 in a paper about the concept of compensatory education, a version of which is reprinted in this volume. These distinctions were further developed in paper nine in this volume. The empirical search for contextual realizations of the codes together with the need to build into their basic definitions sensitivity to the speech realizations of critical socializing contexts, led to a new formulation which brought out into the definition the stress on the social structuring of relevant meanings.

I was always aware of the impossibility of assigning any given stretch of speech or writing to one or other of the codes without some prior knowledge of the evoking social context. Yet it is certainly the case that up to 1968 there are few explicit mentions of the constraints of specific contexts upon the patterning of grammatical and lexical choices. On the other hand, we had built very firmly into the research the possibilities of discovering the contextual constraints on the speech of mothers and children from various social class backgrounds. Clearly it was necessary to make explicit the distinction between the patterning of speech evoked by specific social contexts (speech variants) and the concept of code as a regulative principle controlling speech realizations in diverse social contexts. One of the difficulties created by the distinction between code and speech variant was that a precise statement was required setting out the relationship between the two. For example, if the code was thought to be restricted, what would be the expected linguistic pattern if the context were that of a mother explaining something to her child? The disconnecting of speech variants from the concept of code did permit of the possibility that speakers who had access to an elaborated code would under certain conditions produce *linguistically* restricted speech variants; for example, when offering a fifteen-word summary of a lengthy passage or in giving geographical directions. In the same way, speakers who had access to only a restricted code would produce *linguistically* elaborated variants.

One of the major difficulties of the thesis is that it is necessary to show how socio-linguistic codes are generated, reproduced and changed as a result of macro (institutional) features of the society, and how they are generated, reproduced and changed at the more micro levels of interactions within the family and within the school. As a direct result of the empirical research, more emphasis was given to operationalizing the basic concepts at the micro level. Indeed, if this proved impossible, there was little point in speculations at the macro level. I found it necessary to disconnect the notions of restricted and elaborated speech variants from the concept of code. This immediately raised the question of when it is necessary to evoke the concept of code; that is, when is a restricted or elaborated speech variant no more than a switch in register, and when are such speech variants an indication of code? I suggested that one would have to obtain samples of speech in critical contexts and examine their syntactic and lexical properties in the light of each context according to the explicitness and specificity of the meaning. On this basis, one could only infer code after examination of speech obtained from selected contexts.

So far, the relationship between code and speech variant has not been made clear, nor have I brought the notion of speech variant in relationship with meaning. The first step involved bringing together meanings and their linguistic realization. Here the work of Dr R. Hasan, who was research officer to the Sociological Research Unit for a period of two years, was critical. Dr Hasan, before she came to the Unit, was working on a theory of cohesion (the description of integrative phenomena within and between sentences); Dr Hasan's enquiries offered an important means of obtaining linguistic descriptions of texts above the level of the sentence. Indeed, if I had been aware of the sociological significance of her work earlier, it would have prevented decisions (which were my personal responsibility) which took the research down some very blind alleys. One of the major difficulties of the research has always been the problem of inferring from micro counts of specific linguistic choices to macro characteristics of the speech as a whole.

Both Dr Lawton and myself found that in a discussion context small groups of middle-class children, matched with small groups of working-class children for age, sex and ability, differed from the working-class children in their relative use of certain syntactic choices and lexical selections. Thus we obtained a range of differences between the two groups. It was not the case that one group took up choices that were *never* used by the second group, nor was this expected. The difference on individual measures was always one of relative frequency. It was and still is my view that these differences, across a range of measures, in relative frequency produced an overall difference in the *patterning* of the speech. There was, however, no way of demonstrating the existence, above the level of the sentence, of a distinctive patterning of the speech.

Dr Hasan's work on cohesion led her to explore the various ways meanings between sentences were related or tied through the grammar and lexes. I cannot here go into the details of this work (see Dr Hasan's chapter 'Codes, Register and Dialects', in the accompanying volume) but her researches indicated an important approach to the study of implicit linguistic usage. Very briefly, it is possible to distinguish between forms of speech where the referents of the speech are explicit in the text, or at some point have been made explicit, and forms of speech where the referents are not in the text, but in the *context*. In the latter case, unless the listener has access to critical features of the context in which the speech is imbedded, the meanings are not clear. Dr Hasan calls such context imbedded speech, exophoric. When speech is exophoric, the meanings are highly context dependent. Much of everyday speech with people we know very well takes this form. A mother who can just see out of the corner of her eye her child intent on some piece of domestic sabotage suddenly shouts 'Stop that! You do that again, and you're for it!' If we heard that imperative and threat on a tape recorder, it would be difficult to infer what it was that evoked the imperative, and what, specifically, would happen if the child continued. We all use exophoric or context dependent speech in specific situations, but we also switch to relatively context independent speech when we wish to make our meanings explicit and specific.

The first step towards linking meanings and their linguistic realization involved making a distinction between relatively context independent meanings and relatively context dependent meanings. In this way I returned to the basic ideas of implicitness and explicitness and to the central idea that the form of the social relationship acts selectively upon the meanings to be realized, which in turn activate specific grammatical and lexical choices.

The second step followed readily from the first. If meanings were context-dependent, then only those who possessed a shared, unspoken, implicit understanding of certain relevant features of the context could have access to the meanings realized by the speech. From this point of view, context-dependent meanings are available only to *particular* types of speakers; those who share an implicit understanding of the context. Thus, context-dependent meanings could be considered *particularistic*. On the other hand, context-independent meanings did not rely, to anywhere near the same extent, upon shared, unspoken understandings of critical features of the context, for context-independent meanings are linguistically explicit. From this point of view, context-independent meanings are in principle available to all. Thus, context-independent meanings could be considered *universalistic*. I could now consider speech variants which were context-dependent and so gave rise to particularistic orders of meaning and speech variants which were context-independent and so gave rise to universalistic orders of meaning. (I now had returned to the 1962 paper, published in *Language and Speech*.) Implicit also in the formulation is that these two speech variants are realized by different role relationships. The concepts of universalistic and particularistic orders of meaning could also link the more distinctly sociological features of the theory with the linguistic features.

The third step focused more specifically upon cognitive aspects of context-dependent/independent meanings. I suggested that where meanings are context-independent and so universalistic, then principles may be made verbally explicit and elaborated, whereas where meanings are context-dependent and so particularistic, principles will be relatively implicit, or, as in regulative contexts, simply announced.

I now had distinguished between two types of speech variants. I have suggested that restricted speech variants are context-dependent, give rise to particularistic orders of meaning, where principles are verbally implicit or simply announced; whereas elaborated speech variants are context-independent, give rise to universalistic orders of meaning, where principles are made verbally explicit and elaborated. I have also suggested, that restricted and elaborated speech variants possess distinctive linguistic features and so by implication the resources of the grammar and lexes will be *differently* explored. This formulation also enables one to bring together at a high level of abstraction role, speech and cognitions in causal relationship: that is, sociology, linguistics and psychology.

The fourth step links codes and speech variants. This step was made possible because of what was, to me, a critical paper by Professor Michael Halliday, entitled 'Relevant Models of Language' which is reprinted in *Class, codes and control*, vol. 2. In this paper, Professor Halliday outlines a set of what he calls language functions: (1) instrumental, (2) regulatory, (3) personal, (4) interactional, (5) heuristic, (6) imaginative, (7) informative. He regards these as distinct functions which are realized in the grammatical system and the vocabulary. In learning his mother tongue the child learns to produce integrated structures in which various different functions may be combined. From the point of view of their *initial* acquisition by the child, Professor Halliday goes as far as saying that each function has its own distinctive grammar. I reduced these seven functions, for my purposes, to four—regulative, instructional, inter-personal, imaginative—and conceptualized his functions in terms of critical primary socializing contexts. Thus, as these four critical primary socializing contexts entailed different language functions, then their linguistic realization should also differ. *The concept code now referred to the regulative principle which controlled the form of the linguistic realization of the four primary socializing contexts.* The strength of code restriction could now be assessed in terms of the *socializers'* (parents, peer group, etc.) use of restricted speech variants across the four contexts: regulative, instructional, interpersonal and imaginative. The strength of code elaboration could be assessed in terms of the socializers' use of elaborated speech variants across the same four contexts. This new formulation of codes brings out in the definition both the social structuring of relevant meanings and the *contexts* relevant to the theory. At the same time, the linguistic features of the codes are examined in terms of the code's regulation of the linguistic realization of primary language functions. The formulation also makes explicit the difference in level between speech variants and codes. Codes are not directly observable, only speech variants. Speech variants in the theory represent the surface structure whereas codes represent the deep structure. For in the same way that sentences which look superficially different can be shown to be realizations of the same rule, then differences between the linguistic realizations of different language function may in this theory be seen as superficial in terms of the underlying coding principle.

The work of Professor Halliday on functions of language together with the development of his systemic grammar into network theory, creates exciting possibilities, for both more general and more delicate formulation of the basic concepts, and makes possible the translating of a sociological language into a linguistic language.

The reader may ask what all this has to do with the interaction between research and theory. In the first place, the Sociological Research Unit used initially Halliday's Scale and Category Grammar and, to a lesser extent, inter-personal contexts. A number of the empirical papers in the second volume by Peter Hawkins, Dorothy Henderson, Peter Robinson Susan Rackstraw, and Geoffrey Turner, illustrate aspects of the conceptual development. The penultimate paper in this volume, 'Social class, language and socialization', points to both the past and the future.

Developments also took place on the more distinctly sociological aspects of the theory, but these were more in the direction of elaboration and greater specificity of existing concepts than reformulations. As I have written earlier in this introduction, in 1962, before the research began, an account was given of different types of family structures which were considered to give rise to different communication structures, together with a brief account of the conditions of change in the family structures. This account also contained an approach to social control which emphasized its linguistic realization. Two simple, basic dimensions were at the basis of the conceptualization. The first dimension referred to the selective emphasis placed by the controller (parent, socializer) upon the attributes of the controlled (the child, the pupil, etc.). The controller, or parent, could focus upon general attributes of the child, upon his age, sex or age relational status, in which case the control was termed positional. The controller or parent could focus upon particular attributes of the child, those which were specific to him; in this case the control was called personal. The second dimension referred to the discretion accorded by the controller to the controlled in the control relationship. Thus, if a range of alternatives was made available to the controlled, this would count as high discretion, whereas if the range of alternatives was severely reduced, this would count as low discretion. Although the above formulation appears very coarse, it proved capable of considerable delicacy at the operational level. We believed that the social structuring of meanings and their linguistic realization and emphasis would vary with positional and personal family types. Miss Cook and myself constructed a most delicate coding grid which explored these concepts and which was used to analyse both the mothers' and children's accounts of how they would cope with a series of hypothetical regulative contexts. Miss Cook's analysis and modification of the interpretative framework is to be published as an SRU Monograph. Geoffrey Turner, research officer to the SRU, is attempting to apply Professor Halliday's network theory in order to develop a linguistic specification of types of social control; a very difficult task. We were thus in a position to examine inter- and intra-class phenomena in terms of the distribution of family types and their hypothesized structures of communication, and also the conditions for their change.

At the same time as I was trying to gain greater control over inter- and intra-family interactions as these gave rise to different forms of, and emphasis on, verbal communication, I tried to explore how changes in the wider institutional structure of society affected the symbolic structure and communication processes in, minimally, the family and the school. Parallel to the socio-linguistic papers I wrote four little-known papers, which tried to examine changes in the knowledge and organizational structures of schools. At that time, I was very fortunate to meet and enjoy a continuous relationship with Dr Mary Douglas, now Professor of Social Anthropology at University College, London. As a result, the work on family structures, sociolinguistic codes and their wider institutional relationships became focused upon the idea of the variable strength of boundaries and their relationship to the structuring and realizing of experience. Full circle, apparently back to Durkheim, but if one remembers that power relationships are expressed through boundary relationships, then the Marx, Durkheim, Meadian matrix, may well be able to deal with change.

The greatest sadness is that after twelve years I think the theory is sufficiently explicit to stand detailed exploration at both conceptual and empirical levels, but this is now too late for our own research. For the research was predicated on a much coarser theoretical position and this affected the nature of the data we collected, the methods of analysis and the interpretative principles. Yet one has to get out of the armchair at some point; my own feeling is that one should never be in it in the first place. Whatever the philosophers of science say about the hypothetical-deductive nature of scientific activity, it seems to me that one is continuously experiencing in oneself the experience of society. There are many ways of experiencing this experience and a variety of ways of making it public. Because of the applied nature of much sociological enquiry, because of the critical problems which sociologists both feel they wish to consider, and are expected to consider, I think we are forced into frighteningly complex problems before we have even managed to formulate the problem. And when we can, either the grant has come to an end, or we are exhausted, or both. We have as yet not given enough consideration to the various issues—personal, intellectual, organizational and political—which are entailed in the activity of sociological research.

Research in the social sciences arises out of a social context, is organized within a social context and, of critical significance, is given its various meanings by receiving social contexts. This statement probably sounds like a pompous statement of the obvious. Even more obvious is the discrepancy between the intentions of the researcher and the social interpretations placed upon his research.

In my case, I can distinguish two inter-related strands: the various factors which affect children's experience of formal education, and a more general problem of the structure of cultural transmission and change, with special reference to speech. I think it would be true to say that there has been scant attention paid to the general problem compared to the attention to the applied problem. From a personal point of view, I have never understood how the applied problem could be seen other than against the perspective of the general problem.

It would be true to say that I was almost wholly unaware of any major interest in the work until 1964, when I undertook a series of visits to the USA. Even when I did become aware of general interest, the day-to-day problems of the research kept my head very close to the ground. A number of factors woke me up; ritual references to the work in the literature of a very superficial kind. (I do not refer here to the criticisms of Frederick Williams, Courtney Cazden, Malcolm Coulthard, Alan Grimshaw); the uncritical and curious expositions of students in degree, teacher's certificate, 'A' level, and even 'O' level examinations, who drew only upon very early work; ideological imputations made here, but especially in the USA.

To begin with, the left wing saw the work as another powerful indictment of the class system. In the end, the left wing, especially the new left, saw the work as yet another stereotype of the working class from a middle-class perspective. It represented an attempt at the ideological level at reducing the value of 'natural' forms of communication, and aimed at breaking these in order to impose middle-class values and meanings more successfully in the school. I was responsible, by omission, for failing to draw attention to the material poverty under which communities were forced to live, and for failing to draw attention to the conditions in schools which were responsible for educational failure. The right wing, on the other hand, felt I had given some justification to the curious idea that 'high culture' was not for the working class, or that the thesis offered an approach to their assimilation into the existing middle class. Both left wing and right wing were convinced that the basic model was that of deficit. The concept of restricted code was said to impose a humiliating uniformity upon the diversity and imaginative potential of cultural forms. At the level of the classroom, the same concept was said to have lowered the expectations teachers held of their children, whereas the concept of elaborated code legitimized the teachers' own middle-class conception of appropriate communication. The code definitions are said to have given rise to mechanical grammar and vocabulary drills. Indeed, one able English linguist, in a paper, considers that the thesis is fundamentally misleading and irrelevant to the applied problem.

There are few indications in the papers about changes in the curricula, pedagogy or organizational structures of the school. This omission was deliberate. It has always seemed to me that educational institutions at secondary or primary levels are likely to absorb ideas, and try them out on a fairly large scale, provided that those subject to them are either the very young children or the so-called less able working-class children, before the ideas are sufficiently worked through to be useful. I felt I did not know enough about the problem nor did I have sufficient evidence to make any recommendation to teachers. It was also the case that I was trying to develop an analysis of the social basis of knowledge made available in schools, which I considered was prior to offering suggestions to teachers of pupils of the age group five to seven years. (See the final paper in this volume).

The point I want to make is not one of defence. It is up to the reader to decide as well as the students I have taught and the groups to whom I have lectured. I would rather ask how so much discussion could have arisen when hardly any evidence existed, even at the level of illustration, and when much other research existed which was more fully documented.

Clearly, I must take some responsibility for these conflicting interpretations. The papers are obscure, lack precision and probably abound with ambiguities. In 1969 I tried to clear up some of the ambiguities in a paper called 'A critique of the concept of Compensatory Education'. Since that time, various versions of that paper have appeared in different journals and books. I hope that these two volumes will clear, or at least clarify, the ideological atmosphere. The evidence will not, for theories are rarely refuted: they are explored and replaced by more simple, more explicit, more delicate, more general, indeed, more exciting ideas. It is probably wrong to use the word 'theory'. The most we seem able to do is to construct weak interpretative frames. Perhaps in the end the sole criterion is: do these encourage a shift in perspective so that we can see received frames differently or even a little beyond them?

Introduction to the second edition

I have taken the opportunity afforded by this reprint to make an addendum on the coding of objects and modalities of control and to insert a postscript which first appeared in the Open University Course Unit E262, *Language and Learning*, Block 3, and subsequently in the paperback edition.

Part I Beginnings

Chapter 1 Some sociological determinants of perception

Within the last thirty years in both the fields of sociology and psychology there has been an increasing awareness of sub-cultural and social class influences upon behaviour and, in particular, learning. Many workers have demonstrated correlations between sub-culture or class and educational attainments but there exists no unifying theory to explain the empirical relationships and found discrepancies between potential and actual attainment of working-class children.

While much of this work, especially that of the Chicago School, has been the subject of severe methodological criticism, it is widely agreed that these studies point to critical relationships between social class, behaviour and performance. J. Floud reports Professor P. E. Vernon as saying:

> It is argued that the influence of the environment is cumulative. At each stage in the child's life from birth to maturity its influence must be given increasing weight as a determinant of the differences between individuals and particularly of those differences which are measured by tests of intelligence and attainment on which, in the main, we base our educational decisions about them.

Dr H. Himmelweit, in a discussion of the relations between social class and education, writes, 'None of the facts mentioned here provides more than a hint as to the reasons for the different performance of children from the various social levels.' It is with this gap in the existing knowledge of the relations between social class and educational attainment that this paper is primarily concerned.

It would seem important to understand what underlies 'the complex of attitudes favourable to educational and social mobility'. That is, those factors which influence working-class children who do less well at grammar schools, leave early and fail to assimilate the grammar-school ethos; factors which influence those working-class children who tend to do less well on verbal tests of intelligence than on non-verbal tests, and those factors which influence educational attainment in basic subjects. A framework is also necessary within which much of the existing data can be re-examined and systematized and which would indicate new areas of research.

The purpose of this paper is to indicate a relationship between the mode of cognitive expression and certain social classes. The predisposition to form relationships with objects in a particular way is an important perceptual factor and may be distinguished from cognitive potential.

Different terms, or the same term used to denote the same object, may imply different experiences, which are related to a more general method of ordering relationships. Two types of ordering of relationships will be proposed; that which arises out of sensitivity to the content of objects and that which arises out of sensitivity to the structure of objects. This division between structure and content is analytical and the two predispositions to perceive are not dichotomous but stages on a social continuum. The sociological determinants of these two stages and their implications will be examined in relation to certain formal educational institutions. It is necessary to examine the predisposition and resistance to certain educational processes. It is suggested that the lower the social strata the greater the resistance to formal education and learning, and that this is a function of the social structure of the strata. This resistance is expressed in many different ways and levels, e.g. critical problems of discipline, non-acceptance of the values of the teacher, the failure to develop and feel the need for an extensive vocabulary, a preference for a descriptive rather than an analytical cognitive process. It is suggested that resistance is a function of a mode of perceiving and feeling which is characterized by a sensitivity to the content rather than to the structure of objects. It is contended that members of the unskilled and semi-skilled strata, relative to the middle classes, do not merely place different significances upon different classes of objects, but that their perception is of a qualitatively different order.

Sensitivity to the structure of objects is here defined as a function of learned ability to respond to an object perceived and defined in terms of a matrix of relationships. Sensitivity to content is a function of learned ability to respond to the boundaries of an object rather than to the matrix of relationships and inter-relationships in which it stands with other objects. This distinction, it will be seen, is wholly qualitative.

The basic requirements for the group termed 'middle-class and associative levels' will be a family where the father is more likely to have received grammar-school education, or some form of further education or certificated training for a skill, or one in which the mother is more likely to have received something more than elementary schooling, or before marriage to have followed an occupation superior to that of the father, or a non-manual occupation. Such a family may be found among certain wage-earning manual workers. Middle-class and associative levels include the occupational hierarchy above this base line. The base line is considered the transitional family structure which modifies social perception and orients it to sensitivity to the structure of objects. The term 'working-class' includes all members of the semi-skilled and unskilled group except the type of family structure indicated as the base line for the middle-class and associative levels. The groups are fundamentally distinct because the first possesses:

(1) An awareness of the importance of the relationships between means and ends and of the relevant cognitive and dispositional attributes.
(2) A discipline to orient behaviour to certain values but with a premium on individual differentiation within them.
(3) The ability to adopt appropriate measures to implement the attainment of distant ends by a purposeful means-end chain.

Thus a major characteristic of the middle-class and associative levels is an instrumental attitude to social relations and objects, whilst for the second groups the attitude is non-instrumental. Integral to this paper is the contention that sensitivity to the content or structure of objects varies in degree according to the extent and ramifications of the above factors.

The child in the middle-class and associative levels is socialized within a formally articulated structure. Present decisions affecting the growing child are governed by their efficacy in attaining distant ends. Behaviour is modified by, and oriented to, an explicit set of goals and values which create a more stable system of rewards and punishments; although the psychological implications of this may vary from one family to another. The future is conceived of in direct relation to the educational and emotional life of the child. Consequently, the child grows up in an ordered, rational structure in which his total experience is organized from an early age. Within middle-class and associative levels direct expressions of feeling, in particular feelings of hostility, are discouraged. The word mediates between the expression of feeling and its approved social recognition, that is, a value is placed upon the verbalization of feeling. This is so in all societies but the important determining factor here is the nature of the words and the type of language-use, not necessarily the size of vocabulary, but the degree to which the social emphasis on an aspect of the language structure mediates the relation between thought and feeling. Language exists in relation to a desire to express and communicate; consequently, the mode of a language structure—the way in which words and sentences are related—reflects a particular form of the structuring of feeling and so the very means of interaction and response to the environment.

From this standpoint language facilities and language barriers are of the utmost importance and must be studied in their interplay with a host of other factors that make for ease or difficulty of transmission of ideas and patterns of behaviour. Furthermore the sociologist is necessarily interested in the symbolic significance in a social sense of the linguistic differences which appear in any large community (Sapir, 1956).[1]

Sapir goes on to say:

Peculiar modes of pronunciation, characteristic turns of phrase, slangy forms of speech, occupational terminologies of all sorts—these are so many symbols of the manifold ways in which society arranges itself and are of crucial importance for the understanding of the development of individual and social attitudes.

Again:

Language is heuristic . . . in the much more far reaching sense that its forms predetermine for us certain modes of observation and interpretation (ibid.).

When a middle-class mother says to her child, 'I'd rather you made less noise, darling,' the child will tend to obey because previous disobedience after this point has led to expression of disapproval or perhaps other punitive measures. The operative words in this sentence, which the middle-class child responds to, are 'rather' and 'less'. The child has learnt to become sensitive to this form of sentence and the many possible sentences in this universe of discourse. The words 'rather' and 'less' are understood, when used in this situation, as directly translatable cues for immediate response on the part of the middle-class child. However, if the same statement were made to a child from the family of an unskilled worker it would not be understood as containing the same imperative cues for response. 'Shut up!' may contain a more appropriate set of cues. Of course, the last statement is meaningful to a middle-class child but what is important to stress is the fact that the middle-class child has learnt to be able to respond to *both* statements, and *both* are differentially discriminated within a finely articulated world of meaning. We are discussing two modes of language and the working-class child has learned to respond to only one, and so although he may understand both, he will not differentiate effectively between the two. Further, if the first statement is made by a middle-class person to a working-class child, the child will translate it into 'shut up' and will relate the difference between the statements to the different social levels. What he will not have and what he cannot respond to *directly*, is the different language structure of the first sentence. The working-class child has to translate and thus *mediate* middle-class language structure through the logically simpler language structure of his own class to make it personally meaningful. Where he cannot make this translation he fails to understand and is left puzzled.

In an appendix to *A Study of Thinking* (Bruner, 1957) the author considers that a range of experience may be differentiated in the lexicon of one language and undifferentiated in another. Although the context of the statements is in a discussion of distinctions within and between primitive languages the force of the comment is believed to hold here. Allison Davis (1951) made a contribution to the understanding of the importance of cultural usages and symbolic forms and means, but he did not work out the consequences of his own statements, 'The lower socio-economic groups have a different language structure than the higher groups. They speak various non-standard dialects' (p. 82). Similarly Eells and Murray (1951) seem to be thinking in terms of a different dialect rather than the effects of different modes of language-use which differentiate different ranges of experience and thus modify what is actually responded to in an object. The difference in response between the children in the example involves a different structuring of receptivity to language cues and to relationships and symbolism implied by a language. It has been found by investigation that a value is placed on early verbalization in the middle-class child but this fact, in itself, is not so important as the mode of verbalization or the structure of the language and its functions.

One of the aims of the middle-class family is to produce a child oriented to certain values but individually differentiated within them. The child is born into an environment where he is seen and responded to as an individual with his own rights, that is, he has a specific social status. This early process of individuation is accomplished by two important factors: the scrupulous observation of the child by the parents so that the very fine stages of development and the emergence of new patterns of behaviour are the object of attention and comment; together with recognition and communication in a language structure where personal qualifications are significantly used and which the child learns to use in response. The child's relation to the environment is such that his range and expression of discriminating verbal responses is fostered by the social structure from the beginning. A virtuous circle is set up which is continually reinforced, for the mother will elaborate and expand the embryo personal qualificatory statements that the child makes. It would follow that the greater the differentiation of the child's experience the greater his ability to differentiate and elaborate objects in his environment.

The next fact to consider is the way in which the order of communication, the mode of expression of language, modifies perception. It is necessary to make a distinction between non-verbal expressions of meaning and verbal expressions of meaning in any communication. The role of gesture, facial expression, bodily movement, in particular volume and tone of the speaking voice, will be termed 'immediate' or direct expression, whilst the words used will be termed 'mediate' or indirect expression. What *is* important is the emphasis placed upon one or the other and the nature of the form of the verbal communication. Now if the words used are part of a language which contains a high proportion of short commands, simple statements and questions where the symbolism is descriptive, tangible, concrete, visual and of a low order of generality, where the emphasis is on the emotive rather than the logical implications, it will be called a *public* language.[2]

The language-use of the middle class is rich in personal, individual qualifications, and its form implies sets of advanced logical operations; volume and tone and other non-verbal means of expression, although important, take second place. It is important to realize that initially in the middle-class child's life it is not the number of words or the range of vocabulary which is decisive but the fact that he or she becomes sensitive to a particular form of indirect or mediate expression where the subtle arrangement of words and connections between sentences convey feeling. It is the latter which the child originally strives to obtain in order to experience a full relationship with the mother and in so doing learns to respond to a particular form of language cues. Because of the importance of this type of mediate relation between mother and child a tension is created between the child and his environment so that there is a need to verbalize his relations in a personal, individual way. Thus the child at an early age becomes sensitive to a form of language-use which is relatively complex and which in turn acts as a dynamic framework upon his or her perception of objects. This mode of language-use will be termed *formal*. It was stated earlier that the pressure within a middle-class social structure to intensify and verbalize an awareness of separateness and difference increases the significance of objects in the environment. Receptivity to a particular form of language structure determines the way relationships to objects are made and an orientation to a particular manipulation of words.

The child in the middle-class and associative levels grows up in an environment which is finely and extensively controlled; the space, time, and social relationships are explicit regulated within and outside the family group. The more purposeful and explicit the organization of the environment with reference to a distant future, that is the greater the rationality of the connections and inter-relations between means and distant ends, the greater the significance of objects in the present. Objects in the present are not taken as given, but become centres for enquiry and starting points for relationships. The effect of this on the experience of the child is to make him more generally and specifically aware of a wide range of objects at any one time which will intensify his curiosity and reward his explorations. Here the critical factor is the mode of the relationship and this is a function of his sensitivity to structure. A dynamic interaction is set up: the pressure to verbalize feelings in a personally qualified way, the implications of the language learnt, combine to decide the nature of the cues to which he responds—structural cues. An orientation towards structure allows many interpretations or meanings to be given to any one object, which increases the area and intensity of the child's curiosity and receptiveness. This leads to an awareness of the formal ordering of his environment, notions of its extensions in time and space, and so is the beginning of the formation of primitive interpretative concepts. This, of course, is part of the socializing process of any child but it is the mode of establishing relationships which is of decisive importance, because the mode determines the levels of conceptualization possible. Different children will be able to benefit more from this environment as a result of other factors, e.g. specifically psychological factors, but the means of utilizing and exploiting formal educational facilities are provided.

The school is an institution where every item in the present is finely linked to a distant future, consequently there is not a serious clash of expectations between the school and the middle-class child. The child's developed time-span of anticipation allows the present activity to be related to a future, and this is meaningful. There is little conflict of values between the teacher and child and, more importantly, the child is predisposed to accept and respond to the language structure of communication. The school aims at assisting the development of consciousness of self, cognitive and emotional differentiation or discrimination, and develops and encourages mediate relationships, There is in the child a desire to use and manipulate words in a personal qualifying or modifying way and, in particular, a developing sense of tense (time) which together combine to reduce the problem of the teaching of English: reading, spelling, writing. The middle-class child is predisposed towards the ordering of symbolic relationships and, more importantly, imposing order and seeing new relationships. His level of curiosity is high. There is a conformity to authority and an acceptance of the role of the teacher, irrespective of psychological relationships to his personality. This is not to say that at times feelings of rebellion will not appear. The middle-class child is capable of manipulating the *two* languages—the language between social equals (peer groups), which approximates to a public language, *and* a formal language which permits sensitivity to role and status. This leads to appropriateness of behaviour in a wide range of social circumstances. Finally, the school is an important and socially approved means whereby the developing child can enhance his self-respect. Thus the social structure of the school, the means and ends of education, creates a framework which the middle-class child is able to accept, respond to and exploit.

Before examining certain factors of the working-class environment which have a bearing on the mode of cognition the following study will be presented. The sample is of particular interest because of the class, educational and occupational homogeneity of the subjects. This study was carried out in a London day college on 309 male students with whom the writer has personal contact in the course of teaching. The sample consisted of boys between fifteen and eighteen (with a mean age of sixteen years), all of whom were messenger boys, (young postman grade) employed by the GPO. They came from unskilled and semi-skilled backgrounds and their homes were randomly distributed geographically in inner and outer London. Of this group 295 went to secondary modern schools, five to junior technical schools, three to central schools and six to grammar schools. All boys left at fifteen years and have no recorded examination successes. They were given the Mill Hill vocabulary test 1948, Form I Senior and the Progressive Matrices 1938. It was predicted that the higher the score on the matrices the greater the difference between the matrices and the Mill Hill scores. That is, within this group of subjects there would not be a linear relation between the two scores. (Sixteen points or more was taken as an arbitrary indication of a significant difference between the scores.)

On examination of the results eighty-one boys showed matrices greater than Mill Hill test discrepancy of 16 or more points, the differences ranging between 16 and 37 points. Of these, nineteen boys falling within the matrices range 105–15 IQ points had Mill Hill IQ scores between 83 and 102, while the further sixty-two with a matrices range 116–26 + IQ points had Mill Hill scores within the range 82–110 IQ points. Of the total group only eighteen boys with a matrices score of 116 IQ or more showed a discrepancy of less than 16 points. As predicted (see Table 1) there is non-linear relationship between the scores. There is a clear trend that the higher the matrices score the greater the discrepancy between the Mill Hill and the matrices scores. It will be seen that all Mill Hill means fall within the average range.

Table 1

Number of subjects	3	23	77	64	104	38
Range of IQ matrices	71–80	81–90	91–100	101–10	111–20	121–6
Matrices mean	76	87	97	106	115	124
S.D.	1·41	2·11	2·73	3·03	3·17	2·15
Mill Hill mean	94	94	98	99	101	104
S.D.	10·2	7·9	5·78	6·37	7·63	7·5

Where the matrices IQ is over 101 points, Mill Hill means fall below this. Where the matrices IQ is below 100 points, Mill Hill means rise slightly above this, except for the three lowest scores.

It seems apparent that a great deal of potential ability is being lost as the greater proportion of these boys are functioning at an average or below-average level of ability and educational attainment in formal subjects. Their functioning ability in formal subjects is related to their Mill Hill scores. On matrices scores eighty of the subjects might have been potential candidates for grammar school; in fact only six went to grammar school, five to a technical school and three to central school, and none of this group of fourteen benefited in terms of attainment in examination. Of the total group 20·7 per cent have potential ability for grammar school but would, and perhaps did, fail as a result of educational attainment and showing on verbal tests. (IQ of 116 was considered the minimum required for grammar-school entrance.)

The clustering of the vocabulary scores about the mean, independent of matrices score, indicates the discrepancy between the ability to solve certain non-linguistic *relational* problems involving logical addition and subtraction, and purely linguistic problems of a conceptual or categorizing order. Although no evidence is offered here, the writer's experience with these boys indicates that the level of attainment in formal subjects is related to the vocabulary, not the matrices IQ. It is predicted on the basis of the theory that a comparative group of Mill Hill scores from subjects matched for similar age from middle-class strata would not show this non-linear relationship with the matrices. These results may have greater meaning in the context of the analysis of the working-class environment which follows.

The working-class family structure is less formally organized than the middle-class in relation to the development of the child. Although the authority within the family is explicit, the values which it expresses do not give rise to the carefully ordered universe spatially and temporally of the middle-class child. The exercise of authority will not be related to a stable system of rewards and punishments but may often appear arbitrary. The specific character of long-term goals tends to be replaced by more general notions of the future, in which chance, a friend or relative plays a greater part than the rigorous working out of connections. Thus present, or near present, activities have greater value than the relation of the present activity to the attainment of a distant goal. The system of expectancies, or the time-span of anticipation, is shortened and this creates different sets of preferences, goals and dissatisfactions. This environment limits the perception of the developing child of and in time. Present gratifications or present deprivations become absolute gratifications or absolute deprivations, for there exists no developed time continuum upon which present activity can be ranged. Relative to the middle classes, the postponement of present pleasure for future gratifications will be found difficult. By implication a more volatile patterning of affective and expressive behaviour will be found in the working classes.

The language between mother and child is public: one which contains few personal qualifications, for it is essentially a language where the stress is on emotive terms employing concrete, descriptive, tangible and visual symbolism. The nature of the language tends to limit the verbal expression of feeling. This child learns only a public language from his mother and feeling is communicated by non-verbal means.[3] It must be emphasized that with the use of a public language the child will tend to make and respond to personal qualifications which are expressed by an immediacy of communication whether verbally or non-verbally expressed.

As the nature of the language-use limits the verbal communication of feelings the latter tend to be as undifferentiated as the language. Consequently the emotional and cognitive differentiation of the working-class child is comparatively less developed, and the cues responded to in the environment will be primarily of a qualitatively different order. He is sensitive to the content of objects. Because the language is public, with a corresponding emphasis on emotive content, the very vehicle of communication precludes the structure of objects as major referent points. Of critical importance is the type of language-use upon which value is placed, for once a value is so placed, then that language-use will reinforce the emotional disposition which resulted in the initial preference.

It must be seen clearly that the distinction between structure and content is one of degrees within a conceptual hierarchy. All that is implied is this: where there is sensitivity to content only the simplest logical implications or boundaries of the structure will be cognized. More definitely, certain aspects of an object will not register as meaningful cues; or if they do, the verbal response will be inadequately determined.

It is difficult to distinguish the complex of dynamic factors involved in this order of perception, for the many relationships are mutually dependent and developmentally reinforce each other. The child is born into a world in which personal qualifications are established non-verbally in the sense that the personal qualifications are left out of the structure of the sentences. Relationships are made by the use of an individual selection from a public language, and by gesture, tone, change of volume and physical set, etc., that is, by *expressive symbolism*. Thus the child early learns to respond and make responses to cues which are immediately relevant. Expressive symbolism of this order has no reference other than to itself. Through his relationships to this symbolism the child in turn learns to respond to immediate perceptions and does *not* learn a language other than a public language in his class environment. The stress on the present in the *means* of communication precludes the understanding of the meaningfulness of a time continuum other than of a limited order. Necessarily, the child lives in the here-and-now experience of his world, in which the time-span of anticipation or expectancy is very brief, and this is reinforced by the lack of a rigorous working out of connections between means and distant ends as discussed previously. One important consequence of this patterning of perception is that it produces a descriptive cognitive process, e.g. the recognition of events A, B, C, D as separate unconnected facts or, at best, crude causal connections, are made. Sustained curiosity is not fostered or rewarded, as answers to questions rarely lead beyond the object or further than a simple statement about the object. The social structure continues to reinforce the early patterning of perception.

It is now necessary to show how this mode of perceiving and the attendant structuring of receptivity conflicts with and induces a resistance to formal education. There is an initial conflict between the need to make and to be sensitive to the mediate responses which formal learning requires and the immediate responsiveness the child has learned from his social structure. This creates difficulties at many levels. The appropriate cues which enable a child to establish a personal relationship are absent; from the point of view of the working-class child the teacher's feeling is impersonalized through the language he uses. The public language is, in fact, a language to be used between equals (from a middle-class point of view), for it contains little reference to social status (i.e. a structured object), and the terms used to denote social status within the class environment are often judged unacceptable for use outside it. Thus the use of this language in a superior-inferior situation (to a doctor, teacher, etc.) may often be interpreted by the superior as a hostile or aggressive (rude) response. Because the working-class child can use only, and knows only, a public language, it is often used in situations which are inappropriate. The expressive behaviour and immediacy of response which accompany the use of this language may again be wrongly interpreted by the teacher. This may well lead to a situation where pupil and teacher disvalue each other's world and communication becomes a means of asserting differences.

Fundamentally, it may lead to a breakdown of communications between teacher and child, for two different languages are in fact being used. If the teacher is conscious of a deficiency of his own status this may exacerbate the existing difficulty of communication. In contrast to the middle-class child, who is brought up to respond to the distinction between an office and its content, the working-class child confounds the two, so that if there is no personal relationship with the teacher his function and the subjects connected with it are together disvalued; although the working-class child may still have at the same time a sense of unease and a recognition of failure.

The fact that the working-class child attaches significance to an aspect of language different from that required by the learning situation is responsible for his resistance to extensions of vocabulary, the manipulation of words and the construction of ordered sentences. Because he has previously learned to make personal qualifications through expressive symbolism he has little desire to acquire new words or order his existing vocabulary in a way which expresses this qualification. There is, in fact, from his own standpoint, no *need* to do this. The 'I' of the child is adequately communicated by tone-volume-physical set, not in the language he uses. Unfortunately, within a formal learning situation, this means of communication is not recognized and must necessarily be disvalued. The attempt to substitute a different use of language and to change the order of communication creates critical problems for the working-class child as it is an attempt to change his basic system of perception, fundamentally the very means by which he has been socialized. The introduction of a new word, or a previously known word used differently, may not become a vehicle for future expression, for there exists no emotional and thus cognitive framework in which it can find a place. A situation is created of mechanical learning, with its implication of forgetting when the original stimuli are removed. The working-class boy is often genuinely puzzled by the need to acquire vocabulary or use words in a way that is, for him, peculiar. It is important to realize that his difficulties in ordering a sentence and connecting sentences—problems of qualifying an object, quality, idea, sensitivity to time and its extensions and modifications, making sustained relationships—are alien to the way he perceives and reacts to his immediate environment. The total system of his perception, which results in a sensitivity to content rather than the structure of objects, applies equally to the structure of a sentence.

The mechanical understanding and manipulation of numbers according to elementary rules of addition, subtraction and multiplication may not show a discrepancy between the two classes except in speed. It is believed that the difficulty for the working-class boy will arise with the application of the underlying principles to the new symbols involved in fractions, decimals and percentages. He does not understand the underlying principles and so cannot generalize the operations to different situations. The principles and operations apply only to discrete situations. Further, verbal problems based upon this symbolism, which require an initial ordering of relationships, create difficulties. Finally, the understanding of a language, which for the working-class child has no content, e.g. algebra, transposition of formulae, etc., is a critical step in his understanding of number and often indicates a point in the gradient of difficulty which he is unable to pass.

These critical points of difficulty may not be directly the result of deficiency of intelligence, however this controversial term is defined; rather, because of the nature of an object and its symbolic relations (here the implications of number), much is lost to perception and not cognized. The working-class child will encounter difficulties with basic subjects that are of an order different from those encountered by the middle-class child, and these may inhibit learning, or the exploitation of what is learned, or both. Simply, what is learned by a middle-class child will have a significance to him different from that which it has to a working-class child because of a differing perception of the items within a learning situation.

It has been pointed out that the level of curiosity of the working-class child is relatively low, and as compared with the middle-class child, differently oriented, and this removes a powerful stimulus from the classroom. The working-class child has a preference for descriptive cognitive responses; his response is an immediate one with only vague extensions in time and space, and consequently his attention will be brief or difficult to sustain without punitive measures. Rather than pursuing the detailed implications and relations of an object or an idea, which at once create the problem of its structure and extensions, he is oriented towards the cursory examinations of a series of different items. Hoggart has described, in his book *The Uses of Literacy*, an attitude characterized by fragmentation and the need for logical simplicity (1957).

There is no continuity between the expectancies of the school and those of the child. In the school an activity or a series of activities are meaningful in relation to a distant goal and the present has critical extensions in time and place. The working-class child is concerned mainly with the present, and his social structure, unlike that of the middle-class child, provides little incentive or purposeful support to make the methods and ends of the school personally meaningful. The problems of discipline and classroom-control result not from isolated points of resistance or conflict but from the attempt to reorient a whole pattern of perception with its emotional counterpart; and this may create the disproportion between the intensity of any one response and the specific set of stimuli which occasions it. Finally it may be stated that the school provides an important means by which the middle-class child enhances his self-respect, and that this is not so for the working-class child. His self-respect is in fact more often damaged. It is obtained elsewhere in the careful conformity to the symbols of his class.

An attempt has been made to show the social origins and some implications of two different orders of perception, characterized by sensitivity to structure or sensitivity to content. It must be emphasized that this is a distinction of general orientation. It has been stated that the middle-class child is aware of content through a structure of a different order from the working-class child and responds to qualitatively different perceptual cues. Cues which are meaningful to the middle-class child are not available to the working-class child. The way the receptivity of the working-class child has been structured is such that that which is available to perception is determined by the implications of the language-use of his class environment. Funda-mental to this paper is the assertion that the middle-class child is capable of responding to, manipulating and understanding, a public language, expressive symbolism and a formal language which is structured to mediate personal qualifications as a result of his class environment. It has been shown that a greater complexity of possible relationships is made available to him which permits a systematiza-tion of a high order. Because of the different structuring of the working-class environment the working-class child does not learn a language which is structured to mediate personal qualifications but is limited to expressive symbolism and a public language. This radically narrows the extent and type of his object relationships and has sociologically crucial implications for behaviour. The implica-tions are very wide and only those relevant to formal education have been indicated in this paper.

The dynamics of sensitivity to structure 'underlies the complex of attitudes favourable to educational and social mobility', whereas sensitivity to content, it would seem, is responsible for the poor showing in formal educational subjects by working-class children even if they have a high IQ. This mode of perception (sensitivity to content) would explain some of the discrepancies between verbal and non-verbal tests (see study) and why working-class children tend to do less well on purely verbal tests. Although it has been found that working-class children do not become part of the social and cultural life of the grammar school (Himmelweit, 1954; Oppenheim, 1955) this fact in itself is not explanatory nor need it necessarily lead to poorer educational performance. In fact it has been shown that often working-class children in grammar schools come from homes where there is little divergence between the aims of the school and those of the home. For the reasons given in this paper, the fact that many working-class parents apparently hold middle-class attitudes does not imply that the children are equipped affectively and cognitively to respond to the grammar-school opportunity, despite the level of their measured intellectual potential. It is further important to recon-sider the Hogben model (1938) in the light of this paper, for in order to equate ability with opportunity it is necessary to understand precisely the variables which determine the *expression* of ability. This is necessary at the present moment, when the society in order to survive must be able to profit by the *expressed* potential of all of its members.

It is thought that many aspects of the present controversy relating to the concept 'intelligence' might be seen differently within this conceptual framework. Specifically it might throw some light on the found discrepancies between potential ability and measured attainment of working-class pupils, by indicating how perception is patterned sociologically. A comparative study of middle-class and working-class nursery schools would be invaluable. The psychological causes of difficulties in the basic subjects is a different problem. What appears vital is the separating out of sociological and psychological factors in order that constructive methods may be worked out to prevent the wastage of working-class educational potential. If this theory is valid it is thought that it is possible to systemize many disparate hypotheses and much established data, relating to working-class and middle-class differences in attainment and behaviour.

Finally, although the low mobility rate of the unskilled and semi-skilled strata (Hall and Glass, 1954) may imply educational waste, it is equally important to consider that as a result of the close relationship between education and occupation a situation may soon be reached when the educational institutions legitimize social inequality by individualizing failure. Democratization of the means of education together with the internalizing of the achievement ethic by members of the working-class strata may lead to an individualizing of failure, to a loss of self-respect, which in turn modifies an individual's attitude both to his group and to the demands made upon him by the society. If the theory presented in this paper has practical value then it will also indirectly illuminate this dilemma inherent in present social policy.

Notes

1 In this paper the valuable work of Cassirer (1944, 1953), Whorf (1956) and Sapir (1956) has been used to explore the social implications of language. See also H. Hoijer (1954).
2 Characteristics of a public language are: short, grammatically simple, often unfinished sentences with a poor syntactical construction; simple and repetitive use of conjunctions (so, then, and), thus modifications, qualifications and logical stress will tend to be indicated by non-verbal means; frequent use of short commands and questions; rigid and limited use of adjectives and adverbs; infrequent use of the impersonal pronoun (it, one) as subject of a conditional sentence; statements formulated as questions which set up a sympathetic circularity, e.g. 'Just fancy?' 'Isn't it terrible?' 'Isn't it a shame?' 'It's only natural, isn't it?' A statement of fact is often used as both a reason and a conclusion, e.g. 'You're not going out' 'I told you to hold on tight' (mother to child on bus, as repeated answer to child's 'Why?'). Individual selection from a group of traditional phrases plays a great part. The symbolism is of a

low order of generality. The personal qualification is left out of the structure of the sentence, therefore it is a language of implicit meaning. Feelings which find expression in this language will themselves be affected by the form of the expressions used. Feelings communicated will be diffuse and crudely differentiated when a public language is being used, for if a personal qualification is to be given to this language, it can be done only by non-verbal means, primarily by changes in volume and tone accompanied by gesture, bodily movement, facial expression, physical set. Thus if the language between mother and child is a public one, as it is in the working classes, then the child will tend to become sensitive to the quality and strength of feeling through non-verbal means of expression, for the personal qualification will be made through these means. And this has many implications for the structuring of experience and relationships with objects.

3 It is relevant to quote here a finding of both Greenald (1954) and Floud (1956) that achievement in the grammar school was correlated with the social grading of the mother's occupation before marriage. This finding is of great importance as it indicates the order of the initial communication to the child.

References

BAYLEY, N. (1940), *Mental Growth in Young Children* and *Factors Influencing the Growth of Intelligence in Young Children*, Year Book Nat. Soc. Study Educ. 39, Part II, Ch. II, Ch. III.

BAYLEY, N. (1949), 'Consistency and variability in the growth of intelligence from birth to eighteen years', *J. Genetic Psychol.* 75.

BOGER, J. H. (1952), 'Analysis of factors adversely affecting scholarship of High School pupils', *J. Educ. Res.* 46.

BRENNAN, T., COONEY, E. W. and POLLINS, H. (1954), *Social Change in S.W. Wales*, Watts.

BRUNER, J. S., GOODROW, J. J. and AUSTIN, A. (1957), *A Study of Thinking, Wiley* (Append. on language).

CAMPBELL, W. J. (1951), 'The influence of sociocultural environment upon the educational progress of children at the Secondary School', Unpub. Ph.D. Thesis, University of London.

CASSIRER, E. (1944), *An Essay on Man*, Yale Univ. Press.

CASSIRER, E. (1953), *The Philosophy of Symbolic Forms* I, Yale Univ. Press.

CLARKE, A. D. B. (1953), 'How constant is the I.Q.?' *Lancet* 2, 877, 1953.

CLARKE, A. D. B. and CLARKE, A. M. (1954), 'Cognitive changes in the feeble minded', *Br. J. Psychol.* XLV, 173-9.

DAVIS, A. (1955), *Social Class Influence upon Learning*, Harvard Univ. Press.

DAVIS, A. *et al.* (1951), *Intelligence and Cultural Differences*, Univ. of Chicago Press.

DENNIS, N., HENRIQUES, F. and SLAUGHTER, C. (1956), *Coal is our Life*, Eyre & Spottiswoode.

EELLS, K. and MURRAY, W. (1951), in *Intelligence and Cultural Differences* (eds.), Eells *et. al.*, Univ. of Chicago Press, Part III.

ESTES, B. W. (1953), 'Influence of socioeconomic status on Weschler Intelligence Scale for children: An exploratory study', *Journal of Consulting Psychol.* 17.

FLOUD, J. (ed.) (1956), *Social Class and Educational Opportunity*, Heinemann.

FLOUD, J. and HALSEY, A. H. (1956), 'Education and occupation: English Secondary Schools and the supply of labour', *Year Book of Education*.

GREENALD, G. M. (1954), 'An inquiry into the influence of sociological and psychological factors in trends of achievement in Grammar Schools' (London Univ., LSE), Unpub. M.A. Thesis.

HALL, J. R. and GLASS, D. V. (1954), 'Education and social mobility', Ch. X in *Social Mobility* (ed.) Glass, D. V., Routledge & Kegan Paul,

HALSEY, A. H. and GARDNER, L. (1953), 'Selection for secondary education and achievement in four grammar schools', *Br. J. Soc.* 4.

HAVIGHURST, R. J. (1951), in *Intelligence and Cultural Differences* (eds.) Eells *et. al.*, Univ. of Chicago Press, Ch. III.

HIMMELWEIT, H. (1954), 'Social status and secondary education since the 1944 Act: Some data for London', in *Social Mobility* (ed.) Glass, D. V., Ch. II, Routledge & Kegan Paul.

HOGBEN, L. (1938), *Political Arithmetic*, Allen & Unwin.

HOGGART, R. (1957), *The Uses of Literacy*, Chatto & Windus.

HOIJER, H. (ed.) (1954), *Language in Culture*, Univ. of Chicago Press.

HONZIK, M. P., MACFARLANE, J. W. and ALLEN, L. (1948), 'The stability of mental test performance between two and eighteen years', *J. Exp. Educ.* 17.

JONES, H. E. (1946), 'Environmental influences on mental development' in *Manual of Child Psychology* (ed.) Carmichael, L. (1956), Ch. II, New York: Wiley; London: Chapman & Hall.

JUDGES, A. V. (ed.) (1956), *Looking Forward in Education*, Faber.

OPPENHEIM, A. N. (1955), 'Social status and clique formation among grammar school boys', *Br. J. Soc.* 6.

SAPIR, E. (1956), 'Linguistics as a science', in *Culture, Language and Personality*, ed. Mandelbaum, G., Univ. of California Press.

SHAW, C. F. and MCKAY, H. R. (1942), *Juvenile Delinquency and Urban Areas*, Univ. of Chicago Beh. Res. Fund Monog.

SKODAK, M. and SKEELS, H. M. (1945), 'A follow up study of children in adoptive homes', *J. Genetic Psychol.* 66.

SPINLEY, B. M. (1953), *The Deprived and the Privileged*, Routledge & Kegan Paul.

THRASHER, F. M. (1927), *The Gang*, Chicago Univ. Soc. Series.

WARNER, LLOYD *et al.* (1944), *Democracy in Jonesville*, New York: Harper & Row.

WHORF, B. L. (1956), in Carroll, J. B. (ed.), *Language, Thought and Reality*, New York: Wiley.

WHYTE, W. F. (1943), *Street Corner Society*, Univ. of Chicago Press.

WIRTH, L. (1929), *Community Life and Social Policy*, Univ. of Chicago Press.

WIRTH, L. (1956), *The Ghetto*, Chicago Univ. Soc. Series.

ZORBAUGH, W. H. (1944), *The Gold Coast and the Slum*, Chicago Univ. Soc. Series.

ZWEIG, F., *The British Worker*, Penguin Books.

Chapter 2 A public language: some sociological implications of a linguistic form

In the previous paper an attempt was made to show a relationship between two forms of linguistic expression and the way relationships to objects were established. It was argued that one form of language-use, called a *public language*, facilitated thinking of a descriptive order and sensitivity to a particular form of social interaction. In the earlier paper a *public* language was discussed with reference to its use by the unskilled and semi-skilled strata, but approximations to a public language may well be spoken in such widely separated groups as criminal sub-cultures, rural groups, armed forces and adolescent groups in particular situations. Characteristics of a *public* language are:[1]

(1) Short, grammatically simple, often unfinished sentences, a poor syntactical construction with a verbal form stressing the active mood.

(2) Simple and repetitive use of conjunctions (so, then, and, because).

(3) Frequent use of short commands and questions.

(4) Rigid and limited use of adjectives and adverbs.

(5) Infrequent use of impersonal pronouns as subjects (one, it).

(6) Statements formulated as implicit questions which set up a sympathetic circularity, e.g. 'Just fancy?' 'It's only natural, isn't it?' 'I wouldn't have believed it'.

(7) A statement of fact is often used as both a reason and a conclusion, or more accurately, the reason and conclusion are confounded to produce a categoric statement, e.g. 'Do as I tell you' 'Hold on tight' 'You're not going out' 'Lay off that'.

(8) Individual selection from a group of idiomatic phrases will frequently be found.

(9) Symbolism is of a low order of generality.

42

(10) The individual qualification is implicit in the sentence structure, therefore it is a language of implicit meaning. *It is believed that this fact determines the form of the language.*

These characteristics interact cumulatively and developmentally reinforce each other, and so the effect of any one depends on the presence of the others. The use of a public language is most probably a function of a particular social structure, although psychological and physiological factors will in any given case modify the usage. This language-use is not necessarily the result of a limited vocabulary but arises out of a sensitivity to a way of organizing and responding to experience. Thus two children of four, one of whom comes from an unskilled or semi-skilled home and the other from a middle-class home, might share a similar vocabulary, but the way they relate the words they know will show differences.[2] Further, an individual may have at his disposal two linguistic usages, a *public* language and a *formal*[3] language,[4] or he may be limited to one, a *public* language, depending upon his social group.[5]

Language is considered one of the most important means of initiating, synthesizing, and *reinforcing* ways of thinking, feeling and behaviour which are functionally related to the social group. It does not, of itself, prevent the expression of specific ideas or confine the individual to a given level of conceptualization, but certain ideas and generalizations are facilitated rather than others. That is the language-use facilitates development in a particular direction rather than inhibiting all other possible directions. A *public language* does not imply a common vocabulary. The vocabulary of the Elephant and Castle is different from the Angel, Islington; is different from the Gorbals; and is different from Tiger Bay. *These forms of communication are often finely differentiated with respect to the objects upon which significance is placed.* However, I am concerned with the form or mode of language usage rather than with differences of vocabulary. The term *public language* refers to a common linguistic mode which various forms of communication, dialects, etc., share. I shall examine the behavioural implications of individuals who are *limited* to a *public* language.

The first four characteristics will be considered. The short, grammatically simple, syntactically poor sentence which is the typical unit of a public language does not facilitate the communication of ideas and relationships which require a precise formulation.[6] The crude, simple verbal structure around which the sentence is built points to a possible difficulty inherent in the language-use in the expressing of processes. There may be two important implications of this handicap. An approximate verb of a lower logical order may be used to characterize a given process, whilst the verbal construction may fix the process in an inappropriate time as the result of the insensitivity to tense.[7] This form of language-use is continuously reinforced from the very beginnings of speech, and as the individual learns no other possibility, subjectively, there is little or no experience of inadequate characterization. In fact when a more appropriate formulation is pointed out to the user of a *public* language the latter may insist that this is precisely *what he meant*. In a sense this is true, for what the individual wished to characterize, he did. The reformulation represents a second order characterization (that of a *formal* language), which is alien to the original speaker who will attempt to reduce the second order to the first. When this cannot be done the second order will be considered unnecessary, irrelevant, perhaps silly or the hearer will be bewildered. It may be that the percentage of nouns to verbs is higher in the *public* language than in a *formal* language, quite apart from the fact that a *public* language has a very limiting vocabulary.[8] If this is so, then a *public* language tends to emphasize *things* rather than *processes*.

Because of a simple sentence construction, and the fact that a *public* language does not permit the use of conjunctions which serve as important logical distributors of meaning and sequence, a *public* language will be one in which logical modification and stress can be only crudely rendered linguistically. This necessarily affects the length and type of the completed thought.[9] Of equal importance, the reliance on a small group of conjunctions (and, so, then, because) often means that a wrong conjunction is used or an approximate term is constantly substituted for a more exact logical distinction. The approximate term will then become the equivalent of the appropriate logical distinction. As there is a limited and rigid use of adjectives and adverbs, individual qualifications of objects (nouns) and individual modifications of processes (adverbs) will be severely reduced. Because the choice is restricted, the adjectives and adverbs function as *social counters* through which the individual qualifications will be made. This drastically reduces the verbal elaboration of the qualification which is given meaning by *expressive* symbolism.[10]

The fifth characteristic indicated that there would be infrequent use of impersonal pronouns as subjects of sentences. I am thinking here of the pronoun 'one'. The use of the pronoun 'one' as subject implies the objectification of the experience which is verbalized. The subject is made general and so freed from the confines of a personal experience. 'One' also indicates an attitude to the relationships which confront the individual. In a special sense it involves a reaching beyond the immediate experience, a transcending of the personal, and brings the individual into a particular relationship with objects and persons. Impersonality becomes an important aspect of the possibilities flowing from the language. However with a *public* language it is much more probable that the pronouns 'we' or 'you' will serve an apparently similar function to 'one'. They are in fact not similar, nor are they a simple substitution; for 'we' or 'you' refer to the local experience, the local social relationships, the immediate normative arrangements, and are bounded by the personal. The social and logical frames of reference are different, being insular and restricted. The possibilities inherent in 'one' are absent; possibilities which are of both social and logical importance.

The sixth characteristic of a *public* language refers to the frequency with which a statement of fact is used both as a reason and a conclusion; more accurately, the reason is confounded with the conclusion to produce a categoric statement.[11] Obviously this form of statement will appear in the context of many different forms of language-use but it will often be associated with statements where the reason and the conclusion are clearly demarcated. Here the categoric statement will come at a different point in a behavioural sequence, as it does if the categoric statement is part of *formal* language. However in a *public* language, where this confounding feature frequently occurs, the authority or legitimacy for the statement will reside in the form of the social relationship which is non-verbally present (e.g. by a parent to a child; the lower ranks of a chain of command in an army hierarchy; by a leader to a gang member), rather than in reasoned principles. The categoric statement is used in order to bring about the immediate termination of behaviour or the immediate initiating of new behaviour. When this form of communication takes place between parent and child the reasons for the required change of behaviour are rarely or only briefly given, and so a possible range of behaviour and, more importantly, learning will not occur. Equally as important as the cognitive implications are the social implications. For if this categoric statement is to be challenged, as the reason *is* the authority conferred upon the person, the challenge immediately gives rise to another typical construction: 'Because I tell you' 'Because I'm your father'. The challenger immediately attacks the authority or legitimacy which is an attribute of the form of the relationship and this brings the social relationship into one of an affective type. However, if a *formal* language is used, reasons are separated from conclusions. The reasons can be challenged as inadequate or inappropriate which may initiate a second set of reasons or a development of the original set. With a *formal* language the relationship to authority is mediated by a rationality and the final resort to the categoric statement will come at a different point in the behavioural sequence and possibly in a different situation, depending on the implications of the reasons given to support the conclusion. The frequency of, and dependency upon, the categoric statement in a *public* language reinforces the personal at the expense of the logical, limits the range of behaviour and learning, and conditions types of reaction and sensitivity towards authority.[12]

The seventh characteristic referred to statements which set up a sympathetic circularity, which may be initiated in several ways, but the dialogue always takes the form of a repetition of a thought by the conversants which maximizes the affective element of the relationship and at the same time restricts the ambit and the order of the discussion.[13] Often the circularity is initiated by some strange or alien fact or something which is peculiar to the local group. It may have been provoked by an experience which threatens or consolidates the social principles of the group's arrangements. Again there are two important logical and social implications. The circularity discourages further analysis of the event and processes which provoked it and so discourages the search for reasons other than those which can be formulated in a *public* language. It inhibits the attitude and the verbal implications of this attitude which underlie the 'going beyond what is given'. Curiosity is therefore limited in such a way as to enhance the solidarity of the social relationship.

Characteristics eight and nine follow naturally from the previous point. A *public* language is one which contains a large number of idiomatic, traditional phrases from which the individual chooses. Instead of an individual learning to create a language-use within which he can select to mediate his individual feeling, a *public* language-user tends to attach his feelings to social counters or tags which maximize the solidarity of the social relationship at the cost of the logical structure of the communication, and the specificity of the feeling. For traditional phrases, idioms, etc., tend to operate on a low causal level of generality in which descriptive, concrete, visual, tactile symbols are employed, aimed at maximizing the emotive rather than the logical impact.

Finally, the tenth and most important characteristic may be regarded as the determinant of the previous nine. In a *public* language the individual qualification creates a language of implicit meaning. The individual qualification[14] will be made primarily through expressive symbolism or through a selection from the possibilities inherent in a *public* language, which is tantamount to saying that it rarely occurs at all via the language; for the *public* language is primarily a means of making *social* not *individual* qualifications. If some of the characteristics are examined—short, grammatically simple, syntactically poor sentence construction;

inappropriate verbal forms; simple and repetitive use of conjunctions; rigid and limited use of adjectives and adverbs; selection from a group of traditional phrases—the very means of communication do not permit, and even discourage, individually differentiated cognitive and affective responses. *This is not to say that speakers of this language interact in a completely uniform manner, for the potential of a* public *language allows a vast range of possibilities,* but it provides a language-use which discourages the speaker from verbalizing his discrete relationships with the environment. The individual qualification is realized through a means which offers an immediacy of communication; that is, by expressive symbolism, together with a linguistic form which orients the speaker to a relatively low causal order, to descriptive concepts rather than analytic ones. The result of this mediating process orients the speaker to a distinct relationship with objects in the environment and so to a different *order* of learning from that which accompanies a *formal* language. With a *formal* language meaning is logically explicit and finely differentiated, whilst with a *public* language meaning is implicit and crudely differentiated. By the term 'differentiated' reference is made not simply to the range of objects which are elaborated or significant but to the logical order of the elaboration or significance. That is, to the matrix of relationships which arouse and condition responses.

In fact when an individual learns a *public* language he *learns* to perceive the possibilities symbolized by language in a distinctive way. Language is perceived *not* as a set of possibilities which can be fashioned subtly and sensitively to facilitate the development of a unique, individual experience. Language is *not* a means to verbalize relatively precisely the experience of separateness and difference. Rather, with a *public* language the individual from an early age interacts with a linguistic form which maximizes the means of producing social rather than individual symbols, and the vehicle of communication powerfully reinforces the initial socially induced preference for this aspect of language-use. It is language-use which encourages an immediacy of interaction, a preference for the descriptive rather than the analytic, a linguistic form such that what is not said is equally and often more important than what is said.[15] A critical difference between the two speech forms is that whereas in a *formal* language subjective intent may be verbally elaborated and made explicit, this process is not facilitated in a *public* language.

As the structure of a public language reinforces a strong inclusive relationship, the individual will exhibit through a range of activities a powerful sense of allegiance and loyalty to the group, its forms and its aspirations, at the cost of exclusion and perhaps conflict with other social groups which possess a different linguistic form which symbolizes *their* social arrangements. The structure of a *public* language inhibits the verbal expression of those experiences of difference which would isolate the individual from his group and channels cognitive and affective states which might be a potential threat. For example, curiosity is limited by the low level of conceptualization which is fostered by this form of language-use; the concern with the immediate prevents the development of a reflective experience; and a resistance to change or inherent conservatism is partly a function of a disinterest in processes and a concern with things. Conservatism is also related to the way authority itself is justified or legitimized, for with a public language the authority will inhere in the form of the relationship rather than in reasoned principles. Another important protective function of the *public* language is that other forms of language-use (e.g. *formal* language) will not be directly comprehensible but will be mediated through the *public* language. In other words, a *formal* language will be translated into the *public* language and thus an alternative orientation, which would lead the individual beyond the confines, affective and cognitive, of the *public* language, is neutralized. Where a translation cannot be made at all, there is no communication and thus absolute protection.

A *public* language, because the individual qualification is implicit in the sentence structure, because it is primarily a means for making social qualifications, tends to be what can be called a 'tough' language and will elicit behaviour in accordance with this, both verbally through the language structure and physically through expressive movement and style. Tender feelings which are personal and highly individual will not only be difficult to express in this linguistic form, but it is likely that the objects which arouse tender feelings will be given tough terms—particularly those referring to girl-friends, love, death and disappointments. The experience of tender feelings, as with any situation which forces the need to produce individual qualifications, may produce feelings of acute embarrassment, discomfort, a desire to leave the field and denial or hostility towards the object which aroused the tender feelings. To speakers of a *public* language, tender feelings are a potential threat, for in this experience is also the experience of isolation—social isolation. It is suggested that there are two reasons which underlie the inhibition of the individual qualifications. Firstly, as this has never been encouraged or facilitated by the language-use, any situation which requires it will be one in which the individual's previous learning is inappropriate and inadequate; secondly, a psychological correlate of the producing of an individual qualification is isolation from the group.

Another psychological correlate of this linguistic form is that it discourages the experience of guilt and shame in relation to particular situations. This is not to say that all feelings of guilt are minimized, but they are minimal in relation to certain social acts. Consider these social terms in one type of *public* language for a situation where the individual deliberately avoids an allotted task or duty: 'skive', 'scrounge', 'dodge the column', 'swing the lead', etc. These terms by their very nature are social counters which the individual can attach to a particular class of act. They do not characterize precisely the nature of the act nor the individual's specific relation to it, so that an impersonal sanction is given to the behaviour which the terms designate. The terms take the form of a type of euphemism which disguises or blurs the implications of the intention. Secondly, certain sociological and psychological associations which would follow from the appropriate descriptions of the act—avoiding work deliberately—are neutralized. Perhaps one of the most important is that experiences of guilt are minimized. This is *not* to say that the individual will not be aware that the act is wrong nor that punishment is unjust, but that feelings of guilt are divorced from the notion of wrongness. This would seem to make more likely the recurrence of the behaviour and to create a particular attitude to the punishment. It is not for one moment suggested that if precise terms were used to designate the behaviour that they would, in themselves, inhibit the intended action, but that the action would be accompanied by psychological states which might not be present if the social counters were used. These psychological states may be of great importance in modifying the form and content of the punishment.[16]

Perhaps another example might indicate this process more clearly. The social counter 'lark', e.g. 'I only did it for a lark', covers a dimension of behaviour from a harmless prank to a major delinquency. The term defines the situation as one of play so that if there are any unfortunate consequences these will be regarded as *unintended*, accidental developments, so freeing the doer from individual responsibility. Experiences of guilt are thus minimized, which makes possible a range of activity and, of course, learning attaches to the activity and so conditions future behaviour. Again, the activity made possible by the sanction 'lark' may be evaluated as wrong, yet guilt feelings will be divorced from the evaluation and so the sense of individual responsibility will be neutralized. Probably in *all* forms of language-use, a counterpart to the terms used here as examples will be found as rationalizations for behaviour, but where the speaker is limited to a *public* language those terms are of greatest significance, for they help to reinforce the development of a particular affective and cognitive orientation. It is suggested that speakers limited to a *public* language have more terms which serve to minimize guilt and that these terms are generalized to include a greater range of activities than have speakers of a *formal* language.

It may be helpful to summarize at this point some of the implications of a *public* language. The implications are logical, social and psychological. It is suggested that a correlate of this linguistic form is a low level of conceptualization—an orientation to a low order of causality, a disinterest in processes, a preference to be aroused by and respond to that which is immediately given rather than to the implications of a matrix of relationships, and that this, it is suggested, partly conditions the intensity and extent of curiosity, as well as the mode of establishing relationships. These logical considerations affect what is learned and how it is learned and so affect future learning.[17] A preference for a particular form of social relationship is engendered; a form where individual qualifications are non-verbally communicated, or mediated through the limited possibilities of a *public* language; a preference for inclusive social relationship and a great sensitivity to the demands of solidarity with the group which differs from the relationship to the group which is mediated through a formal language.[18] There will exist a socially induced conservatism and resistance to certain forms of change which contrast with an interest in novelty. There will be a tendency to accept and respond to an authority which inheres in the form of the social relationship rather than in reasoned or logical principles. It fosters a form of social relationship where meaning is implicit, where what is not said, when it is not said and, paradoxically, how it is not said, form strategic orientating cues. It is a form of social relationship which maximizes identifications with the aims and principles of a local group rather than with the complex differentiated aims of the major society. This correspondingly minimizes the expression of differences and individual distinctiveness in the sense of the previous discussion.

A *public* language is a linguistic form which discourages the verbalization of tender feeling and consequently the opportunities for learning inherent in the verbal expression of such feelings. Again it is important to add that this does not imply that tender feelings are not subjectively experienced but that the form and implications of their expression are modified. Conversely it is a linguistic form which will tend to elicit 'tough' responses either through vocabulary or through expressive style or both. Further, it is probable that 'tough' terms will be used to characterize situations or objects rather than the articulation of tender feelings in an individually discrete way. This in its turn modifies the individual's ready entertainment of such feelings. It is a linguistic form which will tend to minimize the experience of guilt in relation to particular classes of situations, so permitting a range of antisocial behaviour (and learning) by divorcing individual responsibility and guilt from the evaluative judgments of the behaviour involved. Finally, and most importantly, a situation which calls for an explicit individual qualification may well be one which engenders critical psychological distress for the speaker of a *public* language. A critical situation of this kind which will be examined later is one typically found in psychiatric treatment.

It is necessary to state at this point that the type of *public* language described and analysed here will rarely be found in the *pure* state. Even if such an 'ideal' language-use were to be spoken it would not be used in all situations within the local group. Modifications *within* the form would occur, most certainly, depending upon whether the situation is defined as social or personal. It is suggested that what is found empirically is an orientation to this form of language-use which is conditioned by socially induced preferences.

Finally, I should like to examine briefly some of the implications of this form of language-use for the psychiatric treatment of those patients who are limited to a *public* language. It is possible that with the development and expansion of the National Health Service and the growing understanding of the psychological determinants of behavioural disorders (to name but two reasons), more individuals who are confined to a *public* language will be treated.

The form of psychiatric treatment relevant here is where the therapy is inherent in a process of communication rather than by the use of physical medicine, e.g. drugs, ECT, insulin and conditioning, etc., and where the patient is neurotic rather than psychotic. It is clear that psychiatrist and patient would be drawn from two distinct cultures and would use two distinct linguistic forms. It is also clear that the speaker of a *public* language defines the doctor in a specific way and also has particular expectations of the forms of treatment. This analysis is directed not to the general cultural differences, but to the rather more specific and limited problems of what is said, and what has to be said, in order that psychotherapy may be accomplished.[19] To begin with the patient is placed in a situation where treatment depends essentially on the extent to which the patient can verbalize, or be brought to verbalize by various techniques, his particular, discrete, personal relationships with the environment and eventually to understand and emotionally accept the implications of the pattern they form. For this makes possible the transformation of affective processes which is the aim of the treatment. This is necessarily a simplified description of the individual psycho-therapeutic situation.

However, this involves for the patient a mode of communication and orientation which he has not only never *learnt* but which has been positively discouraged by his previous learning processes. It is important to realize that reference is *not* made here to the difficulty which patients have about communicating certain personal experiences concerned with sex, etc., but to the fact that the patient is required to make individual qualifications of his own experience and that this is alien to him. For with a *public* language, feelings are mediated through a form which maximizes the possibility of a social rather than individual qualification—to the constructing of social rather than individual symbols. This is not to say that the individual does not possess individual symbols, of course he does, but the form of their expression is limited by the language he uses. Individual differentiation proceeds within the limits of the possibilities set by a public language. To the patient the situation is one of perplexity and bewilderment—he is under pressure to give a response he has never learnt to make. This is entirely different from the situation in which a patient speaking a *formal* language is initially confronted with the psycho-therapeutic situation or where specific problems generated by psychological defences cause temporary blockages. The behaviour of a person speaking a *public* language is, sociologically speaking, normative.

The psycho-therapeutic relationship may also trigger off all the protective devices inherent in a *public* language. Irrespective of the apparent simplicity of the psychiatrist's vocabulary, complex relationships are symbolized to which the patient is neither oriented nor sensitive. It is probable that the patient will translate the psychiatrist's language (where possible) into a *public* language and this mediating process will act to preserve the psychological *status quo* of the patient. For, as was pointed out earlier, the translation involves neutralizing the alternative orientation implicit in the psychiatrist's language. The process of therapy is directed to the establishing of new relationships, often complex ones, and to the seeking of sophisticated connections between events. The user of a *public* language tends to be disinterested in processes and also incurious, as a result of his preference for descriptive concepts of a low order of causality. This may make the whole technique of therapy bewildering, perplexing and seemingly irrelevant to the solution of the patient's particular behavioural problem. Involved in the psycho-therapeutic situation is the need for the verbalization of what have been termed 'tender feelings' with their behavioural implications. The discussion of these feelings at 'surface' level of interpretation may trigger off a powerful response which is seemingly disproportionate to the intended reaction. There are, it is believed, important psycho-therapeutic implications, related to the form of the organization and expression of tender feelings by a speaker of a *public* language.

A patient limited to this linguistic form will be under a different kind of stress to a patient using a *formal* language, because the latter is able to cope better with a situation where the social relationship is mediated through verbally explicit individual qualifications.The customary form of social relationship for a patient speaking a *public* language is explicitly structured; the authority inheres in a non-verbal element and is an attribute of the form of the relationship. Cognitive and affective immediacy tend to be conditions for meaningful arousal and response. The psycho-therapeutic relationship is almost the complete antithesis of this, in that it is apparently non-directed, it has few orientating cues, the authority is ambiguous and relies essentially on a verbal mode which gives little explicit direction to the here-and-now behaviour. It maximizes the pressure on the patient to structure and restructure his experience with the aid of individual verbal symbols. This suggests that the therapy situation would cause great stress for a *public* language patient because of the high level of anxiety generated by the form of the social relationship. It might not be too much to say that the situation itself is felt as persecutory.

Therapy with this class of patient is therefore likely to prove unrewarding for both patient and psychiatrist. The likelihood of the patient breaking off treatment early in therapy seems high.[20] It may seem that the patient is not 'co-operating' or that he is bringing 'insufficient' material forward. On the contrary, according to the view presented here there is an abundance of material which arises from the sociologically normative elements of the therapeutic relationship. Sensitivity to the normative elements which are symbolized by the form of communication may make possible the conditions for the beginning of a successful therapeutic relationship.

I should like to conclude this paper with some general remarks about the method of analysis used. Very clear to any student of the sociology of language is the debt that is owed to Edward Sapir and his followers who pointed the way to the scientific study of the social institution of language. It is the view held here that language is one of the most important intervening variables between the individual and behaviour. Certainly the implications of a given form of language-use are continuously reinforced from the beginning of speech, perhaps even before. The child understands before it can speak. It would seem that a linguistic form orients the individual in one direction rather than another and once this direction is given it is progressively reinforced. The implications of the direction are manifold and subtly modify cognitive, affective and social experiences. Put in another way, the linguistic form is a powerful conditioner of what is learnt and how it is learnt, and so influences future learning. In this paper the behaviour which is facilitated by a *public* language has been analysed. It may seem that there is something inherently circular in the method. One examines the language-use and infers social and psychological behaviour, but the latter originally determines the former—*for the semantic function of a language* is *the social structure*. What one is doing is simply looking at the social structure through a particular institution, the institution of language, and the perspective may be very rewarding. For it enables the observer to catch a glimpse of the unity of behaviour which exists within the manifold activities. It is not thought that any 'new' facts have been found; however, it is hoped that possible relationships have been formed. Perhaps the most important aspect of the approach is that it may throw some light on how the social structure becomes part of individual experience and inasmuch as this is done, it illuminates the relationships between sociology and psychology.

Finally, one major implication of the view held here, which is ethical and political rather than sociological, is that the changing of a form of language-use, in this case a *public* language, involves something more than might be thought at first sight. A *public* language contains its own aesthetic, a simplicity and directness of expression, emotionally virile, pithy and powerful and a metaphoric range of considerable force and appropriateness. Some examples taken from the schools of this country have a beauty which many writers might well envy. It is a language which symbolizes a tradition and a form of social relationship in which the individual is treated as an end, not as a means to a further end. To simply substitute a *formal* language (which is not necessarily a logical, impersonal, emotionally eviscerated language) is to cut off the individual from his traditional relationships and perhaps alienate him from them. This is the old polarity of *Gemeinschaft* and *Gesellschaft* in another guise. The problem would seem to be to preserve *public* language usage but also to create for the individual the possibility of utilizing a *formal* language. And this is no easy task for a society which distributes respect and significance according to occupational achievement. It would seem that a change in this mode of language-use involves the whole personality of the individual, the very character of his social relationships, his points of reference, emotional and logical, and his conception of himself.

Notes

1 Some of these characteristics will occur at certain times in any form of language-use, but the term *public* language is reserved for

a form of communication in which *all* the characteristics are found. It is possible to speak of approximations to a *public* language to the extent that other characteristics do not occur. See characteristics of a *formal* language below.

2 Whilst it is obvious that certain aspects of children's speech development must necessarily hold, irrespective of the social group, the structuring of the language used and responded to is of critical importance whatever the age of the child. The following conversation took place in a middle-class nursery: Two little girls of four were arguing about their respective heights, e.g., 'I'm bigger than *you*' 'No, I'm bigger than *you*', when the dialogue suddenly took this turn:

S: Well, my sister's seven and a half!
K: Well, she's not you!
S: No, everyone's theirselves.

See Templin, Mildred, C. (1957). In a sample of 480 children between three and eight years old, she found significant differences between upper socio-economic and lower socio-economic groups scattered throughout the entire age range. The greatest number of significant differences seem to be concentrated in the articulation of vowels, medial and final consonants, the length of remarks verbalized, the degree of complexity of verbalization and in the vocabulary of recognition at the older ages.

3 Some characteristics of a formal language are:

(1) Accurate grammatical order and syntax regulate what is said.
(2) Logical modifications and stress are mediated through a grammatically complex sentence construction, especially through the use of a range of conjunctions and relative clauses.
(3) Frequent use of prepositions which indicate logical relationships as well as prepositions which indicate temporal and spatial contiguity.
(4) Frequent use of impersonal pronouns (it, one).
(5) A discriminative selection from a range of adjectives and adverbs.
(6) Individual qualification is verbally mediated through the structure and relationships within and between sentences. That is, it is explicit.
(7) Expressive symbolism conditioned by this linguistic form distributes affectual support rather than logical meaning to what is said.
(8) A language use which points to the possibilities inherent in a complex conceptual hierarchy for the organizing of experience.

These characteristics must be considered to give a *direction* to the organization of thinking and feeling rather than to the *establishing* of complex modes of relationships. The characteristics are relative to those of a *public* language.

4 The distinction between *public* and *formal* language-use is not simply a question of an oral and written language. Although a *formal* language will be modified by oral use and situation, the modification will be, it is suggested, within the usage. An oral *formal* language will not be a *public* language. Neither will a written *public* language approximate to *formal* language usage, oral or written. I am indebted to W. H. N. Hotopf for raising this point.

5 The largest of such groups is composed of individuals who come from unskilled and semi-skilled social strata. See Hoggart, R. (1957).

6 See Schatzman, L. and Strauss, A. (1955). The authors describe the difficulty that poor rural respondents had in giving a sequential account of an Arkansas tornado. Examples of this difficulty are the following, given by messenger boys (17 years old) who attend a day-release college: 'They have a novel idea where a gadget breaks (brakes) who on the road safety depends, then you press a button and you are looking at yourself in a mirror,' 'The aim of the motor show is to bring to the public and let them sit in where as they only saw them in the show rooms of car dealers before' 'Only a few men there at one time owing to shift work and mainly waiting for the various brews' 'A new design seen at the motor show was one big side window each side of the car instead of being broken up into two' 'These cars have four doors but the front seat is in two pieces' 'The gas also is for taking a certain place' 'She ended with sea-cadets for training them about the sea'. See also Bossard, J. H. S. (1945); Khater, R. M. (1955).

7 This process of substitution also applies to nouns. A working-class mother's reply to her child on being asked the name of a particular building was, 'It's a police station.' The building was Scotland Yard. For ingenious experiments aimed at testing the relationships between linguistic codification, cognition and recognition, see Lenneberg, E. H. (1953); Brown, R. W. and Lenneberg, E. H. (1954); Brown, R. W. (1957a); Brown, R. W. (1957b); Brown, R. W. and Lenneberg, E. H. (1958), and Carroll, J. B. and Casagrande, J. B. (1958).

8 See McCarthy, D. (1930). The author found that children of the working classes used a greater percentage of nouns than the middle classes, also fewer compound or complex sentences as well as fewer interrogatives, but more exclamations. For a general review of the literature, see McCarthy, D. (1954).

9 See the report (1958) of an address by Mr A. M. Kean, Deputy Director of the Institute of Education, Leeds University, which opened the Conference on the 'Writing of English' in Leeds. Of secondary modern pupils: 'The emission of a complete sentence in it [the written work] may be unusual' 'The pupil must be habituated

to the carrying of a sequence of ideas in words'. The whole report
is pertinent to the discussion.

10 Mr Kean further said that the secondary modern pupil's language
had a small vocabulary, particularly in adjectives. Words like 'nice',
etc., covered almost every reaction. See the role of expressive
symbolism—Miller, D. and Swanson, G. (1956, 1959).

11 Examples of this statement are: Mother to child on bus: 'Hold on
tight.' Child: 'Why?' Mother: 'Hold on *tight*!' Child: 'Why?'
Mother: 'I told you to hold on tight, didn't I?'
    Father to son: 'You're not going out.' Son: 'Why?' Father:
'You're always going out.' Son: 'Why can't I go?' Father: 'I told
you, you're not going out. Now shut up!'

12 See Sarason, S. B. and Gladwin, T. (1958): 'Of great importance
. . . what happens when a child asks "Why?" Is he rewarded or
punished, answered or not answered, in terms of *tradition* or *logic*,
or is he told he is too young, or is he *encouraged* or *discouraged*
to think about it himself?' (my italics). Of course, this categoric
statement will appear at times in any language-use, but in a *public*
language it is not only used more frequently, it also becomes a
part of a language pattern which narrows the range of stimuli to
which the child learns to respond. In a *formal* language, the
categoric statement is simply an isolated statement with a specific
and limited effect. The source of authority, if a *formal* language
is being used, lies both in the status of the speaker *and* in the
reasons given to support conclusions, whilst with a *public* language
the reasons play a much smaller role in the establishment of
authority. This, it is believed, is of great importance for the
implications of early learning. See also Kohn, M. L. (1959 a and b).

13 I am unable to give an example of this usage because it would take
too much space and, of more importance, it is doubtful whether
the example would be more than a parody. This raises the problem
of suitable research techniques. Questionnaire techniques and testing would be of little use, though the methods used by social
anthropologists would be helpful. I have used the term 'sympathetic
circularity' because in such a dialogue the amount of new information made available by the conversants is limited, yet the dialogue
may be sustained for some time by a repetition of the previous
remark, slightly modified, which triggers off another similar
comment. Often many aphorisms are exchanged. It is a sympathetic
circularity because one of the main satisfactions seems to be derived
from the emotional identification of the two speakers in relation to
the topic discussed.

14 The term 'individual qualification' refers to the way an individual
comments or reflects upon, and verbally organizes his responses to,
the environment. In a *public* language, the qualification is limited
to a global rather than a differentiated response. The verbal statement seems to arise out of an abstracting process without a prior

differentiation which leads to a condensation of experience to a word or to the use of a portmanteau term or phrase which blurs the nature of the experience (I am grateful to Professor M. Ginsberg for clarification of this point). The nature of the qualification tends to limit the verbal elaboration of subjective intent. It refers to concrete feeling experiences that have little concern with processes and generalizations except of a low causal order. Meanings are strung together like beads on a frame rather than following a logical sequence.

15 Of course, what is not said plays a great part in most communications. However, if a *formal* language were to be used, what is not said could in many cases be said. With a *public* language this is not so, for verbal inarticulateness results from the language-use, though a strongly uniting culture creates an affective sympathy which fills the gaps. The latter becomes significant when a *formal* language speaker talks to a person limited to a *public* language, and vice versa.

16 There is a tendency for this to be recognized. Punishment of a *public* language user in a school will tend to be frequently corporal, either through threats or direct action, because it is difficult to manipulate a sense of guilt or shame in the boy, or a sense of personal involvement in the act. A mechanical relationship is set up between wrong doing and punishment. Caning exists in public schools where a *formal* language is spoken; however, other methods are also used to modify behaviour. With a *formal* language user, punishment can involve a temporary rejection, or a talking-through of the misdemeanour with an aim to maximize the experience of guilt, shame, responsibility and thus personal involvement. The attempt to interchange the means of social control may lead at first to many difficulties. This is not to be taken to mean that corporal punishment is necessarily an effective means of social control. It is often used as a substitute for the real difficulty of making an interpersonal relationship, and when so used is rarely effective in the long run.

17 A linguistic environment limited to a *public* language is likely to produce (from a formal educational point of view) deleterious effects, both cognitive and affective, which are difficult but not, it is believed, impossible to modify. IQ tests may often yield a correct educational or occupational prediction for members of the unskilled or semi-skilled social strata, not solely because of the presence of some general innate factor, but because of the efficiency of early learning, specifically the learning of forms of language-use in special environments. See the work of Nisbet, J. D. (1953); Scott, E. M. and Nisbet, J. D. (1955); Dawe, H. C. (1942); Worbois, G. M. (1942); Kellmer Pringle, M. L. and Bossio, V. (1958); Kellmer Pringle, M. L. and Tanner, M. (1958); Luria, A. R. and Yudovitch, F. I. (1959); Vygotsky, L. S. (1939), and Bernstein, B. (1959).

18 Support for the social psychological inferences in this and the next paragraph is to be found in Auld, F. (jnr) (1952); Raissman, F. and Miller, S. M. (1958), and in Miller, D. and Swanson, G. (1959).

19 Supportive evidence for this section is to be found in Hollingshead, A. B. and Redlich, F. C. (1958), Part V; also in Nash, E. H. (1957) (although here it was found that patients tended to reject group therapy more frequently than individual therapy, and that this was related to social class and general 'social ineffectiveness'. However, the authors stated that the treatment was carried out under adverse conditions as a result of the research requirements.)

20 It may well be that an additional complicating factor is the result of the patient's perception of mental illness, which is, of course, one of Hollingshead and Redlich's points. The *public* language speaker probably has a deficient perception; consequently, when he is finally treated, he is in fact sicker and therefore more difficult to treat.

References

AULD, F. (jnr) (1952), 'Influences of social class on personality responses', *Psychol. Bull.* 49.

BERNSTEIN, B. (1959), 'Some subcultural determinants of learning: with special reference to language', *Kölner Zeitshrift für Soziologie und Sozialpsychologie* (monograph issue).

BOSSARD, J. H. S. (1945), 'Family modes of expression', *Am. Soc. Rev.* 10.

BROWN, R. W. (1957a), Appendix on Language in *A study of Thinking* J. C. Bruner (eds.) *et. al.*, New York: Wiley.

BROWN, R. W. (1957b), 'Linguistic determinism and parts of speech', *J. Ab. and Soc. Psychol.* 55.

BROWN, R. W. and LENNEBERG, E. H. (1954), 'A study in language and cognition', *J. Ab. and Soc. Psychol.* 49.

BROWN, R. W. and LENNEBERG, E. H. (1958), 'Studies in linguistic relativity', in *Readings in Social Psychology* (eds) Maccoby, E. E. *et al.*, New York: Henry Holt.

CARROLL, J. B. and CASAGRANDE, J. B. (1958), 'Language and classification in behaviour', in *Readings in Social Psychology* (eds) Maccoby, E. E. *et al.*, New York: Henry Holt.

DAWE, H. C. (1942), 'A study of the effects of an educational programme upon language development and related mental function in young children', *J. Exp. Educ.* 11.

HOGGART, R. (1957), *The Uses of Literacy*, Chatto & Windus.

HOLLINGSHEAD, A. B. and REDLICH, F. C. (1958), *Social Class and Mental Illness*, New York: Wiley.

KEAN, A. M. (1958), Report of Opening Address to the Conference on 'Writing of English' (Leeds), *Times Educational Supplement*, 28 November.

KELLMER PRINGLE, M. L. and BOSSIO, V. (1958), 'A study of deprived children: Part II. Language development and reading attainment', *Vita Humana* 1.

KELLMER PRINGLE, M. L. and TANNER, M. (1958), 'The effects of early deprivation on speech development', *Language and Speech* 1.

KHATER, R. M. (1955), 'The influence of social class on the language patterns of kindergarten children', Unpub. Ph.D. Thesis, University of Chicago, reported in De Boer, J. H., 'Oral and written language', *Rev. Ed. Res.* 25.

KOHN, M. L. (1959a), 'Social class and the exercise of parental authority', *Am. Soc. Rev.* 24.

KOHN, M. L. (1959b), 'Social class and parental values', *Am. J. Soc.* 64.

LENNEBERG, E. H. (1953), 'Cognition in ethnolinguistics', *Language* 29.

LURIA, A. R. and YUDOVITCH, F. I. (1959), *Speech and the Development of Mental Processes in the Child*, Staples Press.

MCCARTHY, D. (1930), *The Language Development of the Pre-school Child*, Inst. of Child Welfare Monograph Series No. 4, University of Minnesota Press.

MCCARTHY, D. (1954), 'Language development in children', in *Manual of Child Psychology*, (ed.) Carmichael, L., New York: Wiley.

MILLER, D. and SWANSON, G. (1959), *Inner Conflict and Defense*, New York: Henry Holt.

NASH, E. H. *et al.* (1957), 'Some factors related to patients remaining in group therapy', *Int. J. Group Therapy* 7, 264-74.

NISBET, J. D. (1953), *Family Environment*, Occasional Papers on Eugenics No. 8, Cassell.

RAISSMAN, F. and MILLER, S. M. (1958), 'Social class and projective tests', *J. Projective Techniques.* 28.

SARASON, S. B. and GLADWIN, T. (1958), 'Psychological and cultural problems in mental subnormality: A review of research', *Genetic Psychol. Monogr.* 57.

SCHATZMAN, L. and STRAUSS, A. (1955), 'Social class and modes of communication', *Am. J. Soc.* 60.

SCOTT, E. M. and NISBET, J. D. (1955), 'Intelligence and family size in an adult sample', *Eugenics Review.* 46.

TEMPLIN, MILDRED, C. (1957), *Certain Language Skills in Young Children*, Inst. of Child Welfare, Monograph Series No. 26, Univ. of Minnesota Press; O.U.P.

VYGOTSKY, L. S. (1939), 'Thought and speech', *Psychiatry.* 2.

WORBOIS, G. M. (1942), 'Language development of children in two rural environments', *Child. Dev.* 13.

Chapter 3   Language and social class

It has been suggested in earlier papers that associated with the organization of particular social groups are distinct forms of spoken language. Linguistic differences, other than dialect, occur in the normal social environment and status groups may be distinguished by their forms of speech. This difference is most marked where the gap between the socio-economic levels is very great. There have been many studies of children aimed at measuring this difference. It is suggested that the measurable interstatus differences in language facility result from entirely different *modes* of speech found within the middle class and the lower working class. It is proposed that the two distinct forms of language-use arise because the organization of the two social strata is such that different emphases are placed on language potential. Once the emphasis or stress is placed, then the resulting forms of language-use progressively orient the speakers to distinct and different types of relationships to objects and persons, irrespective of the level of measured intelligence. The role intelligence plays is to enable the speaker to exploit more successfully the possibilities symbolized by the socially determined forms of language-use. There are exceptions to this linguistic determinism which arise under special limiting physiological and psychological conditions.

It is suggested that the typical, dominant speech mode of the middle class is one where speech becomes an object of special perceptual activity and a 'theoretical attitude' is developed towards the structural possibilities of sentence organization. This speech mode facilitates the verbal elaboration of subjective intent, sensitivity to the implications of separateness and difference, and points to the possibilities inherent in a complex conceptual hierarchy for the organization of experience. It is further suggested that this is not the case for members of the lower working class. The latter are *limited* to a form of language-use, which although allowing for a vast range of possibilities, provides a speech form which discourages the speaker from verbally elaborating subjective intent and progres-

61

sively orients the user to descriptive, rather than abstract, concepts.

A study was designed to show that the two speech modes are related to different status groups and, more importantly, to show that the orientation of the two linguistic structures is independent of non-verbal intelligence test scores. It was predicted for the working-class group that the language scores would be severely depressed in relation to the scores in the higher ranges of a non-verbal measure of intelligence.

The design of the study was as follows. Two extreme social groups were selected for linguistic comparison. One group consists of sixty-one subjects between fifteen and eighteen years of age, matched for previous education, general social background, occupation and sex, but whose homes are distributed between inner and outer London. These subjects are students at a day-release college where they attend one day a week to receive a general non-vocational education. They are all employed as messenger boys and none have received a grammar school education. This group will be referred to as working-class. The second group consists of forty-five subjects matched for age and sex with the first group, all pupils of one of the six major public schools. These boys represent a reasonable cross-section of the Upper School in respect of scholastic attainment and educational interests. This group will be referred to as public-school.

The two groups were given the Raven's Progressive Matrices test, 1938 (a non-verbal measure of intelligence), and the Mill Hill Vocabulary Scale Form I Senior. (These tests were selected so as to afford a comparison with 309 working-class subjects who had previously been given the same two tests.) From the two major groups, four sub-groups, each of five members, were originally selected, matched on the Matrices score (119 IQ points—126-plus IQ points). Eight members of the public-school sub-groups had scores within the measurable range of the Matrices test. A tape-recorded, non-directed discussion on the topic of 'The Abolition of the Death Penalty' was taken with each of the sub-groups. It is possible to make a comparative analysis of the distinct speech forms associated with the two major groups on subjects matched for high non-verbal intelligence. This analysis is in progress. The results of the two intelligence tests will be presented here.

The two histograms indicate the mean Matrices and Mill Hill IQ scores. The figure in each block refers to the number of scores within each range. It is quite clear that the relationship found between the mean IQ scores for the two tests on the previous working-class sample is confirmed by this result. Fifty-eight working-class subjects (Figure 1) have language scores which fall within the average

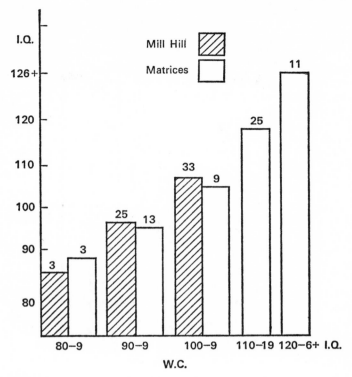

Figure 1

range of the vocabulary test. In relation to the higher ranges of the Matrices test the mean language scores are depressed. The Mill Hill mean scores are zero above the average range of the test. For the public-school group (Figure 2) the relationship between the means of both tests is different. At all ranges the mean scores on both tests are closely matched.

It was considered that this difference in the relationship between the two tests for the two social groups could be closely described by the drawing of regression lines. It should be emphasized that in order to characterize the differences between the two groups a linear regression analysis was employed as a simple descriptive device for the limited ranges involved. Raw scores were used to calculate the regression equations and the correlation coefficient because of the nature of the range of the tests. Figure 3 indicates the position of the regression lines of the tests for both groups. For both the public-

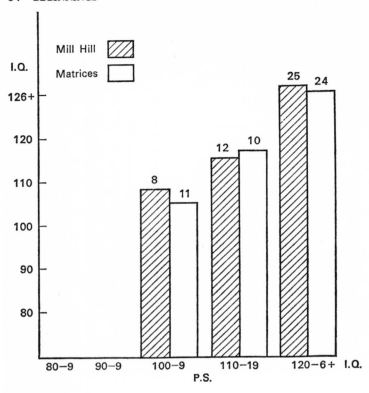

Figure 2

school and the working-class group the slope of the regression lines byx, $b'yx$ (the regression of the vocabulary upon the Matrices score) is similar. This is not the case for bxy, $b'xy$, which indicates the regression of the Matrices upon the language score for the two groups. The difference in the slopes of bxy and $b'xy$ indicates differences in the distribution of the language scores in the two groups. The distribution of the working-class language scores in relation to those of the public school is depressed at the higher ranges of the Matrices score. The regression equations for the public-school group are, $b'yx=0.96$, $b'xy=0.12$; whilst for the working-class group the equations are, $byx=0.3$, $bxy=0.46$.

The correlation coefficient between the Matrices and the Mill Hill for the public-school sample is 0.4, and for the working-class sample is 0.37. The size of the correlations must be seen in relation to the

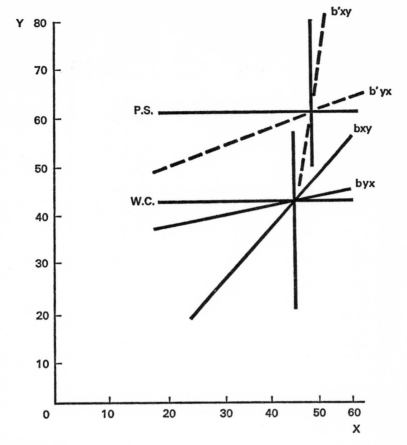

Figure 3

homogeneity of the two samples. Although the two correlations are closely matched, Figure 3 indicates that the conditions for the correlations are very different. It is of interest to compare the mean raw scores for the two tests obtained by both groups. The mean raw score for the total working-class group on the Matrices test is 47·36, whilst for the public school it is 51·4. However, the mean raw vocabulary score for the working-class group is 41·9; for the public-school group it is 60·2. There is a difference of 18·3 on the overall vocabulary mean and 4·04 on the Matrices mean. If one extrapolates these scores for a mean age of sixteen years, then these differences are 8–10 IQ points for the Matrices mean and 23–4 IQ points for the vocabulary means.

There can be no doubt that a different relationship exists between the non-verbal and verbal group measures of intelligence for the two social groups tested in this study. The language scores of the working-class group are depressed in relation to the score at the higher ranges of the Matrices and this relationship is *not* found in the public-school group. The difference between the overall vocabulary mean IQ scores for the two groups is over twice the size of the difference between the overall means of the Matrices IQ scores.

Many studies have reported discrepancies between group verbal and non-verbal measures of intelligence; however, equally as important is the fact that in the studies discussed here almost all members of the working-class sample are confined to the average range of the group verbal test. It may well be that the discrepancy arises *only* with a non-verbal test which is based upon operations of addition and subtraction within a setting where all possibilities are given. It is thought that where a non-verbal measure of intelligence utilizes other operations, such as the need to find a principle and then to deduce the next term in an incomplete series, this discrepancy may be reduced. This does not mean that the Matrices relative to other non-verbal measures is a poor test of 'g' (the evidence indicates quite the contrary), but the question is raised of the relationships between potential and *developed* intelligence.

The high score on the Matrices is not necessarily because the test is non-verbal, for sub-vocal activity may accompany the process of reaching a solution, but because the relational operations required are available to members of the working class, whereas the concepts and principles required for the upper ranges of verbal tests are not. In other words, a score on the Matrices may not indicate anything except the score; but a score on a reliable verbal test often serves as a guide to educational and occupational performance. This leads to one of two possibilities. Either the *mode* of expression of intelligence is a cultural function or the lower working class are genetically deficient in a factor which enables the exploitation of complex verbal relationships. The latter possibility seems improbable especially when one considers that the normal linguistic environment of the working class is one of relative deprivation. It is thought that the *mode* of expression of intelligence, in particular the general factor (g), may well be a matter of learning: in particular the early learning of speech forms, which create and reinforce in the user different dimensions of significance. The different vocabulary scores obtained by the two social groups may simply be one index, among many, which discriminates between two dominant modes of utilizing speech. One mode, associated with the middle class, points to the possibilities within a complex conceptual hierarchy for the organization of experience; the other, associated with the lower working class, progressively limits the type of stimuli to which the child learns to respond.

Acknowledgments

I should like to express my gratitude to the headmaster and second master of the public school, the principal of the day college, and to the London County Council for their courtesy and help in making this study possible. I am also indebted to Miss Elizabeth Brownstein, of the Tavistock Institute, for her assistance in the original testing. I should like to thank Dr R. Audley, Dept of Psychology, University College, London, for his advice in the statistical analysis. Finally a special debt is owed to B.C., without whose initial assistance the study could not have been carried out.

References

BERNSTEIN, B. (1958), 'Some sociological determinants of perception', *Br. J. Soc.* 9.

BERNSTEIN, B. (1959), 'A public language: some sociological implications of a linguistic form', *Br. J. Soc.* 10.

BERNSTEIN, B. (1960), 'Sozio-kulturelle Determinaten des Lernens: mit besonderer Berucksichtigung der Rolle der Sprache' in *Sociologie der Schule: Kölner seitschrift für Soziologie und Sozialpsychologie,* Sonderheft, 4.

WALTON, D. 'Reply to H. Gwynne Jones' comments on D. Walton's paper, "Validity and interchangeability of Terman Merrill and Matrices Test Data" ', *Br. J. Ed. Psych.* 26.

Part II Developments

Chapter 4　A review of 'The Lore and Language of Schoolchildren'*

This book presents a most detailed and comprehensive collection of the oral lore of the early child and the early adolescent in contemporary Britain. The material was gathered, mainly, but not wholly, by teachers from seventy non-fee-paying schools. The authors, however, believe that the collection is representative of the child population. The oral traditions of children in fee-paying schools and the language-use of delinquents are excluded. The language-use of children in residential institutions is not represented. The material is classified under such headings as 'Guile', 'Partisanship', 'The Child and Authority', 'The Code of Oral Legislation', and gives an overwhelming impression of the all-pervasiveness of the speech form used by a child in his peer group. The classification has been used for the purposes of description and provides a linguistic inventory of an age grade from five to fifteen years. Especially interesting are the maps which show the regional distribution of the chief contributing schools and the areas where special terms, rituals and games are to be found. It would have been of great sociological interest if the material had been organized along sex, age and class lines, but this was not the intention of the authors. There can be no doubt that this book provides social scientists with a unique source of reference which is of significance to students of sub-cultures, child development and dynamic psychology.

A big problem is presented. What is the significance of the material? How can it be analysed? Upon what does it throw light? Two courses are open. One can either examine the material in the light of the Opies' classification which would lead to an examination of the speech contents associated with particular games, rituals and special relationships; or one can discuss the psychological and sociological implications of the dominant mode of the speech. To do the latter may do an injustice to the richness of the material and the

* Iona and Peter Opie, Clarendon Press, 1959.

71

scholarship of the authors, but it might provide an illustration of the general significance of the book to social scientists.

A distinction can be made between speech which is specially created to fit a particular referent which an individual uniquely coins to designate an experience, and speech which consists of attaching 'ready-made' words, phrases and sequences as tags or social counters to particular contexts. The latter, according to Dr Eisler, is fluent speech resulting from a habitual combination of words often shared by a language community and is more or less automatic; whilst the former consists of speech in which the sequences cease to be a matter of common or shared conditioning and become highly individual and unexpected. A discussion about the weather or the opening conversational gambit at a cocktail party consists of habitual automatic sequences. These utterances indicate the exchange of previously learned social counters which are operated as moves in a game. It is clear that an individual shifts from one usage to another depending upon the social context of the communication, but there may well be a series of linked social contexts where one form of usage is dominant. Put another way, certain forms of social organization, social structures, may be epitomized by one dominant mode of language-use rather than another. The Opies have given us a most systematic and well documented study of a speech process which is a function of a particular type of sub-culture.

There is, it is thought, a dynamic interaction between the speech form learned, the experiences organized by it and subsequent behaviour. The experience of a speaker is conditioned and differentiated by and through his language. Spoken language is a process and processing phenomenon and is the major means by which an individual becomes self-regulating. An analysis of the typical dominant speech mode learned should give important insights into the psychological effects of linguistic processing and the inter-relationships with the social structure which condition and limit the form of the usage.

The language of children used in the peer group bears all the hallmarks of old, practised, well-organized speech. The speech is not specially created by the child, except by the innovators; rather the child's task is to learn when and how to apply the sequence appropriately and adroitly. The knowledge of the lexicon is, in itself, inadequate. What counts is the correct choice of situation, the timing, tone and fitness of a term. The child when he acquires the language learns to emit and answer a series of signals, both verbal and expressive, which indicate to others the adequacy of his sensitivity to the norms of his sub-culture. And this adequacy is revealed every time he speaks. The appropriateness of the child's behaviour is thus conditioned to a wide variety of situations by means of the vehicle of communication. It is a language which continuously signals the normative arrangements of the group rather than the individual experiences of its members. The speech mode is a public language in its pure form.

The language does not facilitate the unique verbalization of subjective intent. Its use reinforces solidarity with the group, its functions, roles and aims. Certain individual differences, which, if they appeared, would threaten the solidarity of the group, are channelled via the language and rendered innocuous. For example, the bright child, according to the Opies, is the originator of new sequences. The child or young adolescent expresses his individuality *not* through the creation of speech which is unique to him but through his selection from a set of social/public terms and by expressive means. The automatic character of the verbal sequences allows for a high level of emotional excitation which can be triggered off by apparently innocuous stimuli, a passer-by, a pimple on a face, a different pair of socks, a name; in fact anything which signals difference or uniqueness or violates an implicit norm of 'average expectancy'.

Because the speech is public, the language of a group not of an individual, the terms are global, direct, concrete and activity-dominated and refer to a class of contents rather than to a specific one, e.g. teachers, cowards, adults, school dinners, gluttons, etc. A fundamental characteristic of the language, despite its apparent warmth and vitality, is that it is impersonal in the literal sense of the term. It is this very impersonality which enables the child or young adolescent to operate with savage and unfeeling terms quite freely, without a sense of guilt and shame, and also releases behaviour in accordance with these terms. Respectable figures or institutions may be caricatured, denigrated and slandered quite happily with joyous unconcern. Other members of the group may be treated mercilessly or with great sentimentality. The Opies have gathered a rich variety of material illustrating these points.

The impersonality insulates or protects the child from responsibility or guilt for what he has said or done. A whole range of verbal behaviour and actions is made possible, particularly anti-person behaviour. Of equal importance, the impersonality opens the way for rigid adherence to standards and ritualization which reinforce almost a tribal, mechanical solidarity. This channels and focuses the high emotional level which the use of the language itself helps to create. The impersonality may serve other, psychologically important, functions. The rhymes and catch-phrases to do with eating, sex, death and unpopular children are stark and revolting to an adult. The words and rhymes are not the child's *own* words, not specifically created by him, but are taken over by him so that he is freed from the *personal* responsibility of the implications for what he is saying. His fears and anxieties are in this way expressed whilst he is safely insulated from personal concern and retribution. It is not surprising to find that some referents which might normally arouse tender feelings are given tough terms. These feelings may, of course, be expressed, but in a prescribed manner and in a prescribed context.

The language-use makes the child sensitive to the significance of role and status and also to the customary relationships, connecting and legitimizing the social positions within his peer group. As the Opies say, the language is a friend of tradition and in many respects is undemocratic. Mechanical means are used for the settling of disputes, reconciliations, extracting promises, obtaining secrecy and choosing. A word at the right time secures or revokes ownership. Magical forces and omniscient acts are readily incorporated into the stream of activity. The cognitive and affective implications of the speech form narrows yet intensifies the range of stimuli to which the child and young adolescent learns to respond. At the same time it introduces another range of potential behaviour which may be actualized and controlled within a highly organized, rigid, explicit structure, so making a predictable and secure world, distinct and cut off from the shifting and expanding realm of the adult world which the child, in another sphere, is trying to master.

The speech form does not 'cause' the sub-culture. The former is a function of the latter. As the Opies say, the child learns his society through the language and in its use a form of social tie is progressively strengthened. It is as well to remember how different the behaviour of the child is when he is *not* among his peers.

One can only outline how rich the material presented by the Opies is, in rhymes, oral codes, methods of reconciliation and decision-making, including many historical and international comparisons; in fact the whole minutiae of the world of the peer group. It would be interesting to compare this material with the language-use of members of combat units in the armed services and, if we possessed it, anthropological linguistic data for similar age grades drawn from non-literate peoples. Especially interesting is a conclusion of the Opies that, despite the increase in the range and intensity of the mass media, the oral lore of children remains, on the whole, stubbornly traditional in form and content. This is not what one is led to expect by those who are manning the bastions of literary culture. Perhaps this book offers a means of judging the extent to which mass culture is successful in *depth* and of indicating the age group which is most susceptible to its influence. Certainly it would seem that it is the middle and late adolescent rather than the younger child.

The Opies have shown, among many things, what an invaluable aid to the understanding of groups and individuals is the study of language behaviour. There is to be a further volume, a collection of street and playground games, which should be of equal interest. One final word: It is sad that so rich a vein of material should have been overlooked by sociologists and psychologists for so long.

Chapter 5 Linguistic codes, hesitation phenomena and intelligence

Introduction

In the previous papers attempts have been made to find a way of analysing some of the interrelationships between social structure, language-use and subsequent behaviour. In some way the form of the social relationship acts selectively on the speech possibilities of the individual, and again in some way these possibilities constrain behaviour. Luria (1959, 1961) has explored both theoretically and experimentally the regulative function of speech. I take it that a proposition central to his view is that when a child speaks he voluntarily produces changes in his field of stimuli and his subsequent behaviour is modified by the nature of these changes. I shall here propose that forms of spoken language in the process of their learning initiate, generalize and reinforce special types of relationship with the environment and thus create for the individual particular dimensions of significance. One of the tasks of the sociologist would be to seek the social origins of particular linguistic forms and to examine their regulative function. This task would become an attempt to reduce the interrelationships between social structure, language-use and individual behaviour to a theory of social learning. Such a theory should indicate *what* in the environment is available to be learned, the *conditions* of learning and the *constraints* on subsequent learning. From this point of view the social structure transforms language possibility into a specific code which elicits, generalizes and reinforces those relationships necessary for its continuance.

Definition of the codes

Two general types of code can be distinguished: *elaborated* and *restricted*. They can be defined, on a linguistic level, in terms of the probability of predicting for any one speaker which syntactic elements will be used to organize meaning. In the case of an elaborated code, the speaker will select from a relatively extensive range of alternatives and therefore the probability of predicting the pattern of organizing elements is considerably reduced. In the case of a restricted code the number of these alternatives is often severely limited and the probability of predicting the pattern is greatly increased.

On a psychological level the codes may be distinguished by the extent to which each facilitates (elaborated code) or inhibits (restricted code) the orientation to symbolize intent in a verbally explicit form. Behaviour processed by these codes will, it is suggested, develop different modes of self-regulation and so different forms of orientation. The codes themselves are functions of a particular form of social relationship or, more generally, qualities of social structure.

Sociological conditions for the two codes

The pure form of a restricted code would be one where the lexicon and hence the organizing structure, irrespective of its degree of complexity, are wholly predictable. Examples of this pure form would be *ritualistic modes of communication*—relationships regulated by protocol, religious services, the opening gambits at a cocktail party, conversations about the weather, a mother telling her children stories, etc. It is clear that in the pure form of the restricted code individual intent can be signalled only through the non-verbal components of the situation, i.e. intonation, stress, expressive features, etc. Specific verbal planning will be minimal.

What is more often found is a restricted code[1] where prediction is possible only at the structural level. The lexicon will vary from one case to another, but in all cases it is drawn from a narrow range. The social forms which produce this code will also vary, but the most general condition for its development will be based upon some common set of closely shared identifications self-consciously held by the members, where immediacy of the relationship is stressed. It follows that these social relationships will be of an inclusive character. The speech is played out against a background of communal, self-consciously held interests which removes the need to verbalize subjective intent and make it explicit. The meanings will be condensed. Examples of the use of this code are to be found in the peer group of children and adolescents, criminal sub-cultures, combat units in the armed services, senior common rooms, between married couples of long standing, etc. In these social relationships the sequences will tend to be well organized at both the structural and lexicon levels. Verbal planning will tend to be reduced and the utterances fluent. The non-verbal component (expressive features) will be a major source for indicating changes in meaning. These expressive features will tend to reinforce a word or phrase rather than finely discriminate between meanings. The utterances will be well ventilated. They will tend to be *impersonal* in that the speech is not specially prepared to fit a particular referent. How things are said, rather than what is said, becomes important. The intent of the listener may be taken for granted. Finally, the content of the speech is likely to be concrete, descriptive and narrative rather than analytical and abstract. The major function of this code is to reinforce the *form* of the social relationship (a warm and inclusive relationship) by restricting the verbal signalling of individuated responses.[2]

An elaborated code has its origins in a form of social relationship which increases the tension on the individual to select from his linguistic resources a verbal arrangement which closely fits specific referents. The code becomes a vehicle for individual responses. If a restricted code facilitates the construction and exchange of 'social' symbols, then an elaborated code facilitates the construction and exchange of 'individuated' symbols. The verbal planning function associated with this code promotes a higher level of structural organization and lexicon selection. The preparation and delivery of relatively *explicit* meaning is the major purpose of the code. This does not necessarily mean that the content will be abstract, although this is inherent among the possibilities regulated by the code, but that the code will facilitate the verbal transmission and elaboration of the individual's experience. The condition of the listener will *not* be taken for granted, as the individual, through verbal planning, will modify his speech in relation to the specific requirements of the listener. This is not to say that such modification will always occur, but that the possibility exists. The code induces, through its regulation, a sensitivity to the implications of separateness and difference and points to the possibility inherent in a complex conceptual hierarchy for the organization of experience. Finally the expressive features which accompany the speech will tend to discriminate finely between meaning within sequences.

Formal sociological conditions for the emergence of the two codes

A 'restricted' code is particularistic with reference to meaning and to the social structure which controls its inception. The speech model for this code is universalistic as its use depends on the characteristics of a form of social relationship which can arise at any point in the social structure. An 'elaborated' code is universalistic with reference to its meaning and *potentially* universalistic with reference to the social structure which controls its inception. The speech model for this code in contemporary societies is particularistic. This does not mean that its origin is to be sought in the psychological qualities of the model but that the model is an incumbent of a specialized position which is a function of the general system of social stratification. The models for the two codes lie in different sociological dimensions. In principle this is not necessary; it happens to be the case at the moment.

In terms of learning the codes are different. The abbreviated structures of a restricted code may be learned informally and readily. They become well habituated. The greater range of and selection from structural alternatives associated with an elaborated code normally requires a much longer period of formal and informal learning. An elaborated code is universalistic with reference to its meaning inasmuch as it summarizes *general* social means and ends. A restricted code is particularistic with reference to its meaning inasmuch as it summarizes *local* means and ends. The degree of elaboration is thus a function of the generality of the means and ends while the degree of restriction is a function of the parochialness of the social means and ends. Thus, because a restricted code is universalistic with respect to its model, all people have access to the code and to its local condensed meanings, but because an elaborated code is particularistic with respect to its model only some people have access to the code and to the potential universalistic character of its meanings. Access to an elaborated code will depend not on psychological factors but on access to specialized social positions within the social structure, by virtue of which a particular type of speech model is made available. Normally, but not inevitably, these positions will coincide with a stratum seeking, or already possessing, access to the major decision-making area of the social structure.

The distinctions which have been drawn in terms of the availability of the speech model and the subsequent differences in coding are useful in isolating the general conditions for a special case of a restricted code. This is where the speech model is particularistic and the meaning is also particularistic. *In this situation the individual is wholly constrained by the code.* He has access to no other. It is with this situation that this paper is concerned.

The sociological conditions may be summarized as follows:

(1) Restricted code (lexicon prediction): ritualism
    (*a*) restricted code (high structural prediction)

Model: universalistic; meaning particularistic

   (b)   restricted code (high structural prediction)
Model: particularistic; meaning particularistic

(2)   Elaborated code (low structural prediction)
Model: particularistic; meaning universalistic

Definition of the term 'code'

At this point it is necessary to define the sense in which the word 'code' is used. The following is both an attempt at definition and an attempt to show the relationship with verbal planning.

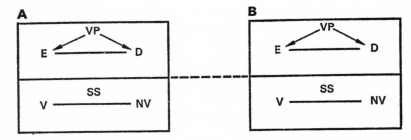

Figure 1

In the model represented in Figure 1, the section below the line represents the signal store in which inter-related verbal and non-verbal signals are contained. Above the line, E and D represent the usual encoding and decoding processes controlled and integrated by the verbal planning function (VP).

When A signals to B it is suggested that at least the following takes place:

ORIENTATION: B scans the incoming message for a pattern of dominant signals (this is the beginning of the verbal planning sequence). ASSOCIATIONS to the pattern of dominant signals control selection from the signal store (V+NV). ORGANIZATION and integration of signals (V+NV) to produce a sequential reply.

The term 'code' as I use it implies the principles which regulate these three processes. It follows that restricted and elaborated codes will establish different kinds of control which crystallize in the nature of verbal planning. The latter is a resultant of the conditions which establish the patterns of orientation, association and organization. The originating determinants of this trio would be the form of the social relationship or, more generally, the quality of the social structure. This would allow the following postulate: the form of the social relationship acts selectively on the type of code which then becomes a symbolic expression of the relationship and proceeds to regulate the nature of the interaction. Simply, the consequences of the form of the social relationship are transmitted and sustained by the code on a psychological level. Strategic learning would be elicited, sustained and generalized by the code which would mark out what has to be learned and would constrain the conditions of successful learning.

It is clear that what is made available to be learned, the conditions of learning and the subsequent constraints are different in the two codes. Individuals will of course shift from one to the other according to the form of the social relationship and so their usage is independent of the personality and intelligence of the speakers. These factors may influence the *level* within each code but the latter is not inevitably a function of these psychological factors. This is a point of some importance, if the situation of an individual who is wholly constrained by a restricted code (structural prediction) is considered. The general condition for this code, it will be remembered, is where both the model and the meaning are particularistic. In this country, it is suggested, this is the situation of the lower working class, including rural groups. Together these groups represent 29 per cent of the population. An elaborated code is associated with the middle-class and adjacent social strata. These codes, however, are not necessarily clear functions of social class, but in advanced industrialized societies the association will have a high degree of probability. Class is only one of many principles of social stratification and differentiation.

Thus in this country children from these respective social strata will be exposed to different orders of learning and so their resultant modes of self-regulation and orientation will be different, irrespective of their levels of innate intelligence. The net effect of the constraint of a restricted code will be to depress potential linguistic ability, raise the relevance of the concrete and descriptive level of response and inhibit generalizing ability at the higher ranges. At the same time it will reinforce the solidarity of the developing child with his peers, which in turn will reinforce the solidarity of the code.

Children from the middle-class and adjacent social strata will be exposed to both a restricted and an elaborated code and so to the possibilities symbolized by both these codes.

An experiment was designed to see whether these two codes were associated with social class and, more particularly, to see whether the orientation to use one or the other was independent of measured intelligence. At this point a problem arose of the measures which would discriminate the two codes in other than linguistic terms. Measures were required which would throw light upon the major controls of the codes, that is, would illuminate the verbal planning functions. The research, originated and systematically developed by Goldman-Eisler (1954, 1958a, b, c, 1961a, b) into the nature of hesitation phenomena, seemed the most promising technique. Her work has demonstrated a relationship between levels of coding activities and hesitation behaviour. She has found that the habit strength of speech sequences can be inferred from the hesitation phenomena. Levels of verbal planning thus become susceptible to objective measurement and discrimination. In terms of this work the following predictions were made about the hesitation phenomena associated with elaborated and restricted codes when speakers were subject to a group discussion situation.

(1) Holding verbal and non-verbal IQ constant, working-class groups would pause less frequently and spend less time pausing than middle-class groups.

(2) Holding non-verbal IQ constant, working-class groups would pause less frequently and spend less time pausing than middle-class groups.

(3) Irrespective of non-verbal IQ the hesitation phenomena of working-class subjects would be similar.

(4) A general relationship would be found between the two IQ tests for the working-class group: the verbal scores would be severely depressed in relation to the scores at the higher ranges of the non-verbal test. It was expected that this general relationship would not hold for the middle-class group.

Description of the experiment

Two extreme social groups were chosen for linguistic comparison. One group consisted of 61 male subjects between fifteen and eighteen years of age, matched for education and occupation but whose homes were distributed between inner and outer London. These subjects were compulsory students at a day-release college where they attended one day a week to receive a general non-vocational education. They were employed as messenger boys and none had received a grammar school education. This group will be referred to as working-class. The second group consisted of 45 male subjects matched for age with the first group, all pupils at one of the six major public schools. These boys represented a reasonable cross-section of the upper school with respect to educational attainment and particular subject interest. This group will be referred to as middle-class.

TABLE 1

Group	Subjects	Verbal IQ	S.D.	Non-verbal IQ	S.D.	Age
Middle class						
1	5	125·0	1·81	123·8	2·75	16·2
2	5	108·0	2·72	123·0	2·24	16·0
Working class						
3	5	105·0	2·14	126·0	0·0	15·6
4	4	97·5	2·60	123·0	3·08	16·5
5	5	100·0	4·60	100·6	3·20	16·2

The two groups were given the Raven Progressive Matrices 1938 (a non-verbal measure of intelligence) and the Mill Hill Vocabulary Scale Form I Senior. These tests were selected so as to afford a comparison with 309 working-class subjects who had previously been tested (Bernstein, 1958). From the two major groups five sub-groups were selected which would permit the following comparisons (see Table 1).

(1) General interclass comparison.

(2) Class comparisons with non-verbal intelligence held constant.

(3) Class comparisons with verbal and non-verbal intelligence held constant.

(4) Comparisons between different IQ profiles holding class constant.

A tape-recorded, relatively undirected discussion was taken with all groups on the topic of the abolition of capital punishment. It was possible to make a comparative analysis of the speech forms associated with the two major groups and the variations associated with the sub-groups. It was thought that the working-class group would find the test situation threatening and that this would interfere with the speech, and consequently all working-class groups had two practice discussions (one a week) before the test discussion. This was not the case for the middle-class groups as such trials were impracticable. The working-class groups were drawn from four different forms and the sub-groups contained members with varying degrees of personal contact. The social and educational contact of the middle-class group was not known. The probability of this highly selected group with varying characteristics containing members all of whom were in the same form or house was low, as the upper school is very large and there are six houses. As far as possible the boys set the level of discussion and the research worker intervened when a particular sequence was exhausted, when a boy was monopolizing the discussion or when voluntary contributions came to an end. The number of such interventions was considerably greater for the working-class groups for the last-mentioned reason. In order to permit maximum freedom little attempt was made to standardize the questions put to the groups. The major aim was to get the boys talking and to permit the groups, themselves, to establish the level of coding difficulty.

Results of the intelligence testing for the major groups

These results have been published in detail elsewhere (Bernstein, 1960) and only a summary will be given here. For the working-class group all the verbal IQ scores are within the average range of the test but thirty-six subjects (59 per cent) scored above average on the non-verbal test while eleven subjects (18 per cent) scored between 120 and 126+ IQ points. In other words, 18 per cent of the group made scores which placed them in the top 5 per cent of the population. A general relationship held. The higher the score on the non-verbal test, the greater the discrepancy between the scores on the two tests. In relation to the higher ranges of the Matrices test the language scores were severely depressed. This general relationship between the two tests for the working-class group was *not* found for the middle-class group. The mean scores for the two tests at different ranges matched each other very closely.

Speech sample

The speech sample consisted, for each group, of the next 1,800 words approximately which followed the first five minutes of the discussion. An utterance was considered to be from the time a subject commenced to talk until he finished. The utterances were divided into long and short. The former were sequences containing forty syllables or more and the latter were sequences of between ten and forty syllables. This division follows from the work of Goldman-Eisler (1954) who found that the hesitation phenomena associated with short utterances are unstable. The two categories of utterance have been analysed separately and only the results of the long utterances will be given here.

Method

Visual recordings of the speech were made on teledeltos paper and the speech on the magnetic tape was then synchronized with these visual records. Measurements were made from them of the following quantities for each utterance:

(1) The number of words.

(2) The number of syllables.

(3) The articulation rate: this time is based on the rate of vocal speech utterance exclusive of pauses.

(4) The mean number of words per pause (W/P). This gives a measure of the phrase length or frequency of pauses.

(5) The mean pause duration per word utterance (P/W).

(6) The mean word length in number of syllables. Pauses with a duration of under 0·25 sec. were ignored.

TABLE 2

Group	Subjects	Number of utterances	Mean No. of utterances	Number of words	Mean No. of words	S.D.
1	5	21	4·2	1,885	99·4	59·33
2	5	19	3·8	1,242	64·4	8·06
3	5	22	4·4	2,205	101·2	46·89
4	3	12	4·0	793	61·9	27·80
5	4	24	6·0	1,329	54·8	5·86

Organization of the sub-groups

Information about the sub-groups is contained in Table 2. The difference in numbers in Groups 4 and 5 arose because one member from each group failed to contribute a long utterance and one member from Group 4 was absent from the college on the day of the study. It is perhaps of interest that the two members who failed to make a long utterance were both members of the working-class group.

The arrangement of the groups for the purpose of the analysis was different from the original grouping. One subject each from Group 1 and Group 2 were exchanged, two subjects were shifted from Group 4 to Group 3 and one from Group 3 was placed in Group 4. This was necessary in order to make a better match between Group 2 and Group 3 and to see whether the lower verbal IQ of Group 4 would affect the hesitation phenomena. Although the original sample was approximately 1,800 words for each group this rearrangement altered considerably the balance of speech analysed for each group. The number of words also differs because the number of short utterances contributing to the total varied with each group. The very large standard deviation for the mean number of words in Group 1 and Group 3 is the result of one subject from each of these groups contributing a mean of 217·3 words and 194·3 words respectively. If these subjects' utterances are subtracted from the totals of their respective groups then the only major significant difference in the mean number of words for each group is between Group 3 and Group 5. The low total of words for Group 2 was because one of the subjects, who in this analysis now appears in Group 1, uttered a total of 652 words. He took up much of the discussion time. The total for Group 4 is low because one of the original members contributed a total of 777 words but for the purposes of the analysis this subject is included in Group 3. As all the measures used in the analysis are ratios, the real differences between the groups in absolute number of words is not so important as differences in the mean number of utterances contributed by each subject. For the critical comparisons there is little difference. In Group 5 the mean number of utterances is somewhat higher.

Finally, the rearranging of the subjects could not in any way alter the results of the major class comparisons. The exchange of one subject between Group 1 and Group 2 made no difference as the scores on all relevant measures corresponded with the scores of the groups to which they were attached. This was also the case for the exchanges between Group 3 and Group 4.

Results

The results are summarized in Table 4. One tail t tests were used, as the direction of the differences was predicted in all comparisons.

Mean differences There is no significant difference between the articulation rates for any of the comparisons, except for the intra-middle-class comparison where the difference is at borderline significance at the 0·05 level of confidence. This is in line with the findings of Goldman-Eisler (1961a) for this measure. She has found that this rate is a constant of great rigidity inasmuch as it does not respond to changes in the level of verbal planning, as do pauses, but only to the effect of practice.

Differences in mean phrase length, mean pause duration per word and mean word length were found for the class groups matched for non-verbal intelligence. The working-class group uses a longer phrase length, a shorter mean pause duration and a considerably shorter word length.

The same pattern of differences was found (at a higher level of confidence for the hesitation phenomena and at a somewhat reduced level of confidence for mean word length) for the overall comparison between the class groups.

The only difference between the working-class groups (3+4 v. 5), two of whom had an advantage of over 20 non-verbal IQ points, was in mean pause duration. The working-class group with the average IQ profile spends less time pausing.

The mean difference of 7·5 verbal IQ points is associated with no difference in the hesitation phenomena and mean word length for the working-class groups matched for non-verbal intelligence.

Differences were found between the two middle-class groups matched for high non-verbal intelligence, for mean phrase length and mean word length. The group with high verbal intelligence used a longer phrase length and word length than the group with low verbal intelligence.

When the IQ profile was held constant and middle- and working-class groups were compared, differences at a high level of confidence were found for mean phrase length and mean pause duration. No differences were found for mean word length. The working-class group used a considerably longer phrase length (3·8 more words to the phrase) and spent much less time pausing (0·06 seconds) than the middle-class group.

Scatter The scatter about the mean for pause duration per word is considerably smaller for all the working-class groups. It is greatest for Group 1, that is the middle-class group with the superior IQ scores on both tests.

The scatter about the mean for phrase length is considerably and significantly less (p> 0·05) for Group 2 when this group is compared with Group 1 or Group 3.

TABLE 3

Group	Articulation rate					Phrase length				
	Mean	S.D.	Mean	S.D.	t	Mean	S.D.	Mean	S.D.	t
1+2 v. 3+4	6·2	0·80	6·3	0·60	0·27 n.s.	6·3	2·00	8·9	1·92	2·69 p> 0·01
1+2 v. 3+4+5	6·2	0·80	6·2	0·58	0·00 n.s.	6·3	2·00	9·3	2·07	3·29 p> 0·005
3+4 v. 5	6·3	0·60	5·8	0·23	1·47 n.s.	8·9	1·92	10·0	2·28	0·87 n.s.
3 v. 4	6·2	0·32	6·7	0·78	1·11 n.s.	8·9	1·91	8·9	1·69	0·00 n.s.
1 v. 2	6·6	0·61	5·8	0·63	1·82 n.s.	7·6	2·14	5·1	0·49	2·33 p> 0·025
2 v. 3	5·8	0·63	6·2	0·32	1·14 n.s.	5·1	0·49	8·9	1·91	3·87 p> 0·005

Group	Pause duration per word					Word length				
	Mean	S.D.	Mean	S.D.	t	Mean	S.D.	Mean	S.D.	t
1+2 v. 3+4	0·12	0·05	0·08	0·02	1·90 p> 0·05	1·30	0·06	1·21	0·06	2·90 p> 0·01
1+2 v. 3+4+5	0·12	0·05	0·07	0·03	2·94 p> 0·005	1·30	0·06	1·23	0·07	2·33 p> 0·025
3+4 v. 5	0·08	0·02	0·05	0·01	2·50 p> 0·025	1·21	0·06	1·25	0·05	0·85 n.s.
3 v. 4	0·08	0·02	0·07	0·02	0·02 n.s.	1·20	0·06	1·23	0·05	0·61 n.s.
1 v. 2	0·11	0·06	0·14	0·04	0·83 n.s.	1·34	0·05	1·26	0·05	2·28 p> 0·05
2 v. 3	0·14	0·04	0·08	0·02	2·74 p> 0·025	1·26	0·05	1·20	0·06	1·50 n.s.

Discussion

The first point of interest is that this technique of analysis discriminates between the groups and that the hesitation behaviour is independent of measured intelligence for this small sample and with reference to a discussion situation.

All predictions were confirmed except that relating to the hesitation pattern associated with the working-class groups independent of the level of non-verbal intelligence of the members. For this group, non-verbal IQ is related to the ability to tolerate delay associated with coding.

As frequency of pauses (phrase length) refers to the amount of monitoring of the sequences[3] and thus to the number of intervals during which alternative possibilities are available and as duration refers to the relative difficulty of selecting the next sequence, the two measures yield an index of coding difficulty. Duration also refers to the ability to tolerate delay and the resulting tension associated with coding difficulty. Word length yields a crude indication of the informational value of the output (Goldman-Eisler, 1958a).

It would follow that the longer the phrase, the more well organized the sequence and the more likely that the units will readily condition each other, their pairing being the result of common verbal conditioning within a community (Goldman-Eisler, 1958a). In a fascinating paper Goldman-Eisler (1961b) has demonstrated that summarizing (abstracting and generalizing from perceived events) requires more time in pausing than does description. Fluency and hesitation would seem to discriminate between two kinds of speech and differentiate levels of verbal planning. These propositions were derived from data obtained in rigorous experimental conditions and checked against the content of the speech. In evaluating the results of the present experiment conducted in relatively free conditions some caution is required. Furthermore the content of the speech has yet to be analysed. The interpretations are therefore expectations about the organization of the content.

In all inter-class comparisons matched or not for non-verbal intelligence, there are clear-cut differences in the hesitation phenomena which presumably indicate differences in verbal planning. In the critical comparison between the classes in which the IQ profile is held constant, the differences are even sharper. This would seem to mean, at least for the middle-class group, in this comparison, the conditions exist for greater lexicon and structural selection and thus greater appropriateness between the speech sequences and their referents. Further, the middle-class group can tolerate the delay normally associated with increasing information even though at this stage the informational value of the speech is not known. This delay was not associated with a marked drop in output.[4] The hesitation behaviour of the working-class group would seem to rule out the possibilities available to the middle-class group. The verbal planning orientations are different. Inasmuch as the word lengths for these groups, as well as their vocabulary scores, are not significantly different, the differences in verbal planning orientation can be considered independent of passive and active vocabulary.

The intra-class comparisons indicate that for the working-class group matched for non-verbal intelligence, but who differ by a mean of 7·5 verbal IQ points, no differences for the hesitation measures and word length occur. It is considered that these groups share a similar verbal planning orientation despite the difference in verbal IQ. There is considerable restriction of the scatter for the measure of mean pause duration. There are very few relatively long pauses, and this is even more pronounced in the working-class group with an average IQ profile. The latter group makes significantly shorter pauses and this is the only measure which discriminates this group from the working-class groups who have an advantage of over 20 non-verbal IQ points. This raises an interesting point. Differences in verbal IQ between the middle-class groups are associated with differences in phrase and word length and possibly articulation rate, while differences in non-verbal IQ are associated with differences in pause duration. The monitoring processes are affected in one case and only the interval between *similar* monitoring in the other. It would seem that for the average working-class group the delay between impulse and verbal signal is very short and the control (selection) of the subsequent sequences is reduced. Presumably the middle-class group with low verbal intelligence, relative to the middle-class group with high verbal intelligence, were in a situation of coding difficulty and responded by shortening the phrase length in order to avail themselves of a greater number of intervals during which alternative selections could be made. The difference between the articulation rates for the middle-class groups may be related to how well-practised the arguments selected were. The low verbal group would appear to have much difficulty at all coding levels but the members persevered in their orientation.

The behaviour of the middle-class group with the superior IQ profile is of interest. In comparison with the working-class groups matched for non-verbal IQ there is no difference in the hesitation pattern but only in word length ($p > 0·005$).[5] However, the scatter for the measure of mean pause duration is significantly different ($p > 0·05$). In fact 52·4 per cent of the utterances made by this middle-class group have a mean pause duration of 0·09 seconds or over. The figure for the working-class is 34·3 per cent. Over half the utterances contain relatively longer pauses. In other words, this middle-class group can avail itself of longer pauses. Although there is no significant difference, the mean phrase length of this middle-class group is shorter by 1·3 words per phrase. These results are taken to mean that the middle-class group produced a higher level of speech organization, lexicon selection and information for similar monitoring (pause frequency), and that where necessary the delay associated with coding could be tolerated.

If now this discussion is related to the theory briefly outlined in the introduction to this chapter, it is clear that the derivations have been confirmed. Middle-class and working-class subjects in this small sample are orientated to different levels of verbal planning which control the speech process. These planning orientations are independent of intelligence as measured by two reliable group tests and of word length. They are thus independent of psychological factors and inhere in the linguistic codes which are available to normal individuals. In psychological terms, the codes are stabilized by the planning functions and reinforced in the speaking. They are highly resistant to change as they encapsulate the major effects of socialization.

From this point of view the general relationship between the verbal and non-verbal intelligence scores attained by members of the lower working-class stratum becomes somewhat more understandable. This does not rule out the role of innate factors; rather it becomes more difficult to evaluate their relationship to behaviour where the individual is limited to a restricted code and the educational process requires, at least, an orientation to an elaborated code. Children who already have this orientation are in a situation of symbolic development; those without it are in a situation of symbolic change.

For various reasons, in particular the occupation of the mother before marriage and the role differentiation within the family, there will not be a one-to-one correlation between the use of a restricted code and the working-class stratum, but the probability is certainly very high.[6]

The analysis of hesitation phenomena developed by Goldman-Eisler has discriminated between the proposed codes, has illuminated the nature of verbal planning processes and has provided an objective means for their assessment.

Conclusions

Two linguistic codes have been proposed, elaborated and restricted. These codes are regarded as functions of different social structures. They are considered to entail qualitatively different verbal planning orientations which control different modes of self-regulation and levels of cognitive behaviour. Social class differences in the use of these codes were postulated and the hesitation phenomena associated with them predicted.

Speech samples were obtained and the hesitation phenomena analysed from a discussion situation involving small groups of middle-class and working-class subjects with varying IQ profiles.

Major results

(1) Overall social class differences were found. The working-class subjects used a longer mean phrase length, spent less time pausing and used a shorter word length.

(2) Holding non-verbal intelligence constant, social class differences were found in the same direction.

(3) Holding verbal and non-verbal intelligence constant, social class differences were again found in the same direction, but not for word length.

(4) Within the middle-class group, the sub-group with superior verbal intelligence used a longer mean phrase length, a faster rate of articulation and a longer word length.

(5) Within the working-class group, the sub-group with the average IQ profile spent less time pausing.

The major predictions were confirmed. The results were considered as supporting evidence for the two codes and the different verbal planning orientations which are entailed.

Acknowledgments

I should like to thank Dr Frieda Goldman-Eisler of the Department of Phonetics, University College London, for the many fruitful discussions I have had with her. I should also like to express my gratitude to the London County Council, the principal of the day college and the headmaster of the public school for their co-operation in making the study possible. Finally, I should like to thank Mrs E. Wolpert of the Tavistock Institute of Human Relations, London, for her assistance in the original testing.

Notes

1 In different ways Vygotsky (1939), Malinowski (1923) and Sapir (1931) have drawn attention to this form of speech.
2 One important channel for individuated responses is humour, wit or the joking relationship. These channels allow an individuated response, but an important effect is to reinforce the solidarity of the social relationship.
3 It is assumed that frequency of pauses is an index of the degree of monitoring.
4 One member of the working-class group in this comparison failed to contribute any long utterances.
5 It is thought that this difference in length of word would be associated with a greater complexity of organization, lexicon selection and informational output.
6 A more general description of the use of this code would be that the speech model is particularistic and the meaning channelled through the model also particularistic.

References

BERNSTEIN, B. (1958), 'Some sociological determinants of perception', *Bri. J. Soc. 9.*

BERNSTEIN, B. (1959), 'A public language: some sociological implications of a linguistic form', *Br. J. Soc. 10.*

BERNSTEIN, B. (1960), 'Language and social class', *Br. J. Soc. 11.*

BERNSTEIN, B. (1961a), 'Aspects of language and learning in the genesis of the social process', *J. Child. Psychol. and Psychiat. 1.*

BERNSTEIN, B. (1961b), 'Social class and linguistic development: a theory of social learning', in *Education, Economy and Society*, eds. Halsey, A. H., Floud, J. and Anderson, C. A., New York: Free Press.

GOLDMAN-EISLER, F., (1954), 'On the variability of the speed of talking, and on its relation to the length of utterances in conversations', *Br. J. Psychol. 45.*

GOLDMAN-EISLER, F. (1958a), 'Speech analysis and mental processes', *Language and Speech. 1.*

GOLDMAN-EISLER, F. (1958b), 'Speech production and the predictability of words in context', *Quart. J. Exp. Psychol. 10.*

GOLDMAN-EISLER, F. (1958c), 'The predictability of words in context and the length of pauses in speech', *Language and Speech. 1.*

GOLDMAN-EISLER, F. (1961a), 'The significance of changes in the rate of articulation', *Language and Speech 4.*

GOLDMAN-EISLER, F. (1961b), 'Hesitation and information in speech', in *Information Theory, 4th London Symposium*, ed. Cherry, C. Butterworth.

LURIA, A. R. (1961), *The Role of Speech in the Regulation of Normal and Abnormal Behaviour*, Pergamon.

LURIA, A. R. and YUDOVITCH, F. (1959), *Speech and the Development of Mental Processes in the Child*, Stapler Press.

MALINOWSKI, B. (1923), 'The problem of meaning in primitive languages', in Ogden, C. K. and Richards, I. A. *The Meaning of Meaning*, Kegan Paul.

SAPIR, E. (1931), 'Communication', in *Encyclopedia of the Social Sciences* 4, 78, New York: Macmillan.

VYGOTSKY, L. S. (1939), 'Thought and speech', *Psychiatry* 2.

Chapter 6 Social class, linguistic codes and grammatical elements

Introduction

In the previous paper, an account was given of differences in the use of hesitations in the speech. In this paper, an analysis of lexical and simple grammatical features will be given. Table 1 and Table 2 which follow give the mean IQ scores for the various groups and the number of long and short utterances.

TABLE 1

Group	Subjects	Verbal IQ	S.D.	Non-verbal IQ	S.D.	Average age
Middle class						
1	5	125·0	1·81	123·8	2·75	16·2
2	5	108·0	2·72	123·0	2·24	16·0
Working class						
3	5	105·0	2·14	126·0	0·00	15·6
4	4	97·5	2·60	123·0	3·08	16·5
5	5	100·0	4·60	100·6	3·20	16·2

TABLE 2 *Utterances (number and type)*

Group:	1	2	3	4	5	1+2	3+4	3+4+5
Long	21	19	22	12	24	40	34	58
Short	24	8	14	9	19	32	23	42
Total	45	27	36	21	43	72	57	100
Mean No. of words	48·8	52·9	68·8	49·6	39·8	50·3	61·8	52·3

Speech sample

The speech sample consisted for each group of the 1,800 words, approximately, which followed the first five minutes of the discussion. Long and short utterances were distinguished according to whether the utterance was between ten and forty syllables or over forty syllables. The distribution is shown in Table 2. In order that close IQ comparisons could be made there was an interchange of one member between Groups 1 and 2 and between Groups 3 and 4. Groups 2 and 3 are matched for verbal and non-verbal IQ. The membership of the original groups differed slightly from the membership shown in Table 1. This shift partly accounts for the differences in the total number of words analysed for each group. The lower number of words in Group 2 is the result of shifting one original member who contributed 590 words and who took up much of the time of the discussion to Group 1. A similar reason accounts for the low number of words in Group 4.

Two members of the working-class sample, one from Group 4 and one from Group 5 were omitted from the analysis as neither contributed a long utterance and the total number of words for each was under 90 words. This results in the difference in the total number of words between Groups 1+2 and Groups 3+4 and reduces the aggregate number of words for Groups 3, 4 and 5.

TABLE 3

Group	Total No. of words	No. of words omitted	No. of words analysed	Percentage omitted
1 (5)	2,194	196	1,998	8·9
2 (5)	1,429	139	1,290	9·7
3 (5)	2,478	283	2,195	11·4
4 (3)	1,042	84	958	8·1
5 (4)	1,709	123	1,586	7·2
1+2 (10)	3,623	335	3,288	9·3
3+4 (8)	3,520	367	3,153	10·5
3+4+5 (12)	5,229	490	4,739	9·4

Not all the words spoken were used for the analysis. All group comparisons, except those for personal pronouns, are based upon a speech sample which excludes all words repeated, fragments (false starts and maze sequences which could be deleted without altering the meaning), sequences such as 'I mean' and 'I think' and terminal sequences such as 'isn't it' 'you know' 'ain't it' 'wouldn't he' etc. One personal pronoun count included the 'I think' and the terminal sequences. The terminal sequences, for reasons which will be given later, are called *sympathetic circularity* sequences and are indicated by the abbreviation S.C. Table 3 contains a summary of the information relating to omission. It can be seen that the percentage of words removed from each group does not vary greatly. The general effect of the words and sequences excluded was to bring the social class speech samples closer together.

Statistical analysis

The nature of the distributions indicated that non-parametric tests of significance were more appropriate as these tests do not require that the data be normally distributed and the variance be homogeneous. The Mann-Whitney u test of significance was used as it is considered the most powerful of the non-parametric tests and a most useful alternative to the parametric t test when the researcher wishes to avoid the t test's assumptions (Siegel, 1956). The grammatical elements were expressed as proportions of the appropriate populations. The distribution of the proportions for the various measures indicate that for the overall sample the scores attained on the various measures are independent of the number of words.

Only when the comparison indicated a significant difference between the major class groupings (1+2 v. 3+4+5) were the sub-groups examined. Intra-class comparisons were made to test the consistency of the inter-class differences. In the previous paper a number of inter-class comparisons were redundant in that given an overall significance between the class groups only a limited inspection may be made of the sub-groups. Thus in this analysis Groups 2 and 3 (the sub-groups matched for verbal and non-verbal IQ but differing in terms of social class) were compared; Group 1 v. 2 and 4 v. 5 were compared, respectively, to test intra-class consistency. Tables of significance are not given (for reasons of space) where no difference exists between the major class comparisons and where the difference is so clear that statistical examination is unnecessary. One-tail tests were used as the direction of the differences was predicted on all tests.

Results

No differences between the major class comparisons (1+2 v. 3+4+5) were found for the proportion of finite verbs, nouns, different nouns, prepositions, conjunctions and adverbs. No count was made for different finite verbs as the writer found it difficult to decide the principle by which these verbs with their attendant stems could be classified.

TABLE 4

Group	I mean	I think	S.C.	I think and S.C.	I think and S.C. as percentage of words
1	10	21	4	25	1·25
2	5	22	4	26	1·82
3	26	11	35	46	2·10
4	2	3	15	18	1·88
5	11	3	17	20	1·26
1+2	15	43	8	51	1·55
3+4	28	14	50	64	2·03
3+4+5	39	17	67	84	1·77

'I mean', 'I think', and S.C. sequences, Table 4

'I mean',

This sequence was excluded from the analysis as it was considered a simple reinforcing unit of the previous or subsequent sequence and likely to be an idiosyncratic speech habit. The Table indicates the findings but of the 26 sequences for Group 3, 22 were contributed by one subject; of the 11 sequences for Group 5, 8 were contributed by one subject; of the 10 for Group 1, 7 were contributed by one subject. The 'I think' and S.C. sequences are not idiosyncratically distributed and their function is different.

'I think',

There is clear evidence that this sequence is used more frequently by the middle-class groups and especially by Group 2.

S.C. sequences,

These sequences are used much more frequently by the working-class groups and, within this group, less frequently by Group 5.

'I think' plus S.C. sequences

If these sequences are added and the result expressed as a percentage of the number of words for each group then the differences between the major class groups is very small. Inspection of the table indicates that this results from the low frequency of these combined sequences in Group 1 and Group 5.

TABLE 5   *Subordination*

Group	n	n	u	P
1+2 v. 3+4+5	10	12	6	0·001
1 v. 2	5	5	8	n.s.
2 v. 3	5	5	1	0·008
4 v. 5	3	4	3	n.s.

Subordination Table 5

The method used to assess the use of subordination was pointed out to the writer in discussion with Dr Frieda Goldman-Eisler. The first step was to isolate a unit which could readily be observed with a minimum of ambiguity in the two major speech samples. This was done by terming a proposition any sequence which contained a finite verb whether or not the subject was implicit or explicit. The implicit verb at the beginning of an utterance was not counted, e.g. 'Not really. . . .' When two finite verbs were associated with the same subject this counted as two propositions. If the number of such finite verbs is then divided into the total number of analysed words for each group a mean proposition length is obtained. There was no difference between the major class groups on this measure. The number of subordinations linking two finite verbs was counted and the proportion of subordinations to finite verbs was assessed for each subject. In this analysis the role of the 'I think' and S.C. sequences becomes important. The latter would tend to decrease the proportion and the former to increase it. Inasmuch as these sequences are class patterned the results would be prejudiced. They were omitted in both the finite verb and subordination counts. The effect of this omission brought the two speech samples closer together.

Table 5 indicates that the difference in use of subordination when Groups 1+2 are compared with Groups 3+4+5, is significant at above the 0·001 level of confidence. The difference between Groups

2 and 3 is significant at the 0·008 level of confidence. The intra-class differences are not significant.

No comparison was made of differences in sentence length as no reliable method for distinguishing the samples on this measure was available. A method appropriate for Groups 1 and 2 would have been inappropriate for Groups 3, 4 and 5. The method of double juncture was too sophisticated to be used in terms of the skills of the research worker.

TABLE 6   *Complexity of verbal stem*

Group	n	n	u	P
1+2 v. 3+4+5	10	12	23	0·02
1 v. 2	5	5	12	n.s.
2 v. 3	5	5	3	0·028
4 v. 5	3	4	5	n.s.

Complexity of the verbal stem Table 6

This count was based upon the number of units in the verbal stem excluding the adverbial negation. Verbal stems containing more than three units were counted for each subject and expressed as a proportion of the total number of finite verbs uttered (excluding the verbs in the 'I think' and S.C. sequences). A verb plus an infinitive was counted as a complex verbal stem. The results indicate that Groups 1 and 2 select more complex verbal stems than do Groups 3, 4 and 5. The difference is significant beyond the 0·02 level of confidence. Group 2 selects more complex stems than does Group 3 and the difference is significant at the 0·028 level of confidence. The intra-class differences are not significant.

TABLE 7   *Passive voice*

Group	n	n	u	P
1+2 v. 3+4+5	10	12	21	0·02
1 v. 2	5	5	5	n.s.
2 v. 3	5	5	4	0·048
4 v. 5	3	4	4	n.s.

Passive voice Table 7

Major class differences in the proportion of passive verbs to total finite verbs was found and the difference is significant beyond the 0·02 level of confidence. The middle class use a greater proportion of passive verbs and this holds when Group 2 is compared with Group 3 at the 0·048 level of confidence. The intra-class differences are not significant.

Uncommon adverbs Table 8

An arbitrary classification was used to distinguish uncommon adverbs. Adverbs of degree and place, 'just' 'not' 'yes' 'no' 'then' 'how' 'really' 'when' 'where' 'why' were excluded from the total number of adverbs and the remainder, excluding repetitions, was expressed as a proportion of the total number of analysed words used by each subject. This remainder was termed 'uncommon adverbs'.

TABLE 8   *Uncommon adverbs*

Group	n	n	u	P
1+2 v. 3+4+5	10	12	2	0·001
1 v. 2	5	5	12	n.s.
2 v. 3	5	5	0	0·004
4 v. 5	3	4	3	n.s.

TABLE 9   *Total adjectives*

Group	n	n	u	P
1+2 v. 3+4+5	10	12	16	0·01
1 v. 2	5	5	11	n.s.
2 v. 3	5	5	0	0·004
4 v. 5	3	4	3	n.s.

A greater proportion of the adverbs of the middle class are uncommon and the difference is significant beyond the 0·001 level of confidence. This difference, at the 0·004 level of confidence, holds when Group 2 is compared with Group 3. The intra-class differences are not significant.

Total adjectives Table 9

The proportion of all adjectives to total analysed words is greater for the middle-class group and the difference is significant beyond the 0·01 level of confidence. This difference holds at the 0·004 level of confidence when Group 2 is compared with Group 3. The intra-class differences are not significant.

TABLE 10   *Uncommon adjectives*

Group	n	n	u	P
1+2 v. 3+4+5	10	12	4	0·001
1 v. 2	5	5	11	n.s.
2 v. 3	5	5	1	0·008
4 v. 5	3	4	5	n.s.

Uncommon adjectives Table 10

An arbitrary classification was again used to distinguish uncommon adjectives. Numerical and demonstrative adjectives and 'other' and 'another' were excluded from the total number of adjectives and the remainder, excluding repetitions, was expressed as a proportion of the total number of analysed words used by each subject. The middle-class groups use a higher proportion of uncommon adjectives to total analysed words than do the working-class groups and the difference is significant beyond the 0·001 level of confidence. This difference holds at the 0·008 level of confidence when Group 2 is compared with Group 3. The intra-class differences are not significant.

TABLE 11   *Of*

Group	n	n	u	P
1+2 v. 3+4+5	10	12	19	0·01
1 v. 2	5	5	11	n.s.
2 v. 3	5	5	1	0·008
4 v. 5	3	4	0	0·028

Prepositions, 'of' Table 11

No difference was found, it will be remembered, in the proportion of prepositions to total analysed words. For reasons to be given in the discussion the use of 'of' was of interest. The prepositions 'of' and 'in' combined account for over 34 per cent of the total prepositions used. The relative use of 'of' in relation to 'in' and 'into' was assessed by expressing the proportion of 'of' (excluding 'of' in 'sort of') to the total of 'of' and 'in' and 'into'. The middle-class groups use a higher proportion of 'of' than do the working-class groups and the difference is significant beyond the 0·01 level of confidence. The difference holds at the 0·008 level of confidence when Group 2 is compared with Group 3. No difference is found when the two middle-class groups are compared but Group 5 uses a higher proportion of this preposition than does Group 4. The difference between these two groups is at the 0·028 level of confidence.

TABLE 12   *Uncommon conjunctions*

Group	n	n	u	P
1+2 v. 3+4+5	10	12	18	0·01
1 v. 2	5	5	12	n.s.
2 v. 3	5	5	1	0·008
4 v. 5	3	4	3	n.s.

Uncommon conjunctions Table 12

An arbitrary division was made. All conjunctions other than 'and' 'so' 'or' 'because' 'also' 'then' 'like' were classified uncommon and the result was expressed as a proportion of total conjunctions. The middle-class groups use a higher proportion of uncommon conjunctions than do the working-class group and the difference is significant beyond the 0·01 level of confidence. The difference holds at the 0·008 level of confidence when Group 2 is compared with Group 3. The intra-class differences are not significant. Much less faith is placed on this finding than on any of the others as the numbers are small and whether certain conjunctions are classified as types of adverbs will affect the result.

Personal pronouns

Two different assessments of the proportion of personal pronouns were made. The first included all personal pronouns and therefore those to be found in the 'I think' and S.C. sequences. The second excluded those personal pronouns contained in the 'I think', S.C. and direct speech sequences. Two different assessments were also made of the relative proportions of 'I' and 'you' combined with 'they'. The first expressed these pronouns as proportions of total pronouns and the second as proportions of the total number of analysed words. The latter assessment was necessary to see whether these particular pronouns were used more frequently; the former merely establishes which of these pronouns *within* the personal pronoun group is selected more frequently.

All personal pronouns Table 13

The middle-class groups use a smaller proportion of all personal pronouns than do the working-class groups, Table 13 (a). The difference is significant beyond the 0·05 level of confidence. The intra-class differences are not significant, neither is the difference in the proportions when Group 2 is compared with Group 3. The middle-class groups use a higher proportion of the pronoun 'I' to total personal pronouns (Table 13 (b)) and the difference is significant beyond the 0·001 level of confidence. This difference holds when Group 2 is compared with Group 3 at the 0·028 level of confidence. The intra-class differences are not significant. These differences hold when 'I' is expressed as a proportion of the total number of words but at a lower level of significance (0·05) for the major class comparison (Table 13(c)).

When 'you' and 'they' are combined and expressed as a proportion of the total number of personal pronouns (Table 13 (d)) it is found that the working-class group use a higher proportion of the combined pronouns. The difference is significant beyond the 0·01 level of confidence. No significant differences are found for the intra-class comparisons nor between Groups 2 and 3. However, when 'you' and 'they' are expressed as a proportion of the total number of *words* it is found that the working-class groups use a higher proportion and this difference is now significant beyond the 0·001 level of confidence. The difference holds when Group 2 is compared with Group 3 and is significant beyond the 0·028 level of confidence. The intra-class differences are not significant (Table 13(e)).

TABLE 13

(*a*) *All personal pronouns*

Group	n	n	u	P
1+2 v. 3+4+5	10	12	29	0·05
1 v. 2	5	5	5	n.s.
2 v. 3	5	5	6	n.s.
4 v. 5	3	4	4	n.s.

(*b*) *I: Personal pronouns*

Group	n	n	u	P
1+2 v. 3+4+5	10	12	13	0·001
1 v. 2	5	5	5	n.s.
2 v. 3	5	5	3	0·028
4 v. 5	3	4	5	n.s.

(*c*) *I: Words*

Group	n	n	u	P
1+2 v. 3+4+5	10	12	30	0·05
1 v. 2	5	5	7	n.s.
2 v. 3	5	5	3	0·028
4 v. 5	3	4	5	n.s.

(*d*) *You and they: personal pronouns*

Group	n	n	u	P
1+2 v. 3+4+5	10	12	23	0·01
1 v. 2	5	5	11	n.s.
2 v. 3	5	5	6	n.s.
4 v. 5	3	4	2	n.s.

(e) You and they: words

Group	*n*	*n*	*u*	*P*
1+2 v. 3+4+5	10	12	14	0·001
1 v. 2	5	5	12	n.s.
2 v. 3	5	5	3	0·028
4 v. 5	3	4	4	n.s.

Selected personal pronouns (minus pronouns in 'I think', S.C. sequences, and direct speech sequences) Table 14

The middle-class groups use a smaller proportion of total selected pronouns than do the working-class groups (Table 14(a)) and the difference is significant beyond the 0·05 level of confidence. No significant difference is found for the intra-class comparisons nor when Group 2 is compared with Group 3. The middle-class groups use a higher proportion of the pronoun 'I' to total selected personal pronouns (Table 14(b)) and the difference is significant beyond the 0·05 level of confidence. The difference holds when Group 2 is compared with Group 3 at the 0·028 level of confidence. No significant difference is found for the intra-class comparisons.

No significant difference is found when 'I' is expressed as a proportion of words.

When 'you' and 'they' are combined and expressed *either* as a proportion of selected personal pronouns or of words (Table 14 (d) and (e)) the proportion of these combined pronouns is higher for the working-class group and the difference for both assessments is significant beyond the 0·01 level of confidence. In neither case are the intra-class differences significant nor is the inter-class difference significant when Group 2 is compared with Group 3.

The exclusion of personal pronouns in the above sequences brings the speech samples closer together. Direct speech sequences were excluded from the count because their content tends to be concrete, e.g. 'The judge says, "I shall send you away for six months" '. It is thought that the proportion of selected personal pronouns to words gives a better indication of the degree of concreteness of the speech.

Personal pronouns—summary

In both counts of total personal pronouns the combined middle-class groups use a smaller proportion. In both counts the middle-class groups more frequently select 'I' among the personal pronouns but only in the case of *all* personal pronouns does this group use 'I' *more frequently*. In both counts and for both words and personal pronouns the working-class groups use 'you' and 'they' more frequently. These groups both *select* and *use* these personal pronouns more often. The lack of significance in the case of 'I' when expressed as a proportion of *selected* pronouns to words is the result of the exclusion of the 'I think' sequences. The critical result is that the differences in the overall use of personal pronouns and the selections made within them holds when the two speech samples are brought close together by excluding the 'I think' and S.C. sequences. No overall class differences were found for the remaining personal pronouns. The relatively low level of significance both for total personal pronoun counts and for the use of 'I' must be taken to mean that these findings are only suggestive.

TABLE 14

(*a*) *Selected personal pronouns*

Group	n	n	u	P
1+2 v. 3+4+5	10	12	33	0·05
1 v. 2	5	5	5	n.s.
2 v. 3	5	5	11	n.s.
4 v. 5	3	4	4	n.s.

(*b*) *I: Personal pronouns*

Group	n	n	u	P
1+2 v. 3+4+5	10	12	31	0·05
1 v. 2	5	5	12	n.s.
2 v. 3	5	5	3	0·028
4 v. 5	3	4	4	n.s.

(*c*) *I: Words*

NOT SIGNIFICANT

(d) *You and they: personal pronouns*

Group	n	n	u	P
1+2 v. 3+4+5	10	12	23	0·01
1 v. 2	5	5	11	n.s.
2 v. 3	5	5	6	n.s.
4 v. 5	3	4	2	n.s.

(e) *You and they: words*

Group	n	n	u	P
1+2 v. 3+4+5	10	12	19	0·01
1 v. 2	5	5	12	n.s.
2 v. 3	5	5	5	n.s.
4 v. 5	3	4	3	n.s.

Discussion

The results will be discussed in relation to the two general linguistic codes mentioned at the beginning of this paper. For a more detailed account of the social origins and behavioural implications of these codes the reader is referred to previous papers (Bernstein, 1961a; 1961b; 1962).

The codes are defined in terms of the probability of predicting which structural elements will be selected for the organization of meaning. The structural elements are highly predictable in the case of a restricted code and much less so in the case of an elaborated code. It is considered that an elaborated code facilitates the verbal elaboration of subjective intent whilst a restricted code limits the verbal explication of such intent. The codes themselves are thought to be functions of different forms of social relations or more generally qualities of different social structures. A restricted code is generated by a form of social relationship based upon a range of closely shared identifications self-consciously held by the members. An elaborated code is generated by a form of social relationship which does not necessarily presuppose such shared, self-consciously held identifications with the consequence that much less is taken for granted. The codes regulate the area of discretion available to a speaker and so differently constrain the verbal signalling of individual difference.

The community of like interests underlying a restricted code removes the need for subjective intent to be verbally elaborated and made explicit. The effect of this on the speech is to simplify the structural alternatives used to organize meaning and restrict the range of lexicon choice. A restricted code can arise *at any point* in society where its conditions may be fulfilled but a special case of this code will be that in which the speaker is *limited* to this code. This is the situation of members of the lower working class, including rural groups. An elaborated code is part of the life chance of members of the middle class; a middle-class individual has access to the two codes, a lower working-class individual access to one.

It follows from this formulation that orientation towards the use of these codes is independent of measured intelligence and is a function of the form social relationships take.

The results of this study clearly indicate that the class groups are differently oriented in their structural selections and lexicon choices. Furthermore, this difference is relatively consistent within the social class sub-groups. Within the working-class sub-groups (3, 4, and 5) the difference of over 20 non-verbal IQ points does not produce any major disturbances in the consistency of the results. Similarly the difference of 17 verbal IQ points between the two middle-class groups (1 and 2) does not affect the *orientation* of the speech as reflected in the measures used. This does not mean that within the middle-class groups there are no differences in content but that the low verbal middle-class group is at least oriented to making types of selection at both the lexicon and organizational level which are in the same direction as those made by the high verbal middle-class group.[1] It is very clear that Group 2 and Group 3 (the class groups matched for verbal and non-verbal intelligence) are oriented to different selection and organization procedures.

It is thought that the constraints on selection procedures found in the working-class speech samples may well be found in speech samples of a restricted code *independent of the class membership of the speakers*. The data will now be discussed in more detail.

The restriction on the use of adjectives, uncommon adjectives, uncommon adverbs, the relative simplicity of the verbal form and the low proportion of subordinations supports the thesis that the working-class subjects relative to the middle-class do not explicate intent verbally and inasmuch as this is so the speech is relatively non-individuated. The difference in the proportion of selected personal pronouns to words suggests that the content of the speech is likely to be descriptive and narrative and this possibility is increased by the low proportion of subordinations.

The class differences in the relative preference for 'I' and 'you' and 'they' is of interest. Even when the speech samples are brought close together (that is when the 'I think' and S.C. sequences are omitted) the middle class select 'I' more frequently among the personal pronouns than do the working class; whilst the working-class select 'you' and 'they' more frequently among personal pronouns and these pronouns are *used* more frequently in the speech. These relative preferences reach a higher level of significance when they are expressed as proportions of *all* personal pronouns and words.

The use of 'they' is not simply the result of the tension between in-group and out-group. It is not the case that 'they' is used solely to distinguish non-members of the group. Inasmuch as referents are not finely differentiated then the global term 'they' will be adopted as a general label. The non-specificity implied by 'they' is a function of the lack of differentiation and the subsequent concretizing of experience which characterizes a restricted code as a whole. On the one hand, too high a level of abstraction is used ('they'), yet on the other, speakers are often involved in the consideration of a series of individual concrete cases. What appears to be lacking is the inter-vening series of successive levels of abstraction. The lack of specifica-tion also implies that there is possibly some *implicit agreement about the referent* such that the elaboration is redundant. In this sense 'they' is based upon 'we'. How much is redundant will depend upon the community of interests generated by 'we'.

The use of 'you' (second person plural) may also arise out of the concretizing of experience. It offers a formal subject which facilitates a ready identification on the part of the listener. The content of the statement is presented in such a way that the listener can translate this in terms of his experience. Contrary to expectation, 'one' was not used by the middle-class groups. Even if 'one' is used, it is often not the psychological equivalent of 'you'; for 'one' may involve a differentiation of own experience from that which is the subject of the discourse. This is not to say that 'one' may not be reduced to 'me', but 'one' at least extends the invitation to an objective consideration.

The constraint on the use of 'I' is not easy to understand nor is it easy to demonstrate what is thought to be understood. It may be that if an individual takes as his reference point rigid adherence to a wide range of closely shared identifications and expectations, the area of discretion available is reduced and the differentiation of self from act may be constrained. Looked at from another point of view the controls on behaviour would be mediated through a res-tricted self-editing process. If, on the other hand, the controls are mediated through a less constrained self-editing process the area of discretion available to the individual in particular areas is greater. It may well be that such different forms of mediation, in themselves functions of the form social relationships take, are responsible for the differential use of the self-reference pronoun. If this were to be the case then the relative infrequency of 'I' would occur whenever the form of social relationship generated a restricted code. The degree of restriction of the code would affect the probability of the use of 'I'. If individuals are limited to a restricted code one of its general effects may be to reduce the verbal differentiation of self.

The data indicated that although no difference was found in the proportion of prepositions to words the middle-class group selected a higher proportion of the preposition 'of' to 'of' plus 'in' and 'into'. These prepositions account for a much greater proportion of the total prepositions than do any other three. In earlier work it has been suggested that an elaborated code would be associated with greater selection of prepositions symbolizing logical relationships than with prepositions indicating spatial or temporal contiguity. 'Of' has also an adjectival quality and it may be that the restraint on this form of qualification is also responsible for the relatively infrequent use of the preposition 'of' in the working-class groups. There is a hint that this may be the case. Within the working-class groups the average group (5) selected a higher proportion of this preposition and it is this group which uses a higher proportion of adjectives although the difference is not significant.

Of particular interest is the class distribution of the S.C. sequences. It is thought that these sequences will occur more frequently whenever a restricted code is used. The meanings signalled in this code tend to be implicit and so condensed, with the result that there is less redundancy. A greater strain is placed upon the listener which is relieved by the range of identification which the speakers share. The S.C. sequences may be transmitted as a response of the speaker to the condensation of his own meanings. The speaker requires assurance that the message has been received and the listener requires an opportunity to indicate the contrary. It is as if the speaker is saying 'Check—are we together on this?'. On the whole the speaker expects affirmation. At the same time, by inviting agreement, the S.C. sequences test the range of identifications which the speakers have in common. The agreement reinforces the form of the social relationship which lends its objective authority to the significance of what is said. This also acts to reduce any uncertainty which the speaker may have had when the message was first planned. This uncertainty may not only arise out of the change in the level of coding. Inasmuch as a restricted code is generated by the sense of 'we-ness' then at the point where a speaker is giving reasons or making suggestions the form of the social relationship undergoes a subtle change.

A shift from narrative or description to reflection—from the simple ordering of experiences to abstracting from experience—also may signal a shift from we-centred to *individuated* experience. If this is so, then this shift introduces a measure of social isolation for the speaker which differentiates the speaker from his group in a way similar to a figure-ground relation. Inasmuch as the group is based upon a closely-shared self-consciously held identification the change in the role relationships of the members is clearly indicated. The unspoken affirmation which the S.C. signal may receive, reduces the sociological strain upon the speaker. In a discussion situation which invites the verbal signalling of individuated experience, the 'we-ness' of the group is modified in direct relation to such individuated signalling. The S.C. sequences may then function as feelers towards a new equilibrium for the group; that is towards a new balance in the role relationship of the members. This analysis is wholly consistent with the use of these sequences as an idiosyncratic speech habit of an individual. The point here is that they are released relatively frequently by all individuals if they are constrained by a particular form of social relationship which generates a restricted linguistic code.

Thus Groups 3, 4 and 5, the working-class groups, who it is considered are limited to a restricted code, will use such sequences frequently. The uncertainty of the appropriateness of the message, for these groups, in a discussion situation will probably be relatively great. This will add to the sociological strain inherent in producing a verbally individuated message. As a consequence, the frequency of S.C. sequences may be expected to be great.

The middle-class groups are oriented to an elaborated code which is appropriated to a formal discussion situation. This code facilitates the verbal explication of meaning and so there is more redundancy. In a sense, any speaker is less dependent upon the listener because he has taken into account the requirements of the listener in the preparation of his speech. The form of the social relationship which generates this code is such that a range of discretion must be available to the members if it is to be produced at all. Further, the members' social history must have included practice and training for the role which such social relationships require. Role does not refer to the specific role within a discussion group but more generally to the particular role relationships consequent upon the use of an elaborated code. These role relationships receive less support from implicit identifications shared by the participators. The orientation of the individual is based upon the expectation of psychological difference, his own and others. Individuated speech presupposes a history of a particular role relationship if it is to be prepared and delivered appropriately. Inasmuch as difference is part of the expectation, there is less reliance or dependency on the listener; or rather this dependency is reduced by the explication of meaning. The dependency under-pinning the use of a restricted code is upon the closely shared identifications which serve as a back-cloth to the speech. The dependency under-pinning the use of an elaborated code is upon the verbal explication of meaning. The sources of strain which inhere in these codes, and so in the social relationships which generate them, are different. Thus the use of S.C. sequences in an elaborated code will tend to be relatively infrequent.

In the light of this argument, of what significance is the frequency of 'I think' sequences which are associated, it is thought, with the use of an elaborated code and so differentiates Groups 1 and 2 from Groups 3, 4 and 5?

The preface 'I think' is probably as much an indication of semantic uncertainty as the S.C. sequences are in a restricted code. The former sequence does not usually require affirmation; in fact such return signalling is often inappropriate. It invites a further 'I think' on the part of the listener. The sequence signals difference and relates the sequence to the person. It symbolizes the area of discretion which the form of the social relationship permits. It translates in palpable form the sociological relationship constraining the participators. The egocentric basis of the interaction is raised like a flag. At the same time this sequence, just like the S.C. sequences, may indicate the strain in the social interaction but in this case the strain is taken wholly by the *individual*.

Table 4 indicates that Group 2 used more 'I think' sequences than Group 1, the high verbal middle-class group.[2] In the previous report the analysis of hesitation phenomena indicated that Group 2 relative to Group 1 used a shorter phrase length and a slower rate of articulation. This was taken to mean that Group 2 were in a situation of coding difficulty. If the S.C. and 'I think' sequences are functional equivalents in different codes then the total number of such sequences might give an index of coding difficulty. Table 4 indicates the percentage occurrence of this combination. Group 1, the high verbal middle-class group, and Group 5, the average working-class group, have very much lower percentages. There is little objective data which can be used to support the hypothesis that these groups were under less coding difficulty. However, Group 5 in relation to all the other sub-groups used a much shorter pause duration per word which suggests that the speech was well organized and of a high habit strength.

Finally, these sequences may set up different constraints on the flow of communication, particularly on its logical development and elaboration. Inasmuch as the S.C. sequences, which are generated basically by uncertainty, invite implicit affirmation of the previous sequence then they tend to close communication in a particular area rather than facilitate its development and elaboration. The sequences tend to act to maintain the reduction in redundancy and so the condensation of meaning. The 'I think' sequence, on the other hand, allows the listener far more degrees of freedom and may be regarded as an invitation to the listener to develop the communication on his own terms. The sequence facilitates the development and elaboration of the communication and so the logical development and exploration of a particular area. The content analysis of the speech samples may throw some light upon this function of the 'I think' and S.C. sequences. These sequences then, in the light of the above argument, play an important role in maintaining the equilibrium which characterizes the different codes.

If this analysis is appropriate then the role of 'I think' and the S.C. sequences (where they are not idiosyncratic habits) can be understood only in terms of the two codes of which they are a part. As the codes are functions of different forms of social relationships or, more generally, qualities of different social structures, then the function of these sequences must receive sociological analysis. Different orienting media, different forms of dependency, different areas of discretion inhere in these codes and thus the sources of strain in the relationships are also different. Psychological factors will affect the frequency with which different individuals take up the options represented by the sequences. At this point it would be better to conceptualize these sequences as *egocentric* and *sociocentric* signals.

As language is a patterned activity, the consistency of the findings for the two codes is partly to be expected. To attempt to assess the relative contribution of the various measures to the stability of the code is beyond the scope of this report. It is thought that the best single indicator of the two codes is the proportion of subordinations to finite verbs and this measure is, of course, implied in the original definition of the codes.

It may seem that this discussion of the results is somewhat un-balanced in the sense that it has been almost limited to the personal pronouns and the egocentric and sociocentric sequences. This is because in previous papers attention has been given to the findings on the other measures. An attempt has been made to relate the results to conditions more general than social class. Class is a particular but not a necessary exemplar of the codes. The latter are more strictly functions of social hierarchy.

Conclusion

The findings clearly indicate that for this small sample of subjects speech orientation to the two codes and the verbal planning processes which they entail are independent of measured intelligence indicated by the tests used. The mean difference of over 20 non-verbal IQ points between the working-class Groups 3, 4, and 5 does not disturb the orientation of the speech. The mean difference of 17 verbal IQ points between the middle-class Groups 1 and 2 again does not disturb the orientation of the speech of these groups. This does not mean that the quality of the speech is necessarily the same but that the class groups differ in terms of the level of structure and lexicon from which selections are made.

The results fall into two main groups in terms of the direction of the differences found for the various measures; *m* after the finding on a particular measure indicates that the result holds only for the major class comparison (1+2 v. 3+4+5).

Group A

Middle-class groups used a high proportion of the following:

Subordinations
Complex verbal stems
Passive voice
Total adjectives
Uncommon adjectives
Uncommon adverbs
Uncommon conjunctions
Egocentric sequences
'of' as a proportion of the sum of the prepositions 'of', 'in' and 'into' (this finding is *not* consistent within the working-class group)
'I' as a proportion of all personal pronouns
'I' as a proportion of total number of words
'I' as a proportion of total selected pronouns

Where the level of significance of the difference for the major class comparisons is 0·05, the finding should be regarded only as suggestive. In the above group results this applies to 'I' as a proportion of total selected personal pronouns and 'I' as a proportion of words.

Group B

The working-class groups use a higher proportion of the following:

Total personal pronouns (*m*)
Total selected personal pronouns (*m*)
'You' and 'they' combined as a proportion of total personal pronouns (*m*)
'You' and 'they' combined (total personal pronouns) as a proportion of total number of words
'You' and 'they' combined as a proportion of total selected personal pronouns (*m*)
'You' and 'they' combined (selected personal pronouns) as a proportion of total number of words (*m*)
Sociocentric sequences

The significance of the difference for the above results is at the 0·05 level of confidence in the case of total personal and selected pronouns.

No significant differences were found for the proportion of finite verbs, nouns, adverbs, prepositions, conjunctions, and the proportion of the selected personal pronoun 'I' to number of words.

It should be remembered, when assessing the results that the working-class sample was reduced by two subjects as these subjects contributed too few words to justify analysis.

Although the findings for the class comparisons are not related to the number of words, the results must be placed in the perspective of a very small speech sample. The consistency of the findings for the two class groups suggests that if the speech samples were increased it would be a little unlikely for the working-class groups to change their level of verbal planning and maintain it. The topic of the discussion may also have affected some of the elements measured and the relationship with the researcher could have affected probably the quality and amount of speech. The topic may have had a different significance for the two class groups. The working class may have tended to identify with the criminal and the middle class with law and principles of justice. The point is not that such identifications may occur but their effect on speech. One can identify with the criminal but not necessarily be limited to speech with the characteristics associated with the present findings.

It will be remembered that the arrangement of the original groups was different from the arrangement for this analysis. In the case of Groups 1 and 2 and Groups 3 and 4 internal exchanges within the class groups were made in order to control more adequately for verbal IQ. Whilst the scores the exchanged members received were appropriate to the groups to which they were attached, the possibility that the middle-class group of average verbal ability (Group 2) may have been affected by the presence of the high verbal subject cannot be ruled out. On the other hand the original Groups 3 and 4 contained the possibility of a similar disturbance, but perhaps more limited in its effect as the verbal IQ range was narrower. The important question is whether the groups were sufficiently stretched by the discussion to allow for the possibility of changes in the level of the speech. The researcher is confident that the conditions for changes in the level existed in all groups. The measures used in this report are too insensitive to allow the measurement of variations within a given level. It is clear, however, that a longer speech sample, obtained from many more subjects under different conditions, including written work, is required.

With these reservations in mind, it is considered that the results of the analysis of the hesitation phenomena and of the simple grammatical analysis presented in this paper are supportive evidence for the two codes and their social class relationship.

Notes

1 This sub-group used longer words as measured by syllable length (Bernstein, 1962).
2 The number of S.C. sequences produced are too small for comparison.

References

BERNSTEIN, B. (1961a), 'Social class and linguistic development: a theory of social learning', in *Education, Economy and Society*, (eds.) Halsey, A. H., Floud, J. and Anderson, C. A., New York: Free Press.

BERNSTEIN, B. (1961b), 'Social structure, language and learning', *J. Educ. Res.* 3, 163.

BERNSTEIN, B. (1962), 'Linguistic codes, hesitation phenomena and intelligence', *Language and Speech* 5, 31.

SIEGEL, S. (1956), *Non-Parametric Statistics*, New York: Wiley.

Chapter 7   A socio-linguistic approach to social learning

This paper is concerned with:

(1) The neglect of the study of speech by sociologists;
(2) The role of speech as a major aspect of culture and the means of its transmission;
(3) The relations between forms of speech and forms of social relation;
(4) The social and educational consequences of differential access to forms of speech.

The reader may well think that the early discussion in this paper bears little relation to education. It is relevant but the argument is a complex one.

Perhaps one of the most important events that has taken place in scientific endeavour in the twentieth century is the convergence of both the natural and social sciences upon the study of linguistic aspects of communication. The consequences of this convergence and the new relations between the disciplines which it has brought about may well be worthy of a chapter in the next book on the sociology of knowledge. Through the study of language the link between biological and socio-cultural orders is gradually being established. The clarification of this link and the resultant theories may well have consequences for control as exciting as the progress in our understanding of the genetic code. This is not the place to discuss the trends in separate disciplines which have led to this convergence, but a number of works may serve as guides for the reader. What is a little odd is the negligible contribution of sociology to the study of language. The textbooks celebrate the fact of man's symbolic possibilities in chapters on culture and socialization and then the consequences are systematically ignored. One might go as far as saying that the only time one is made aware that humans speak in the writings of contemporary sociologists is incidentally through the statistical relations induced from social-survey enquiries. And here all that is required is that the subjects can read: speech confounds the later arithmetic. Even when what a person says is considered to be relevant, what is actually said is rarely, in itself, singled out as worthy of systematic study. The origins and consequences of forms of saying, linguistic forms, their conditions, formal patterning, regulative functions, their history and change are not included in the sociologist's analysis. And yet long ago both Durkheim and Weber drew attention to the social significance of language.

In its struggle for recognition, sociology has continuously insisted upon the fact that there exists an order of relations, arising out of the interactions of members of a society, which constrains and directs behaviour independent of the unique characteristics of its members. Sociologists have been concerned to explain the nature of this order, in particular the processes making for its diversity and change, and to develop on a formal level a grammar or syntax which controls the conceptualizing of this order. They have studied the major complexes of social forms which shape the social order, their interrelations, and the factors responsible for their change. Language is seen as an integrating or divisive phenomenon; as the major process through which a culture is transmitted; the bearer of social genes. However, this has rarely given rise to a study of language as a social institution comparable to the analyses made of, say, the family, religion, etc. As far as speech is concerned this has been viewed as a datum, taken for granted, and not as an object of special enquiry. It is, of course, true that through the writings of George Mead the role of language, really the role of speech, has been explicitly recognized in the formation of a distinctly social self. And yet, in the study of socialization, it is not possible to find an empirical study which systematically examines the role of speech as the process by which a child comes to acquire a specific *social* identity. In fact, in the numerous studies of child-rearing with the exception of very few, there is no account of the patterning of the linguistic environment.[1] Groups are studied, their formal ordering elegantly discussed, but the implications and consequences of *linguistic* aspects of their communications seem to be unworthy of sociological consideration. Graduates are trained to conduct surveys, to construct questionnaires, to interview, without, at least in England, any explicit and systematic training in what Dell Hymes has called the ethnography of speech—although there is an intuitive or unsystematic recognition of differences in the patterning and consequences of speech events in various sub-cultures.

Sociologists, who focus upon social dynamics as these are expressed through changes in the major institutional forms, have thrown a shadow on problems implicit in the work of the great nineteenth-century theorists. Weber, for example, discusses various types of rationality, and their associated institutional orders and forms of authority. Complex societies involve various forms of rationality which may be differentially distributed among their members. Weber's typology of rationality bears some resemblance to cultural themes which determine modes of action. How does an individual come to acquire a particular form of rationality? Weber's concept of rationality requires an explicit formulation of the inter-relations between institutional and cultural orders *and* of the process whereby individual experience manifests itself in special modes of social action. Durkheim's analysis of the origins and consequences of mechanical and organic solidarity presuppose the same problem.[2] The concept of the individual in Durkheim is reduced to an unstable state of appetites—an instinct-system tending towards disintegration in conditions where the energies are not subordinate to a nor-mative order of a particular kind. His formulation has the distinct merit of stating the problem of the relationship between biological and socio-cultural orders.

A major attempt to relate biological, institutional and cultural orders has been made with the use of the writings of Freud. Indeed, much work on socialization, on the relation between culture and personality, both in anthropology and sociology, implicitly or ex-plicitly attempts a solution of Durkheim's problem in these terms. However, this approach precludes the study of language and speech. As a result of working with the Freudian theory certain elements within the theory limited interest in linguistic phenomena. The gains of this approach are partly outweighed by the tendency to reduce the social to the psychological by means of a theory of unconscious motivation giving rise to an affective theory of learning. Although the ego in psychoanalytic theory is essentially a linguistically dif-ferentiated organization, speech tends to be regarded epi-phenomen-ally as a process shaped by the patterning of the mechanisms of de-fence. It is, of course, true that in this theory reality-testing is accom-plished essentially through verbal procedures, but the patterning of speech is accorded no independence in this theory nor in the behaviour which the theory illuminates.[3] As a result, anthropologists and sociolo-gists who used Freudian theory in their attempts to understand the transformation of the psychic into the social paid little attention to either language or speech, and so carried over into their work the dichotomy between thought and feeling implicit in Freud. Further, the institutional and cultural order are often interpreted in terms of projections of unconscious formations within the individual.

It would seem then that sociologists, because of their emphasis on changes in the major institutional forms in industrial society, have tended to neglect until very recently the study of the transmission of culture. Where this has been attempted, for example in the study of socialization, the influence of Freud has diverted attention from the linguistic environment. The influence of George Mead, who stressed the role of speech in the formation of a distinct social identity, assisted the rise of what has been called interaction theory, but paradoxically not to any special study of the medium of interaction, i.e. speech. The net effect of these movements has been to weaken the possibility of connection between sociology and linguistics and the cross-fertilization of theories and methods between the two disciplines.

This neglect of the study of language and speech in sociology has certainly not been typical of a school of anthropologists who have firmly and boldly stated a controversial relation between language and the interpretation of reality. William von Humboldt's statement in 1848 that 'man lives with the world about him principally indeed . . . exclusively as language presents it' was echoed by Boas who claimed that a purely linguistic analysis 'would provide the data for a thorough investigation of the psychology of the peoples of the world'. However, it was with Sapir, a student of Boas, that a new elegance, clarity, subtlety and originality, was introduced into the discussion of the inter-relations between language, culture and personality, and which has deeply affected all work in this area. Language, according to Sapir, 'does not as a matter of fact stand apart from or run parallel to direct experience but completely interpenetrates it'. Hoijer succinctly stated Sapir's thesis as follows: Peoples speaking different languages may be said to live in different 'worlds of reality' in the sense that the languages they speak affect to a considerable degree both their sensory perceptions and their habitual modes of thought.

Sapir writes: Language is a guide to 'social reality'. Though language is not ordinarily thought of as of essential interest to the students of social science, it powerfully conditions all our thinking about social problems and processes . . . It is quite an illusion to imagine that one adjusts to reality essentially without the use of language and that language is merely an incidental means of solving specific problems of communication or reflection. The fact of the matter is that the real world is to a large extent unconsciously built up on the language habits of the group . . . We see and hear and otherwise experience very largely as we do because the language habits of our community predispose certain choices of interpretation. Whorf, a student of Sapir, went further and attempted to derive from the morphological syntactic and lexical features of Hopi the 'habitual thought' or 'thought world' of the people. The thought world is 'the microcosm that each man carries about inside himself by which he measures and understands what he can of the macrocosm'. Hoijer, one of the major interpreters of Whorf, states that 'the fashions of speaking peculiar to a people, like other aspects of their culture, are indicative of a view of life, a metaphysics of their culture, compounded of unquestioned and mainly unstated premises which define the nature of the universe and man's position within it'.

This is not the place to follow the many twists and turns of the controversy these writings give rise to, or to examine the empirical support for the theory, but the reader will find in the bibliography a guide to this literature. This thesis had repercussions for psychology and has been an important factor in bringing about a relationship between linguistics and psychology. One of the many difficulties associated with it is that it focuses upon *universal* features of the formal patterning of language. Although Whorf insists that 'the influence of language upon habitual thought and behaviour does not depend so much on *any one system* (e.g., tense or nouns) within the grammar as upon ways of analysing and reporting experience which have become fixed in the language as integrated "fashions of speaking" which cut across the typical grammatical classifications, so that a "fashion" may include lexical, morphological, syntactic, and otherwise systematically diverse means co-ordinated in a certain frame of consistency'. These fashions of speaking, the frames of consistency, are not related to an institutional order, nor are they seen as emerging from the structure of social relations. On the contrary, they are seen as determiners of social relations through their role in shaping the culture. In Whorf's later writings, and in the writings of his followers, it is certain morphological and syntactic features of the *language* made psychologically active through the fashion of speaking which elicit habitual and characteristic behaviour in the speakers. In other words, the link between language, culture and habitual thought is *not* mediated through the social structure.

The view to be taken here is different in that it will be argued that a number of fashions of speaking, frames of consistency, are possible in any given language and that these fashions of speaking, linguistic forms, or codes, are themselves a function of the form social relations take. According to this view, the form of the social relation or, more generally, the social structure generates distinct linguistic forms or codes and *these codes essentially transmit the culture and so constrain behaviour.*

This thesis is different from that of Whorf. It has more in common with some of the writings of Mead, Sapir, Malinowski and Firth. Whorf's psychology was influenced by the writings of the *gestalt* school of psychology whereas the thesis to be put forward here rests on the work of Vygotsky and Luria. In a sense the Whorfian theory is more general and more challenging; although, perhaps, it is less open to empirical confirmation, for it asserts that owing to the differential rates of change of culture and language *the latter determines the former*. The thesis to be developed here places the emphasis on changes in the social structure as major factors in shaping or changing a given culture through their effect on the consequences of fashions of speaking. It shares with Whorf the controlling influence on experience ascribed to 'frames of consistency' involved in fashions of speaking. It differs and perhaps relativizes Whorf by asserting that, in the context of a common language in the sense of a general code, there will arise distinct linguistic forms, fashions of speaking, which induce in their speakers *different* ways of relating to objects and persons. It leaves open the question whether there are features of the *common culture* which all members of a society share which are determined by the specific nature of the general code or language at its *syntactic* and *morphological* levels. It is, finally, more distinctly sociological in its emphasis on the system of social relations.

Elaborated and restricted codes

A general outline of the argument will be given first. This will be followed by a detailed analysis of two linguistic forms or codes and their variants. The discussion will be linked to the problem of educability as this is conceived in industrial societies.

Introduction

To begin with, a distinction must be made between language and speech. Dell Hymes (1961) writes: 'Typically one refers to the act or process of speech, but to the structure, pattern or system of language. Speech is a message, language is a code. Linguists have been preoccupied with inferring the constants of the language code.' The code which the linguistic invents in order to explain speech events is capable of generating *n* number of speech codes, and there is no reason for believing that any one language or general code is in this respect better than another, whether it is English or whether it is Hopi. On this argument language is a set of rules to which all speech codes must comply, but which speech codes are generated is a function of the system of social relations.

The particular form a social relation takes acts selectively on what is said, when it is said, and how it is said. The form of the social relation regulates the options which speakers take up at both syntactic and lexical levels. For example, if an adult is talking to a child he or she will use a speech form in which both the syntax and the vocabulary is simple. Put in another way, the consequences of the form the social relation takes are often transmitted in terms of certain syntactic and lexical selections. Inasmuch as a social relation does this, then it may establish for speakers principles of choice, so that a certain syntax and a certain lexical range is chosen rather than another. The specific principles of choice which regulate these selections entail from the point of view of both speaker and listener planning procedures which guide the speaker in the preparation of his speech and which also guide the listener in its reception.

Changes in the form of certain social relations, it is argued, act selectively upon the principles controlling the selection of both syntactic and lexical options. Changes in the form of the social relation affect the planning procedures used in the preparation of speech and the orientation of the listener. The speech used by members of an army combat unit on manoeuvres will be somewhat different from the same members' speech at a padre's evening. Different forms of social relations can generate quite different speech-systems or linguistic codes by affecting the planning procedures. These different speech-systems or codes create for their speakers different orders of relevance and relation. The experience of the speakers may then be transformed by what is made significant or relevant by the different speech-systems. This is a sociological argument, because the speech-system is taken as a consequence of the form of the social relation or, to put it more generally, is a quality of the social structure.

As the child learns his speech or, in the terms used here, learns specific codes which regulate his verbal acts, he learns the requirements of his social structure. The experience of the child is transformed by the learning which is generated by his own apparently voluntary acts of speech. The social structure becomes the substratum of his experience essentially through the consequences of the linguistic process. From this point of view, every time the child speaks or listens the social structure of which he is a part is reinforced in him and his social identity is constrained. The social structure becomes the developing child's psychological reality by the shaping of his acts of speech. Underlying the general pattern of his speech are, it is held, critical sets of choices, preferences for some alternatives rather than others, which develop and are stabilized through time and which eventually come to play an important role in the regulation of intellectual, social and affective orientations.

The same process can be put rather more formally. Individuals come to learn their roles through the process of communication. A role from this point of view is a constellation of shared learned meanings, through which an individual is able to enter into persistent, consistent and recognized forms of interaction with others. A role is thus a complex coding activity controlling the creation and organization of specific meanings *and* the conditions for their transmission and reception. Now, if it is the case that the communication system which defines a given role behaviourally is essentially that of speech, it should be possible to distinguish critical roles in terms of the speech forms they regulate. The consequences of specific speech forms or codes will transform the environs into a matrix of particular meanings which becomes part of psychic reality through acts of speech. As a person learns to subordinate his behaviour to a linguistic code, which is the expression of the role, different orders of relation are made available to him. The complex of meanings which a role-system transmits reverberates developmentally in an individual to inform his general conduct. On this argument it is the linguistic transformation of the role which is the major bearer of meanings: it is through specific linguistic codes that relevance is created, experience given a particular form, and social identity constrained.

Children who have access to different speech-systems (i.e, learn different roles by virtues of their status position in a given social structure) may adopt quite different social and intellectual procedures despite a common potential.

Elaborated and restricted codes: definitions and brief description

Two general types of code can be distinguished: *elaborated* and *restricted*. They can be defined, on a linguistic level, in terms of the probability of predicting for any one speaker which syntactic elements will be used to organize meaning across a representative range of speech. In the case of an elaborated code, the speaker will select from a relatively extensive range of alternatives and the probability of predicting the organizing elements is considerably reduced. In the case of a restricted code the number of these alternatives is often severely limited and the probability of predicting the elements is greatly increased.

On a psychological level the codes may be distinguished by the extent to which each facilitates (elaborated code) or inhibits (restricted code) an orientation to symbolize intent in a verbally explicit form. Behaviour processed by these codes will, it is proposed, develop different modes of self-regulation and so different forms of orientation. The codes themselves are functions of a particular form of social relationship or, more generally, qualities of social structures.

A distinction will be made between verbal or linguistic, and extra-verbal or para-linguistic components of a communication. The linguistic or verbal component refers to messages where meaning is mediated by words: their selection, combination and organization. The para-linguistic or extra-verbal component refers to meanings mediated through expressive associates of words (rhythm, stress, pitch, etc.) or through gesture, physical set and facial modification.

Restricted code (lexical prediction)

The pure form of a restricted code would be one where all the words, and hence the organizing structure irrespective of its degree of complexity, are wholly predictable for speakers and listeners. Examples of this pure form would be ritualistic modes of communication: relationships regulated by protocol, types of religious services, cocktail-party routines, some story-telling situations. In these relations individual difference cannot be signalled through the verbal channel except in so far as the *choice* of sequence or routine exists. It is transmitted essentially through variations in extra-verbal signals.

Consider the case of a mother telling her child stories which they both know by heart. 'And Little Red Riding Hood went into the wood' (ritualistic pause). 'And what do you think happened?' (rhetorical question). If the mother wishes to transmit her discrete experience, her uniqueness, she is unable to do this by varying her words. She can do it only by varying the signals transmitted through extra-verbal channels; through changes in intonation, pitch, speech rhythm, facial set, gesture, or even through changes in muscular tension, if she is holding the child. The code defines the channels through which new information (i.e. learning) can be made available. The discrete intents of mother and child, interpersonal aspects of the relation, can be transmitted only extra-verbally.

Given the selection of the sequence, new information will be made available through the extra-verbal channels, and these channels are likely to become the object of special perceptual activity. The code defines the form of the social relationship by restricting the *verbal* signalling of individual differences. Individuals relate to each other essentially through *the social position or status they are occupying*. Societies differ in terms of the use made of this code and the conditions which elicit it.

It is suggested that where there is an *exchange* of verbal message of maximal predictability, such as social routines, the context will be one where the participants have *low* predictability about each other's individual attributes. The code offers here the possibility of deferred commitment to the relationship. Decisions about its future form will be based upon the significance given to the exchange of extra-verbal messages.

Consider a cocktail party. Two people are introduced who have never met before. A social routine is likely to develop. This establishes mutual predictability and so the basis of a social relation. What is said is impersonal in that the verbal messages are all previously organized. The individuals will be highly sensitive to extra-verbal signals and so these signals are likely to become the object of special perceptual activity. How the social relation will develop initially depends upon the choice of social routine and the significance accorded to extra-verbal signals. Here, orientation is towards the extra-verbal channels: there is a minimal level of planning involved in the preparation of speech; the exchange of verbal sequences presupposes a shared cultural heritage which controls the verbal communications offered by the occupants of this cocktail-party status.

It is important to note that:

(1) The status or positional aspect of the social relationship is important.

(2) Orientation is likely to be towards the extra-verbal channels as new information will pass through these channels.

(3) Specifically verbal planning is confined to choice of sequence, rather than involving the selection and organization of the sequence.

(4) The code restricts the verbal signalling of individual difference.

Restricted code (syntactic prediction)

What is more often found is a restricted code, where prediction is only possible at the syntactic level.[4] The lexicon will vary from one case to another, but in all cases it is drawn from a narrow range. It is necessary to point out that because a lexicon is drawn from a narrow range this is no criterion for classifying the code as a restricted one. The most general condition for the emergence of this code is a social relationship based upon a common, extensive set of closely-shared identifications and expectations self-consciously held by the members.[5] It follows that the social relationship will be one of an inclusive kind. The speech is here refracted through a common cultural identity which reduces the need to verbalize intent so that it becomes explicit, with the consequence that the structure of the speech is simplified, and the lexicon will be drawn from a narrow range. The extra-verbal component of the communication will become a major channel for transmitting individual qualifications and so individual difference. The speech will tend to be impersonal in that it will not be specially prepared to fit a given referent. *How* things are said, *when* they are said, rather than what is said, becomes important. The intent of the listener is likely to be taken for granted. The meanings are likely to be concrete, descriptive or narrative rather than analytical or abstract. In certain areas meanings will be highly condensed. The speech in these social relations is likely to be fast and fluent, articulatory clues are reduced; some meanings are likely to be dislocated, condensed and local; there will be a low level of vocabulary and syntactic selection; *the unique meaning of the individual is likely to be implicit.*

Restricted codes are not necessarily linked to social class. They are used by all members of a society at some time. The major function of this code is to define and reinforce the form of the social relationship by restricting the verbal signalling of individual experience.[6]

Elaborated code (low syntactic prediction)

An elaborated code, where prediction is much less possible at the syntactic level, is likely to arise in a social relationship which raises the tension in its members to select from their linguistic resources a *verbal* arrangement which closely fits specific referents. This situation will arise where the intent of the other person cannot be taken for granted, with the consequence that meanings will have to be expanded and raised to the level of *verbal* explicitness. The verbal planning here, unlike the case of a restricted code, promotes a higher level of syntactic organization and lexical selection. The preparation and delivery of relatively explicit meaning is the major function of this code. This does not mean that these meanings are necessarily abstract, but abstraction inheres in the possibilities. The code will facilitate the *verbal* transmission and elaboration of the individual's unique experience. The condition of the listener, unlike that in the case of a restricted code, will *not* be taken for granted, as the speaker is likely to modify his speech in the light of the special conditions and attributes of the listener. This is not to say that such modifications will always occur, but that this possibility exists. If a restricted code facilitates the construction and exchange of communalized symbols, then an elaborated code facilitates the verbal construction and exchange of individualized or personal symbols. An elaborated code, through its regulation, induces in its speakers a sensitivity to the implications of separateness and differences and points to the possibilities inherent in a complex conceptual hierarchy for the organization of experience.

An example at this point is necessary to show how these various codes control social relations. Imagine a man is at a party where he finds a large number of people whom he has never met before. He goes up to a girl. He will then use, initially, a restricted code (lexicon prediction), which will provide the basis for the social relation. He will attempt to improve upon his understanding of her specific attributes by the meaning he gives to her presence and extra-verbal transmissions. He is then likely to move towards an elaborated code (if he possesses one) so that they may both have a means for elaborating verbally their distinctive experience. The possibility of discovering common ground is in this way increased, and the man may then move into a restricted code (syntactic prediction). The quality of the relationship at this point has shifted, and the girl may then regard this as slightly presumptuous and so force the man back to an elaborated code, or, if he is very unfortunate, to a restricted code (lexicon prediction). On the other hand she may accept the change in the social relation. The important points here are that the codes are induced by the social relation, are expressing it, *and* are regulating it. *The ability to switch codes controls the ability to switch roles.* This is a very simple example but it illustrates all the points made earlier.

Formal sociological conditions for the emergence of the two codes

It is possible to state the formal sociological conditions for the emergence of the two codes by distinguishing between the generality of the meanings controlled by the codes and the availability of the speech models from whom they are learned. To the extent that meanings are made explicit and are conventionalized through language, meanings may be called *universalistic*, whilst if they are implicit and relatively less conventionalized through language, meanings can be called *particularistic*. Similarly, if the speech models are potentially generally available, such models can be called universalistic, whilst if the speech models are much less available they can be called particularistic.

Using these concepts, a restricted code is *particularistic* with reference to its meaning and so to the social structure which it presupposes. However, it is *universalistic* with reference to its models, as such models are generally available. It is important to note here that the concern is with the availability of a *special syntax*. An elaborated code is *universalistic* with reference to its meanings and so to the social structure which it presupposes. However, it is likely that the speech models for this code will be *particularistic*. This does not mean that the origin of this code is to be sought in the psychological qualities of the models but that the models are incumbents of specialized social positions located in the system of social stratification. In principle this is not necessary, but it is likely to be empirically the case.

Thus, because a restricted code is universalistic with reference to its models, all people have access to its special syntax and to various systems of local condensed meanings; but because an elaborated code is very likely to be particularistic with respect to its models, only some people will have access to its syntax and to the universalistic character of its meanings. Following this argument, the use of an elaborated code or an orientation to its use will depend *not* on the psychological properties of a speaker but upon access to specialized social positions, by virtue of which a particular type of speech model is made available. Normally, but not inevitably, such social positions will coincide with a stratum seeking or already possessing access to the major decision-making areas of the society.

In terms of learning the codes, the codes are different. The syntax of a restricted code may be learned informally and readily. The greater range of, and selection from, the syntactic alternatives of an elaborated code normally requires a much longer period of formal and informal learning.

These distinctions are useful in isolating the general conditions for a special case of a restricted code (syntactic prediction). This is where the speech model is particularistic and the meaning is also particularistic. In this situation the individual is wholly constrained by the code. *He has access to no other.* The consequences of this are thought to be relevant to the problem of educability in developed or emergent industrialized societies. The sociological conditions may be summarized as follows:

Restricted code (lexical prediction)

Ritualistic components of status or positional relationships

Restricted code (high syntactic prediction)

(1) Model: universalistic; meaning: particularistic
(2) Model: particularistic; meaning: particularistic

Elaborated code (low syntactic prediction)

Model: particularistic; meaning: universalistic

Verbal planning, linguistic codes and social structures

The codes have now been defined, briefly described, and their formal sociological determinants specified. It is necessary to show how these codes may become established on a psychological level and this will be done by looking more closely at the process called verbal planning.

When one person talks to another it is suggested that the following processes at different levels occur in the listener before he is able to produce a sequential reply.

Orientation: The listener first scans the communication for a pattern of dominant signals. Not all the words and extra-verbal signals will carry the same value; some will carry greater significance than others for the listener.

Selection: There will be associations to the patterns of dominant signals which will control the selections the listener makes from his potential stock of words, sequences and extra-verbal signals.

Organization: The listener will then have to fit the selected words and sequences into a grammatical frame and integrate them with the extra-verbal signals.

On a psychological level codes are generated by specific kinds of verbal planning. It follows that restricted and elaborated codes will establish different kinds of regulation which crystallize in the nature of verbal planning. The originating determinant of the kind of orientation, selection and organization is the form of the social relation or, more generally, it is a quality of the social structure. The codes, linguistic translations of the meanings of the social structure, are nothing more than verbal planning activities at the psychological level and *only at this level can they be said to exist.*

The consequences of the form of the social relationship are transmitted and sustained by codes which at the individual level consist of verbal planning processes. Particular orders of relationship to objects and persons inhere in linguistic codes. These orders of relation are then spontaneously generated by the individual as the verbal planning processes become stabilized. Following this argument, changes in the social structure, in the organization of forms of social relation, modify speech systems or linguistic codes. These in turn, by virtue of verbal planning procedures, change the order of significance which individuals spontaneously create as a consequence of their acts of speech and which in their creation transform them. Clearly not all aspects of social structure are translated into elements of the linguistic code, but it is considered that the major aspects are so translated.

The following diagram[7] might be helpful in distinguishing the levels of analysis:

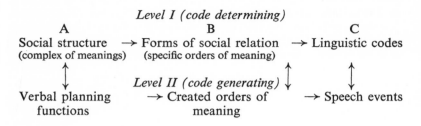

Level I (code determining)

A	B	C
Social structure	→ Forms of social relation	→ Linguistic codes
(complex of meanings)	(specific orders of meaning)	

Level II (code generating)

| Verbal planning functions | → Created orders of meaning | → Speech events |

The arrows indicate reciprocal influence as it is possible for a verbal planning function to develop which creates novel orders of meaning and social relation.

Some implications of restricted[8] and elaborated codes

An elaborated code generated originally by the form of the social relation becomes a facility for transmitting individuated verbal responses. As far as any one speaker is concerned, he is not aware of a speech-system or code, but the planning procedures which he is using both in the preparation of his speech and in the receiving of speech creates one. These planning procedures promote a relatively higher level of syntactic organization and lexical selection than does a restricted code. What is then made available for learning, by an elaborated code, is of a different order from that made available in the case of a restricted code. The learning generated by these speech-systems is quite different. By learning, the reference is to what is significant, what is made relevant: socially, intellectually and emotionally. From a developmental perspective, an elaborated code user comes to perceive language as a set of theoretical possibilities available for the transmission of unique experience. The concept of self, unlike the concept of self of a speaker limited to a restricted code, will be verbally differentiated, so that it becomes in itself the object of special perceptual activity. In the case of a speaker limited to a restricted code, the concept of self will tend to be refracted through the implications of the status arrangements. Here there is no problem of self, *because the problem is not relevant.*

As a child learns an elaborated code he learns to scan a particular syntax, to receive and transmit a particular pattern of meaning, to develop a particular verbal planning process, and very early *learns to orient towards the verbal channel*. He learns to manage the role requirements necessary for the effective production of the code. He becomes aware of a certain order of relationships (intellectual, social and emotional) in his environment, and his experience is transformed by these relations. As the code becomes established through its planning procedures, the developing child voluntarily, through his acts of speech, generates these relations. He comes to perceive language as a set of theoretical possibilities for the presentation of his discrete experience to others. An elaborated code, through its regulation, induces developmentally in its speakers an expectation of separateness and difference from others. It points to the possibilities inherent in a complex conceptual hierarchy for the organization of experience.

It is possible to distinguish two modes of an elaborated code. One mode facilitates the verbal elaboration of *interpersonal relations*, and the second facilitates the verbal elaboration of relations between *objects*. These two modes of an elaborated code would differentiate different ranges of experience and would presuppose learning to manage different role relations. The two modes possess the general features of an elaborated code. They both carry low syntactic prediction; they both serve as facilities for the verbal elaboration of discrete intent; they orient their users to the expectation of difference; they point to logically similar conceptual orders: *but the referents of the relationships are different.*

An individual going into the arts is likely to possess an elaborated code oriented to the person; whilst an individual going into the sciences, particularly the applied sciences, is likely to possess an elaborated code oriented to object relations. C. P. Snow's two cultures may be related to the experiences differentiated through these two modes of an elaborated code. To be able to switch from one mode to the other may involve a recognition of, and an ability to translate verbally, different orders of experience. It may also involve a *recognition* of and an *ability to manage* the different types of role relations which these modes of speech promote. Over and above genetic dispositions towards person or object relations, it may well be that certain kinds of family settings and schools can orient the child towards, and stabilize, the use of one or both of these two modes of an elaborated code. It is possible for an individual to be limited to an elaborated code and to the role relations of either of its two modes, or to possess both modes, or to possess all forms of elaborated and restricted codes. These alternatives may be subject to considerable environmental influence.

A child *limited* to a restricted code will tend to develop essentially through the regulation inherent in the code. For such a child, speech does not become the object of special perceptual activity, neither does a theoretical attitude develop towards the structural possibilities of sentence organization. The speech is epitomized by a low-level and limiting syntactic organization and there is little motivation or orientation towards increasing vocabulary.

There is a limited and often rigid use of qualifiers (adjectives, adverbs, etc.) and these function as social counters through which individual intent is transmitted. This drastically reduces the verbal elaboration of intent which instead tends to be given meaning through extra-verbal means. Words and speech sequences refer to broad classes of contents rather than to progressive differentiation within a class. The reverse of this is also possible; a range of items within a class may be listed without knowledge of the concept which summarizes the class. The categories referred to tend not to be broken down systematically. This has critical implications if the reference is to a subjective state of the speaker. Although the speech possesses a warmth and vitality, it tends to be impersonal in the literal sense of that word. The original social relation between mother and child exerted little pressure on the child to make his experience relatively explicit in a verbally differentiated way. Speech is not perceived as a major means of presenting to the other inner states. The type of learning, the conditions of learning and the dimensions of relevance initiated and sustained through a restricted code are radically different from the learning induced through an elaborated code.

The rigid range of syntactic possibilities leads to difficulty in conveying linguistically logical sequence and stress. The verbal planning function is shortened, and this often creates in sustained speech sequences a large measure of dislocation or disjunction. The thoughts are often strung together like beads on a frame rather than following a planned sequence. A restriction in planning often creates a high degree of redundancy. This means that there may well be a great deal of repetition of information, through sequences which add little to what has already been given. The following passages may illustrate these points:

It's all according like these youths and that if they get into these gangs and that they must have a bit of a lark around and say it goes wrong and that they probably knock someone off I mean think they just do it to be big getting publicity here and there.

Boy, age sixteen. IQ verbal 104, non-verbal 100

Well it should do but it don't seem to nowadays, like there's still murders going on now, any minute now or something like that they get people don't care they might get away with it then they all try it and it might leak out one might tell his mates that he's killed someone it might leak out like it might get around he gets hung for it like that.

Boy, age seventeen. IQ verbal 99, non-verbal 126+

Role relations may be limited and code switching may be hampered by the regulative consequences of a restricted code. An individual limited to a restricted code will tend to mediate an elaborated code through the regulation of his own.

The structure and function of the speech of children and adults limited to a restricted code is of the *same general order* as the speech induced by social relations generating a restricted code outlined earlier. Some children have access to no other code; their only code is a restricted one. Clearly one code is not better than another; each possesses its own aesthetic, its own possibilities. Society, however, may place different values on the orders of experience elicited, maintained and progressively strengthened through the different coding systems.

The orientation towards these codes, elaborated and restricted, may be independent of the psychology of the child, independent of his native ability, although the *level* at which a code is used will undoubtedly reflect purely psychological attributes. The orientation towards these codes may be governed entirely by the form of the social relation, or more generally by the quality of the social structure. The intellectual and social procedures by which individuals relate themselves to their environment may be very much a question of their speech models within the family and the codes these speech models use.

I should like to draw attention to the relations between social class and the two coding systems. The sub-cultural implications of social class give rise to different socialization procedures. The different normative systems create different family-role systems operating with different modes of social control. It is considered that the normative systems associated with the middle-class and associated strata are likely to give rise to the modes of an elaborated code whilst those associated with some sections of the working class are likely to create individuals limited to a restricted code. Clearly social class is an extremely crude index for the codes and more specific conditions for their emergence have been given in this paper. Variations in behaviour found within groups who fall within a particular class (defined in terms of occupation and education) within a mobile society are often very great. It is possible to locate the two codes and their modes more precisely by considering the orientation of the family-role system, the mode of social control and the resultant linguistic relations. Variations in the orientation of the family-role system can be linked to the external social network of the family and to occupational roles. It is not possible to do more than mention the possibilities of these more sensitive indices.

Children socialized within middle-class and associated strata can be expected to possess *both* an elaborated and a restricted code, whilst children socialized within some sections of the working-class strata, particularly the lower working-class, can be expected to be *limited* to a restricted code. If a child is to succeed as he progresses through school it becomes critical for him to possess, or at least to be oriented towards, an elaborated code.

The relative backwardness of lower working-class children may well be a form of culturally induced backwardness transmitted to the child through the implications of the linguistic process. The code the child brings to the school symbolizes his social identity. It relates him to his kin and to his local social relations. The code orients the child progressively towards a pattern of relationships which constitute for the child his psychological reality, and this reality is reinforced every time he speaks.

Conclusion

Two general linguistic codes or speech-systems have been discussed, their social origins explored and their regulative consequences briefly discussed. It is thought that the theory might throw some light on the social determinants of educability. Where a child is sensitive to an elaborated code the school experience for such a child is one of symbolic and social development; for the child limited to a restricted code the school experience is one of symbolic and social change. It is important to realize that a restricted code carries its own aesthetic. It will tend to develop a metaphoric range of considerable power, a simplicity and directness, a vitality and rhythm; it should not be disvalued. Psychologically, it unites the speaker to his kin and to his local community. A change of code involves changes in the *means* whereby social identity and reality are created. This argument means that educational institutions in a fluid society carry within themselves alienating tendencies. To say this is *not* to argue for the preservation of a pseudo-folk culture but is to argue for certain changes in the social structure of educational institutions; it is also to argue for increased sensitivity on the part of teachers towards both the cultural and cognitive requirements of the formal educational relationship. The problem goes deeper than this. It raises the question of a society which measures human worth, accords respect and grants significance by means of a scale of purely occupational achievement.

From a more academic point of view it is tentatively thought that the thesis might well have a more general application. Elaborated and restricted codes and their variants should be found in any society where their originating conditions exist. The definitions should, in principle, be capable of application to a wide range of languages (and to other symbolic forms, e.g. music), although in any one case elaboration and restriction will be relative. The theory might be seen as a part, but clearly not the whole, of the answer to the problem of how the psychic is transformed into the social. The theory is sociological and is limited by the nature of these assumptions. Individual differences in the use of a particular code cannot be dealt with except on an insensitive more-or-less basis. It is also clear that there is more to culture and communication than what might be revealed by a consideration of limited aspects of speech. Finally, it is thought imperative that sociologists recognize in their analyses the fact that man speaks.

Notes

1 I am ignoring here the many studies limited to the development of speech in children. (It is important to remember that this was written in 1964.)
2 Durkheim tends to leap from types of social integration to the quality of a series of individual acts.
3 The major interest has been concerned with symbolism. It is important to note work done in the area of schizophrenic thought disorder and the stress on communication emphasized by the existential school.
4 Prediction here refers to an ability of a special observer *not* of the speakers.
5 Restricted codes will arise in prisons, combat units of the armed forces, in the peer group of children and adolescents, etc.
6 A restricted code does not necessarily affect the *amount* of speech, only its form.
7 I am grateful to Miss J. Cook, Sociological Research Unit, University of London Institute of Education, for her help in this formulation.
8 The reference here and throughout is to a restricted code (high syntactic prediction).

References

AKHAMANOVA, O. S. *et al.* (1963), *Exact Methods in Linguistic Research*, Univ. of California Press.

BERNSTEIN, B. (1960), 'Language and social class', *Br. J. Soc.* 11.

BERNSTEIN, B. (1962), 'Linguistic codes, hesitation phenomena and intelligence', *Language and Speech.* 5.

BERNSTEIN, B. (1962), 'Social class, linguistic codes and grammatical elements, *Language and Speech.* 5.

BERNSTEIN, B. (1964), 'Family Role Systems, Socialization and Communication', paper given at the Conference on Cross-Cultural Research into Childhood and Adolescence, Univ. of Chicago, 1964.

BOAS, F. (1911), *Handbook of American Indian Languages*, Part 1, Washington, D.C.: Government Printing Office.

BOSSARD, J. H. S. (1945), 'Family modes of expression', *Am. Soc. Rev.* 10.

BRONFENBRENNER, U. (1958), 'Socialization and social class through time and space', in Maccoby, E. E. *et al.* (eds), *Readings in Social Psychology*, Methuen.

BROWN, R. (1958), *Words and Things*, New York: Free Press.

CHERRY, C. (1957), *Language and Human Communication*, New York: McGraw-Hill.

COHEN, M. (1956), *Pour une Sociologie de langage*, Paris: Albin-Michel.

FISHMAN, J. A. (1960), 'A systematization of the Whorfian hypothesis', *Behavioral Science* (University of Michigan Publication) 5.

GELLNER, E. (1946), 'The crisis in the humanities and the mainstream of philosophy', in Plumb, J. H. (ed.), *Crisis in the Humanities*, Penguin.

HERTZLER, J. O. (1953), 'Towards a sociology of language', *Social Forces* 32.

HOIJER, H. (ed.) (1954), 'Language in Culture', *American Anthropological Association Memoir* No. 79; also published by Univ. of Chicago Press.

HOIJER, H. (1962), 'The relation of language to culture', in Tax, S. (ed.), *Anthropology Today: Selections*, Univ. of Chicago Press; Phoenix Books.

HYMES, D. H. (1961), 'Linguistic aspects of cross-cultural personality study', in Kaplan, B. (ed.), *Studying Personality Cross-Culturally*, New York: Row Peterson.

HYMES, D. H. (ed.) (1962), 'The ethnography of speaking', in Gladwin T. and Sturtevant, W. C. (eds), *Anthropology and Human Behavior*, Anthropological Society of Washington, D.C. (A.S.W. Smithsonian Institution).

HYMES, D. H. (ed.) (1964), 'The ethnography of communication', *American Anthropologist*, special issue (December).

KOHN, M. L. (1959a), 'Social class and the exercise of parental authority', *Am. Soc. Rev.* 24.

KOHN, M. L. (1959b), 'Social class and parental values', *Am. J. Soc.* 64.

LAWTON, D. (1963), 'Social class differences in language development: A study of some samples of written work', *Language and Speech* 6.

LAWTON, D. (1964a), 'Social class language differences in group discussions', *Language and Speech* 7.

LAWTON, D. (1964b), Social class language differences in individual interviews' (private circulation).

LURIA, A. R. (1961), *The Role of Speech in the Regulation of Normal and Abnormal Behaviour*, Pergamon.

LURIA, A. R. and YUDOVITCH, F. I. (1959), *Speech and the Development of Mental Processes in the Child*, Staples Press.

MEAD, G. H. (1936), *Mind, Self, and Society: From the standpoint of a social behaviorist*, Univ. of Chicago Press.

MILLER, D. R. and SWANSON, G. E. (1959), *Inner Conflict and Defense*, New York: Henry Holt.

MILLER, G. (1951), *Language and Human Communication*, New York: McGraw-Hill.

NEWSON, J. and NEWSON, E. (1963), *Infant Care in an Urban Community*, Allen & Unwin; Penguin.

RAVENETTE, T. (1963), 'Intelligence, personality and social class: an investigation into the patterns of intelligence and personality of working-class secondary school children', Unpub. Ph.D. Thesis, Univ. of London.

REISSMAN, F. (1963), *The Culturally Deprived Child*, New York: Harper & Row.

SAPIR, E. (1929), 'The status of linguistics as a science', in Mandelbaum, D. G. (ed.), *Selected Writings of Edward Sapir*, Univ. of California Press.

SAPIR, E. (1933), *Encyclopaedia of the Social Sciences*, Vol. 9, 155-69.

SAPORTA, S. (ed.) (1961), *Psycho-linguistics: A Book of Readings*, New York: Holt, Rinehart & Winston.

SCHATZMAN, L. and STRAUSS, A. L. (1955), 'Social class and modes of communication', *Am. J. Soc.* 60.

TRIANDIS, H. C. (1964), 'The influence of culture on cognitive processes', in Berkowitz, L. (ed.), *Advances in Experimental Social Psychology*, New York: Academic Press.

VYGOTSKY, L. S. (1962), *Thought and Language*, New York: Wiley.

WHORF, B. L. (1941), 'The relation of habitual thought and behavior to language', in Spier, L. (ed.), *Language, Culture, and Personality: essays in memory of Edward Sapir*, Sapir Memorial Publication Fund, Menasha, Wisconsin.

WHORF, B. L. (1956), in Carroll, J. B. (ed.), *Language, Thought, and Reality: selected writings of Benjamin Lee Whorf*, New York: Wiley.

Part III Explorations

Chapter 8   A socio-linguistic
approach to socialization: with
some reference to educability

I

If a social group by virtue of its class relation, that is as a result of its common occupational function and social status, has developed strong communal bonds; if the work relations of this group offers little variety or little exercise in decision-making; if assertion, if it is to be successful, must be a collective rather than an individual act; if the work task requires physical manipulation and control rather than symbolic organization and control; if the diminished authority of the man at work is transformed into an authority of power at home; if the home is over-crowded and limits the variety of situations it can offer; if the children socialize each other in an environment offering little intellectual stimuli; if all these attributes are found in one setting, then it is plausible to assume that such a social setting will generate a particular form of communication which will shape the intellectual, social and affective orientation of the children.

I am suggesting that if we look into the work relationships of this particular group, its community relationships, its family role systems, it is reasonable to argue that the genes of social class may well be carried less through a genetic code but far more through a communication code that social class itself promotes. Such a communication code will emphasize verbally the communal rather than the individual the concrete rather than the abstract, substance rather than the elaboration of processes, the here and now rather than exploration of motives and intentions, and positional rather than personalized forms of social control. To say this about a communication system is not to disvalue it, for such a communication system has a vast potential, a considerable metaphoric range and a unique aesthetic capacity. A whole range of diverse meanings can be generated by such a system of communication. It happens, however, that this communication code directs the child to orders of learning and relevance that are not in harmony with those required by the school. Where the child is sensitive to the communication system of the school and thus to its orders of learning and relation, then the

143

experience of school for this child is one of symbolic and social development; where the child is not sensitive to the communication system at school then this child's experience at school becomes one of symbolic and social change. In the first case we have an elaboration of social identity; in the second case, a change of social identity. Thus between the school and community of the working-class child, there may exist a cultural discontinuity based upon two radically different systems of communication.

The social origins of linguistic codes

I shall spend the rest of this section examining how different forms of communication arise. I shall argue that the particular form of a social relation acts selectively upon what is said, when it is said and how it is said. The form of the social relation regulates the options that speakers take up at both syntactic and lexical levels. For example an adult talking to a child will use a form of speech in which both the syntax and vocabulary are relatively simple. The speech used by members of an army combat unit on manoeuvres will clearly be different from the same members' speech at a padre's evening. To put it another way, the consequences of the form the social relation takes are transmitted in terms of certain syntactic and lexical selections.[1] Thus different forms of social relation can generate very different speech systems or linguistic codes.

I shall argue that different speech systems or codes create for their speakers different orders of relevance and relation. The experience of the speakers may then be transformed by what is made significant or relevant by different speech systems. As the child learns his speech or, in the terms I shall use here, learns specific codes which regulate his verbal acts, he learns the requirements of his social structure. The experience of the child is transformed by the learning generated by his own, apparently, voluntary acts of speech. The social structure becomes, in this way, the sub-stratum of the child's experience essentially through the manifold consequence of the linguistic process. From this point of view, every time the child speaks or listens, the social structure is reinforced in him and his social identity shaped. The social structure becomes the child's psychological reality through the shaping of his acts of speech.

The same argument can be stated rather more formally. Individuals come to learn their social roles through the process of communication. A social role from this point of view is a constellation of shared, learned meanings through which individuals are able to enter stable, consistent and publicly recognized forms of interaction with others. *A social role can then be considered as a complex coding activity controlling both the creation and organization of specific meanings and the conditions for their transmission and reception.* Now if the communication system which defines a given role is essentially that of speech, it should be possible to distinguish critical social roles in terms of the speech forms they regulate. By critical social roles I mean those through which the culture is transmitted. These roles are learned in the family, in the age or peer group, in the school and at work. These are the four major sets of roles learned in the process of socialization. As a person learns to subordinate his behaviour to the linguistic code through which the role is realized, then orders of meaning, of relation, of relevance are made available to him. The complex of meanings, for example, generated within the role system of a family, reverberates developmentally in the child to inform his general conduct. Children who have access to different speech systems or codes, that is children who learn different roles by virtue of their family's class position in a society, may adopt quite different social and intellectual orientations and procedures despite a common potential.

The concept code, as I shall use it, refers to the principle which regulates the selection and organization of speech events. I shall briefly outline two fundamental types of linguistic codes and consider their regulative functions. These codes will be defined in terms of the relative ease or difficulty of predicting the syntactic alternatives which speakers take up to organize meanings. If it is difficult to predict across a representative range the syntactic options or alternatives taken up in the organization of speech, this form of speech will be called an elaborated code. In the case of an elaborated code, the speaker will select from a wide range of syntactic alternatives and these will be flexibly organized. A restricted code is one where it is much less difficult to predict across a representative range the syntactic alternatives, as these will be drawn from a narrow range. Whereas there is flexibility in the use of alternatives in an elaborated code, in the case of a restricted code the syntactic organization is marked by rigidity. Notice that these codes are not defined in terms of vocabulary or lexes. Jargon does not constitute a restricted code. However, it is likely that the lexical differentiation of certain semantic fields will be greater in the case of an elaborated code.

It is clear that context is a major control upon syntactic and lexical selections, consequently it is not easy to give general linguistic criteria for the isolation of the two codes. Derivations from the theory would be required in order to describe syntactic and lexical usage by any one speaker in a specific context.[2] The definitions given in the text would have increasing relevance to the extent that speakers could freely determine for themselves the nature of the constraints upon their syntax and lexes. In other words, the less rigid the external constraints upon the speech the more appropriate the general definitions. The more rigid the external constraints then the more specific the criteria required. It is also important to point out that the codes refer to cultural *not* genetic controls upon the options speakers take up. The codes refer to *performance* not to competence in the Chomsky sense of these terms. They may be different *performances* for every degree of competence. It is certainly the case that these codes can be seen as different kinds of communicative competence as this concept is expounded by Dell Hymes.[3]

If a speaker is oriented towards an elaborated code, then the code will facilitate the speaker in his attempts to make explicit (verbally) his subjective intent. If a speaker is oriented towards a restricted code, then this code will not facilitate the verbal expansion of the speaker's intent. In the case of an elaborated code the speech system requires more complex planning than in the case of a restricted code. For example, in the case of an elaborated code the time dimension of the verbal planning of the speech is likely to be longer (provided that the speaker is not quoting from himself) than in the case of a restricted code.[4]

It will be argued that the events in the environment which take on significance when these codes are used, are different, whether the events be social, intellectual or affective. These two codes, elaborated and restricted, are generated by a particular form of social relation. Indeed they are likely to be a realization of different social structures. They do not necessarily develop solely because of a speaker's innate ability.

We can now ask what is responsible for the simplification and rigidity of the syntax of a restricted code. Why should the vocabulary across certain, semantic fields be drawn from a narrow range? Why are the speaker's intentions relatively unelaborated verbally? Why should the speech controlled by a restricted code tend to be fast, fluent, with reduced articulatory clues, the meanings often discontinuous, condensed and local, involving a low level of syntactic and vocabulary selection where the 'how' rather than the 'what' of the communication is important; above all, why should the unique meaning of the person be implicit rather than verbally explicit? Why should the code orient its speakers to a low level of causality?

A restricted code will arise where the form of the social relation is based upon closely shared identifications, upon an extensive range of shared expectations, upon a range of common assumptions. Thus a restricted code emerges where the culture or sub-culture raises the 'we' above 'I'.[5] Such codes will emerge as both controls and transmitters of the culture in such diverse groups as prisons, the age group of adolescents, army, friends of long standing, between husband and wife. The use of a restricted code creates social solidarity at the cost of the verbal elaboration of individual experience. The type of social solidarity realized through a restricted code points towards mechanical solidarity, whereas the type of solidarity realized through elaborated codes points towards organic solidarity.[6] The form of communication reinforces the *form* of the social relation rather than creating a need to create speech which uniquely fits the intentions of the speakers. Restricted codes do not give rise to verbally differentiated 'I's'. If we think of the communication pattern between married couples of long standing, then we see that meaning does not have to be fully explicit, a slight shift of pitch or stress, a small gesture, can carry a complex meaning. Communication goes forward against a backcloth of closely shared identifications and affective empathy which removes the need to elaborate verbal meanings and logical continuity in the organization of the speech. Indeed, orientation in these relationships is less towards the *verbal* but more towards the extra-verbal channel. For the extraverbal channel is likely to be used to transmit intentions, purposes and qualifications. It follows from this that speakers limited to a restricted code may well have difficulty in switching from this form of communication to other forms of communication which presuppose different role relations and so different social orientations. Thus a restricted code may limit certain kinds of role switching. However, it must be pointed out that a restricted code may be entirely appropriate for certain contexts.

An elaborated code will arise wherever the culture or sub-culture emphasizes the 'I' over the 'we'. It will arise wherever the intent of the other person cannot be taken for granted. In as much as the intent of the other person cannot be taken for granted, then speakers are forced to elaborate their meanings and make them both explicit and specific. Meanings which are discreet and local to the speaker must be cut so that they are intelligible to the listener, and this pressure forces upon the speaker to select both among syntactic alternatives and encourages differentiation of vocabulary. In terms of what is transmitted verbally, an elaborated code encourages the speaker to focus upon the experience of others, as different from his own. In the case of a restricted code, what is transmitted verbally usually refers to the other person in terms of a common group or status membership. What is said here epitomizes the social structure and its basis of shared assumptions. Thus restricted codes could be considered status or positional codes whereas elaborated codes are orientated to persons. An elaborated code, in principle, pre-supposes a sharp boundary or gap between self and others which is crossed through the creation of speech which specifically fits a differentiated 'other'. In this sense, an elaborated code is oriented towards a person rather than a social category or status. In the case of a restricted code, the boundary or gap is between sharers and non-sharers of the code. In this sense a restricted code is positional or status *not* person oriented. It presupposes a generalized rather thàn a differentiated other.

In the case of an elaborated code the orientation is towards the verbal channel, for this channel will carry the elaboration of the speaker's intentions. In the case of restricted codes, to varying degrees it is the extra-verbal channels which become objects of special perceptual activity. It is important to point out that restricted code users are not non-verbal, only that the speech is of a different order from that controlled by an elaborated code. If an elaborated code creates the possibility for the transmission of individuated symbols, then a restricted code creates the possibility for the transmission of communalized symbols. I now want to turn for a moment to discuss differences in the type of social roles which are realized through these two codes.

Open and closed role systems

Let us first consider the range of alternatives that a role system (say that of the family) makes available to individuals for the verbal realization of different meanings. Here we need to distinguish between two basic orders of meaning, one which refers to inter-personal and intra-personal relationships and one which refers to relationships between objects; thus object meanings and person meanings. We could call a role system which reduced the range of alternatives for the realization of verbal meanings a closed type. It would follow that the greater the reduction in the range of alterna-tives, the more communal or collective the verbal meanings and the lower the order of complexity and more rigid the syntactic and vocabulary selections—thus the more restricted the code. On the other hand, we could call a role system which permitted a range of alternatives for the realization of verbal meanings an open type. It would follow that the greater the range of alternatives permitted by the role system, the more individualized the verbal meanings, the higher the order and the more flexible the syntactic and vocabulary selection and so the more elaborated the code.[7]

We can now take this simple dichotomy a little further by picking up the distinction between object and person orders of meaning. A role system may be open or closed with respect to the alternatives it permits for the verbal realization of object or person meanings.

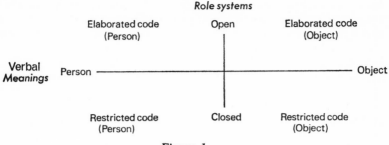

Figure 1

Now in the area where the role system is open, novel meanings are likely to be encouraged and a complex conceptual order explored. In the area where the role system is closed, novel meanings are likely to be discouraged and the conceptual order limited. Where the role system is of the closed type, verbal meanings are likely to be assigned. The individual (or child) steps into the meaning system and leaves it relatively undisturbed. Where the role system is of the open type, the individual is more likely to achieve meaning on his own terms and here there is the potential of disturbing or changing the pattern of received meanings. We can begin to see that in the area where the role system is open, there is an induced motivation to explore and actively seek out and extend meanings; where the role is closed there is little induced motivation to explore and create novel meanings. Let us take this a little further. Where the role system is open, the individual or child learns to cope with ambiguity and isolation in the creation of verbal meanings; where the role system is closed the individual or child foregoes such learning. On the contrary, he learns to create verbal meanings in social contexts which are unambiguous and communalized. Such an individual or child, may experience considerable tension and role conflict if he persistently attempts to individualize the basis of his syntactic and vocabulary selections, and thus attempt to create or point towards an open role system. Notice that what is a source of strain here, is precisely that which an individual or child learns to do if he is socialized into an open role system. Thus a source of role strain in restricted codes is precisely the role relationship appropriate to an elaborated code.

We have now outlined a framework which shows a causal connection between role systems, linguistic codes and the realization of different orders of meaning and relevance. Emphasis has been laid upon the relationship between roles and codes. It is possible for a person to be able to write in an elaborated code but not to be able to speak it, for he may not be able to manage the face to face requirements of the role (over and above the matter of dialect). This may apply, for example, to a bright working-class' boy whose early socialization has offered little training in the social role. In the same way, object and person forms of an elaborated code not only create different orders of meaning; they are realized through different role relations. It may well be that the cultural tension between the sciences, especially the applied sciences, and the arts reflects the different role relations which control object and person forms of the elaborated code.

The organization of education often produces cleavage and insulation between subjects and levels and this serves to reduce role and code switching between person and object modes of the elaborated code and from restricted to elaborated codes.

If we ask what are the general social forces which influence the development of elaborated and restricted codes and their two modes, the answer is likely to be found in two sources. These shape the culture and role systems of the four major socializing agencies, the family, the age group (or peer group), the school and work. One major source of the movement from restricted to elaborated codes lies in increases in the complexity of the division of labour. This changes both the nature of the occupational roles and their linguistic bases. The two modes of the elaborated code may well be affected by the movement of economies from goods to service types. The shift from a goods to a service economy may well promote the development of the person mode of an elaborated code. The second major source of code orientation is likely to be the character of the central value system. Pluralistic societies are likely to produce strong orientations towards the person mode of an elaborated code, whereas monolithic societies are likely to strengthen the orientation towards the object mode. It should be remembered that persons can be treated as objects.

Linguistic codes and educability

I have been trying to show how the nature of the division of labour and the character of the central value system affects linguistic codes through the way they affect the culture and role systems of the major socializing agencies, especially the family and school. Social class position regulates the occupational function, the intra-familial and inter-familial relationships and responsiveness to the school. Thus we can expect, broadly speaking, to find both modes of an elaborated code within the middle class together with restricted codes. In the lower working class we could expect to find a high proportion of families limited to a restricted code. We might further expect that upwardly mobile working-class children would move towards the object rather than the person mode of the elaborated code.

Where children are *limited* to a restricted code, primarily because of the sub-culture and role systems of the family, community and work, we can expect a major problem of educability whose source lies not so much in the genetic code but in the culturally determined communication code.

Children limited to a restricted code learn a code where the extra-verbal tends to become a major channel for the qualification and elaboration of individual experience. *This does not mean that such children's speech output is relatively reduced.* The verbal planning of the speech, relative to an elaborated code, involves a relatively low order and a rigidity in syntactic organization. The inter-personal and intra-personal, although clearly *perceived* and *felt*, are less verbally differentiated. The concept of self developed through a restricted code does not, itself, become an area of enquiry as in the case of an elaborated code, particularly one whose orientation is towards persons. In the case of an elaborated code, such a code points to the possibilities which inhere in a complex conceptual hierarchy for the organization and expression of inner experience. This is much less the case where experience is regulated by a restricted code, for this code orients its speakers to a less complex conceptual hierarchy and so to a lower order of causality. What is made available for learning through elaborated and restricted codes is radically different. Social and intellectual orientations, motivational imperative and forms of social control, rebellion and innovation are different. Thus the relative backwardness of many working-class children who live in areas of high population density or in rural areas may well be a culturally induced backwardness transmitted by the linguistic process. Such children's low performance on verbal IQ tests, their difficulty with 'abstract' concepts, their failures within the language area, their general inability to profit from the school, all may result from the limitations of a restricted code. For these children the school induces a change of code and with this a change in the way the children relate to their kin and community. At the same time we often offer these children grossly inadequate schools with less than able teachers. No wonder they often fail—for the 'more' tend to receive more and become more, while the socially defined 'less', receive less and become less.

I want to make one final point. A restricted code contains a vast potential of meanings. It is a form of speech which symbolizes a communally based culture. It carries its own aesthetic. It should not be disvalued. We must ensure that the material conditions of the schools we offer, their values, social organizatiop, forms of control and pedagogy, the skills and sensitivities of the teachers are refracted through an understanding of the culture the children bring to the school. After all, we do no less for the middle-class child. The problem does not stop there. Housing conditions must be improved, social services extended and pre-school education developed.

We cannot say what a child is capable of, as we do not have a theory of what an optimum learning environment looks like; and even if such a theory existed, we are unwilling to re-direct national expenditure towards physically creating it for children on the scale required.

II

Family role systems, social control and communication

I shall now look more closely at the relationships between role systems and linguistic codes, as the connection between social class and linguistic codes is too imprecise. Such a relationship omits the dynamics of the causal relationship. In order to examine these dynamics it is necessary to look at the nature of the role system of a family and its procedures of social control. The basic requirement of such an analysis is that it is predictive and so gives rise to measurable criteria for evaluating the interrelationships between role systems, forms of social control and linguistic orientations.

It is possible to evaluate family role systems by reference to the principles which for any one family control the allocation of decision-making. Thus we could consider the effect of the allocation of decision-making on the extent and kind of interactions between members of the family.

Let us postulate two types of families—positional and person-oriented families.[8]

1 Positional families

If the area of decision-making is invested in the member's forma status (father, mother, grandfather, grandmother, age of child or sex of child), this type of family will be called positional. (It is not necessarily authoritarian or 'cold' rather than 'warm'.) In such a family there would be a clear separation of roles. There would be formally defined areas of decision-making and judgments accorded to members of the family in terms of their formal status. In such a family type we could expect close relationships and interactions between the parents and grandparents. Further, we could expect that the parents would closely regulate the child's relationships with his age peers (if middle-class) or the child's relationship with his peers would be relatively independent of the parents' regulation (if working-class). Thus, in certain positional families, the socialization of the child might well be through his own age mates. Positional families, it is suggested, would give rise to a weak or *closed* communication system.

2 Person-oriented families

By contrast we could consider a family type where the range of decisions, modifications and judgments was a function of the psychological qualities of the person rather than a function of the formal status. In such families there is clearly a limit to the inter-actions set by age development and status ascription. However, status ascription would be reduced (age, sex, age relations) compared to positional families. Unlike certain positional families the socialization of the children would never be left to the child's age group. The behaviour of the child in his peer group would be subject to discussion with parents rather than to their legislation. Person-oriented families would give rise to a strong or 'open' communication system.

Discussion: positional-personal family types and open and closed communication systems

1 Person-oriented families—open communication system

In these families the limits on the extent to which decisions may be open to discussion would be set by the psychological characteristics of the person rather than by his formal status. Simply, the ascribed status of the member, for many activities, would be weakened by his *achieved* status. The children, for example, would achieve a role within the communication system in terms of their unique social, affective and cognitive characteristics. Clearly, if there is reduced segregation of role and less formal definition, then the parents *and* the children operate with a greater range of alternatives, that is, with greater role discretion. Inasmuch as the role discretion (the range of alternatives of the role in different social situations) is wide, then individual choices can be made and offered. Verbal communication, of a particular kind, is generated. It is not just a question of more talk but talk of a particular kind. Judgments, their bases and consequences, would form a marked content of the communications. The role system would be continuously eliciting and reinforcing the verbal signalling and the making explicit of individual intentions, qualifications and judgments. The role system would be continuously accommodating and assimilating the different intents of its members. Looked at from another point of view, the children would be socializing the parents as much as the parents were socializing the children; for the parents would be very sensitive towards the unique characteristics of the children. These would be verbally realized and so enter into the communication system. Thus there would develop an 'open' communication system which would foster and provide the linguistic means and role learning for the verbal signalling and making explicit of individual differences, together with the explication of judgments, their bases and consequences. Of fundamental importance, the role system would promote communication and orientation towards the motives and dispositions of others.[9] Note also that in such a family the child learns to *make* his role rather than this being formally assigned to him. Children socialized within such a role and communication system learn to cope with ambiguity and ambivalence, although clearly there may well be pathological consequences if insufficient sense of boundary is provided.

2 Positional families—closed communication systems

In this type of family we said that judgments and the decision-making process would be a function of the *status* of the member rather than a quality of the person. There would be segregation of roles and a formal division of areas of responsibility according to age, sex, and age relation status. Boundary areas instead of generating discussion and accommodation might well become border disputes settled by the relative power inhering in the respective statuses. The children's communication system might well be 'open' only in relation to their age mates who would then become a major source of learning and relevance. If socialization is reciprocal in person-oriented families it tends to be unilateral in positional families. The role system here is less likely to facilitate the verbal elaboration of individual differences and is less likely to lead to the verbal elaboration of judgments, their basis and consequences; it does not encourage the verbal exploration of individual intentions and motives. In a person-oriented family the child's developing self is differentiated by the continuous adjustment to the verbally realized and elaborated intentions, qualifications and motives of others. In positional families the child takes over and responds to status requirements. Here he learns what can be called a communalized role as distinct from the individualized role of person-oriented families. In positional families, the range of alternatives which inhere in the roles (the role discretion) is relatively limited, consequently the communication system reduces the degree of individual selection from alternatives. Of course, within positional families, there is sensitivity towards persons but the point is that these sensitivities are less likely to be raised to a level of verbal elaboration so that they can become objects of special perceptual activity and control. Within positional families the child develops either within the unambiguous roles within his family *or* within the clearly structured roles of his agemate society or both. Thus these children are less likely to learn to cope with problems of role ambiguity and ambivalence. They are more likely to avoid or foreclose upon activities or problems which carry this potential.

Social control and family types

It is clear that these two family types generate radically different communication systems which we have characterized as open and closed. It has been suggested that there are important socializing and linguistic consequences. I want now to outline differences in their forms of social control with again special reference to uses of spoken language.

We have said that inasmuch as a role system is personal rather than positional in orientation, then it is a relatively more unstable system. It is continuously in the process of assimilating and accommodating the verbally realized but different intentions, qualifications and motives of its members. Tensions will arise which are a function of the characteristics of the role system. Special forms of arbitration, reconciliation and explanation will develop. These tensions only in the last resource will be managed in terms of relative power which inheres in the respective statuses. Social control will be based upon linguistically elaborated meanings rather than upon power. However, it is clearly the case that power in the end is still the ultimate basis of authority.

In positional families where the status arrangements reduce the instability which inheres in person-oriented families, social control will be affected either through power or through the referring of behaviour to the universal or particular norms which regulate the status. Thus, in person-oriented families, social control is likely to be realized through verbally elaborated means oriented to the person; whilst in positional families, social control is likely to be realized through less elaborated verbal means, less oriented to the person but more oriented towards the formal status of the regulated (child).

It is of crucial importance to analyse the procedures of social control for I want to show, amongst other things, that person-oriented families, very early in the child's life, sensitize him towards and actively promote his language development in order that they can apply their favoured modes of control. In positional families the modes of social control depend less upon individually created and elaborated verbal meanings and so within these families there is less need to sensitize the child towards, and promote the early development of, verbally elaborated forms of speech.

Modes of social control [10]

I shall distinguish initially between imperative modes of control and control based upon appeals. Two forms of appeal will be further distinguished. Underlying these distinctions in modes of control is the role discretion (the range of alternatives) accorded.

1 Imperative mode

This mode of control reduces the role discretion accorded to the regulated (child). It allows the child only the external possibilities of rebellion, withdrawal or acceptance. The imperative mode is realized through a restricted code (lexicon prediction): 'Shut up' 'Leave it alone' 'Get out' or extra-verbally through physical coercion.

2 Appeals

These are modes of control where the regulated (child) is accorded varying degrees of discretion in the sense that a range of alternatives, essentially linguistic, are available to him. Thus social control which rests upon appeals does permit, to different degrees, reciprocity in communication and hence linguistically regulated learning. These appeals may be broadly broken into two types and each type further classified into sub-types. The two broad types are positional and personal appeals.

(a) *Positional appeals*. Positional appeals refer the behaviour of the regulated (child) to the norms which inhere in a particular or universal status. Positional appeals do not work through the verbal realization of the personal attributes of the controllers (parents) or regulated (children). Some examples now follow:

'You should be able to do that by now' (age status rule)
'Little boys don't cry' (sex status rule)
'People like us don't behave like that' (sub-cultural rule)
'Daddy doesn't expect to be spoken to like that' (age relation rule)

Positional appeals are not necessarily disguised forms of the imperative mode. Consider the following situation where a child is learning his sex role. A little boy is playing with a doll:

Mother: Little boys don't play with dolls.
Child: I want the dolly.
Mother: Dolls are for your sister.
Child: I want the doll (or he still persists with the doll).
Mother: Here, take the drum instead.

Compare this with a situation where the mother says: 'Why do you want to play with the doll—they are so boring—why not play with the drum?'

The essence of positional appeals is that in the process of learning the rule the child is explicitly linked to others who hold a similar universal or particular status. The rule is transmitted in such a way that the child is reminded of what he shares in common with others. Where control is positional, the rule is communalized. Where control is positional, the 'I' is subordinate to the 'we'. Positional control is realized through a specific linguistic variant. As will be shown later, positional appeals can be given in restricted *or* elaborated codes. They can be complex linguistically and conceptually as in the case of a West Point or public school boy who is reminded of his obligations and their origins. Where control is positional, the child (the regulated) learns the norms in a social context where the relative statuses are clear-cut and unambiguous. Positional appeals may lead to the formation of shame rather than guilt. In the case of positional appeals, however, certain areas of experience are less verbally differentiated than in the case of personal appeals. Positional appeals transmit the culture or sub-culture in such a way as to increase the similarity of the regulated with others of his social group. They create boundaries. If the child rebels he very soon challenges the bases of the culture and its social organization and this may force the controller (parent/teacher) into the imperative mode.

(b) *Personal appeals*. In these appeals the focus is upon the child as an individual rather than upon his formal status. Personal appeals take into account interpersonal or intra-personal components of the social relationship. They work very much at the level of individual intention, motive and disposition and consequently are realized through a distinctive linguistic variant. This again can be within restricted or elaborated codes. It will be the case that the areas of experience verbally differentiated through personal appeals are very different from the experiences controlled by positional appeals. The following example might help to bring out the distinctions.

Imagine a situation where a child has to visit his grandfather who is unwell and the child does not like to kiss him because the grandfather has not shaved for some time. One mother says to the child before they go:

Mother: Children kiss their Grandpa (positional)
Child: I don't want to—why must I kiss him always?
Mother: He's not well (positional reason)—I don't want none of your nonsense (imperative)

Another mother says in the same context: 'I know you don't like kissing Grandpa, but he is unwell, and he is very fond of you, and it makes him very happy.'

The second example is perhaps blackmail, but note that the child's intent is recognized explicitly by the mother and linked to the wishes of another. Causal relations at the interpersonal level are made. Further, in the second example, there is the appearance of the child having a choice (discretion). If the child raises a question more explanation is given. The mother, so to speak, lays out the situation for the child and the rule is learned in an individualized interpersonal context. The rule is, so to speak, *achieved* by the child. The child, given the situation and the explanation, opts for the rule. In the first example, the rule is simply *assigned* in a social relationship which relies upon latent power for its effectiveness. Here we see another difference between positional and personal appeals in that rules are assigned in positional control and achieved in personal control.

Where control is personal, whole orders of learning are made available to the child which are not there if control is positional. Where control is personal, each child learns the rule in a context which, so to speak, uniquely fits him, and a language through which this is realized. Where control is positional, learning about objects, events and persons is reduced and the child comes to learn that the power which inheres in authority may soon be revealed. Where control is personal, as distinct from where it is positional, the status differences are less clear-cut and ambiguities and ambivalences are verbally realized. I should point out, although I have no time to develop this, that there may well be pathological consequences of extensive use of personal appeals.

Finally, if positional appeals do lead to the development of shame, personal appeals may lead to the formation of guilt.

In the case of person-oriented appeals, the rights of the controller or parent which inhere in his formal status are less likely to come under attack than in the case of positional appeals. For in the case of personal appeals, what may be challenged are the reasons the controller gives or even a specific condition of the controller or parent (e.g. 'Do you always have a headache when I want to play?'). Thus personal appeals may act to protect the normative order from which the controller derives his rights. For here there is an attenuation of the relationship between power and the rule system. In the case of positional appeals which shift rapidly to the imperative mode of control, the formal rights of the controller or parent may well be challenged, and with this the whole normative order from which the controller derives his rights can come under attack. Imperative/positional forms of control under certain conditions may lead the socialized to turn to alternative value systems. Further, where control is personal, the basis of control lies in linguistically elaborated individualized meanings. This may lead to a situation where the child attains autonomy although his sense of social identity may be weakened. Such ambiguity in the sense of social identity, the lack of boundary, may move such children towards a radical closed value system and its attendant social structure. On the other hand, where control is positional and, even more, where it is imperative, the child has a strong sense of social identity but the rules which he learns will be tied to specific contexts and his sense of autonomy may well be reduced. Finally, a child socialized by controllers who favour positional or imperative procedures becomes highly sensitive to specific role relations in the context of control. Such a child may be bewildered, initially, when placed in a context of control where personal procedures are used, as he may lack the orientation and the facility to take up the different options or alternatives which this form of control makes available. Person-oriented forms of control may induce role strain where the child has been socialized through imperative or positional forms of control.

I have briefly outlined, with special reference to communication, imperative, positional and personal modes of social control. It is very clear that in any one family, or even in any one context of control, all three modes may be used. It is also likely to be the case within a family that parents may share control modes or each may use a different mode. We can, however, distinguish between families, or at a greater level of delicacy between parents, in terms of their preferred modes of control. It follows that we could also distinguish the modes of control which are used in any one context. We can summarize the consequences for learning which inhere three modes as follows:

Mode	Learning	Level of learning
Imperative	Hierarchy	Restricted code
Positional	Role obligation and Differentiation	{ Restricted code Elaborated code
Personal	Interpersonal Intra-personal	{ Restricted code Elaborated code

We can now link positional families with closed systems of communication with positional, imperative modes of control. We could, in principle, distinguish between positional families whose preferred mode of control was imperative (the lower working class?) from positional families where the preferred mode was positional appeals with relatively little use of physical coercion. We could distinguish between positional families according to whether the dominant code was elaborated or restricted. In the same way, we could link person-oriented families with open communication systems operating with personal appeals. We could again distinguish between such families in terms of the dominant general code, elaborated or restricted. The latter tells us about the degree of openness of the communication system and its conceptual orientation. Thus the roles which children learn in these various families, their conceptual orientations, their perception of and use of language, should differ.[11]

Social class, positional and personal families and social change

On this analysis we might find positional families who were deeply embedded in their community operating essentially with imperative modes of control and where the children were socialized through unsupervised age peers or mates. Here we could expect the development of restricted codes (object), the hard core of the language/educability problem. It should also be possible to locate, within the working class, families who were moving towards personal forms of control within the general rubric of a restricted code. These families, we would expect, would be less tightly embedded within their local community, perhaps through rehousing or where the parents were actively confronting the complex relationships between their local sub-culture and the cultures of the wider society. Here we might find an orientation towards a restricted code (person) or a movement towards an elaborated code (person).

A further point is worth making. Within working-class positional large families we should expect a marked difference between boys and girls in their use of language. Girls, especially older girls in such families, tend to take on mothering roles. They also, of equal relevance, mediate between parents and sibs. Their role then is more complex as it combines a normal sib role with that of mediator, and with that of controller. Further, girls are less tied to the activity-oriented, group-dominated peer group social structure such as that of the boy. Thus girls, especially older girls in such families, are likely to be person-oriented and to have to rely more upon forms of control based upon linguistically elaborated meanings than upon physical coercion. Finally, they are placed in a situation involving a variety of role and code switching, e.g. girl-girl, girl-boy, girl controlling girls, girl controlling boys, girl mediating between parents and other sibs. These factors are likely to develop the girl's orientation towards a more differentiated, more individualized use of language.[12]

Within the middle class we should be able to isolate positional and person-oriented families, who, on this argument, should orientate their children *initially* (formal education could change this) to the two modes of object and person of an elaborated code. In the earlier section of this paper suggestions were made as to the social origins of elaborated and restricted codes in terms of the increases in the complexity of the division of labour and the character of the central value system. We shall now turn our attention to the social conditions which may produce positional- and person-oriented families within the middle class and the working class.[13]

The literature strongly suggests that the traditional working-class family is of the positional type. For here we find insulation between working-class and middle-class sub-cultures and social relationships (a product of the class system); high population density within limited territories; low rate of social mobility (through educational failure) producing intra-group marriage; social solidarity arising out of similarity of economic function and interests; unemployment; reciprocity of services and mutual help between families arising partly out of low income (in the USA common ethnic origin and sub-culture) sustaining the transmission of this particular sub-culture. The weakening of the positional family type, closed systems of communication limited to a restricted code, would result from the play of forces which would differentiate the family from its community and so weaken the transmission of collective beliefs, values and the subsequent detailed regulation of behaviour.

In England, since the war, this has begun to happen as a result of:

(1) Greater affluence, greater geographical mobility and, therefore, greater responsiveness to a wide range of influences which has been partly assisted by mass media.

(2) Rehousing into areas of relatively low population density.

(3) A change in the power position of the wife through her independent earning capacity.

(4) A change in attitude both towards education and child development on the part of the working-class groups and therefore greater responsiveness to education and subsequent social mobility.

(5) A change in the solidarity between workers arising out of, until recently, full employment and higher earnings.

(6) A shift in the division of labour away from goods to that of a services economy. This is part of a long-term trend from a goods to a service economy, an economy which is now more person- than object-oriented.

These different forces are beginning to weaken the transmission of the communally-based, socially-insulated, working-class sub-culture and have created the conditions for more individualized family systems.[14] This is not to say that the working-class sub-culture has been eroded and replaced by middle-class beliefs, values and norms; only that there now exist the *conditions* for more individualized and less communalized relationships.

In the USA (and one is really not entitled to discuss this) the situation is much more complex. Apart from attempts of the school which so far have not been outstandingly successful, the most important influence upon change of linguistic code is probably the Civil Rights Movement. This movement and its various organizations are bringing about a change in the negro's view of his own sub-culture, his relation to the white culture and his attitude towards education. This movement has produced powerful charismatic leaders at both national and local levels, who are forcing negroes to reassess, re-examine their structural relationship to the society. This confrontation (despite the violence) is likely to make new demands upon linguistic resources and to challenge the passivity of the old sub-culture and its system of social relationships. The language of social protest, with its challenging of assumptions, its grasping towards new cultural forms, may play an important role in breaking down the limitations of sub-culturally bound restricted codes.

On the other hand, middle-class changes in the orientations of family types might well reflect changes in the character of middle-class occupations; in particular, the movement from entrepreneurial to managerial, professional and service type occupations. At the same time, the indeterminacy of the value system has individualized choice and changed the basis of authority relationships within the family. The 'science' of child development and its popularization through books, papers and journals, has also had an important influence, given the above conditions, in shaping role relationships and communication within middle-class families. It is likely that the personalizing of socialization agencies has gone further in the USA than in the UK. It is important to point out that family types may also be very influenced by the nature of religious and political beliefs. On the whole, pluralistic societies like the USA and UK are likely to produce strong tendencies towards personalized socialization agencies, whereas societies with monolithic centrally planned and disseminated value systems are likely to develop highly positional socializing agencies generating object-oriented linguistic codes.

Let me now retrace the argument. We started with the view that the social organization and sub-culture of the lower working class would be likely to generate a distinctive form of communication through which the genes of social class would be transmitted. Secondly, two general types of linguistic codes were postulated and their social origins and regulative consequences analysed. Thirdly, it was suggested that the sub-culture of the lower working class would be transmitted through a restricted code whilst that of the middle class would realize both elaborated and restricted codes. This causal link was considered to be very imprecise and omitted the dynamics of the process. The fourth step entailed the construction of two types of family role systems, positional and personal, their causally related 'open' and 'closed' communication systems and their procedures of social control. The fifth step made the causal link between restricted and elaborated codes and their two modes with positional- and person-orientated family role systems. Finally, factors affecting the development and change of family types were discussed.

III

Some consequences of change of habitual linguistic code

I should like finally to consider some possible consequences of linguistic code switching. In contemporary societies, both in the West and in the newly developing societies, educational institutions are faced with the problem of encouraging children to change and extend the way they normally use language. In terms of this paper, this becomes a switch from restricted to elaborated codes. A change in linguistic code implies more than a change in syntactic and lexical selection. The view taken here and in other papers is that linguistic codes are basic controls on the transmission of a culture or sub-culture and are the creators of social identity. 'Changes in such codes involve changes in the *means* whereby order and relevance are generated. Changes in codes involve changes in role relationships and in procedures of social control.

In another paper I have distinguished my position from that of Whorf[15], but I believe that there are distillations or precipitations from the general system of meanings which inhere in linguistic codes which exert a diffuse and generalized effect upon the behaviour of speakers. What I am tentatively putting forward is that imbedded in a culture of sub-culture may be a basic organizing concept, concepts or themes, whose ramifications may be diffused throughout the culture or sub-culture. The speech forms through which the culture or sub-culture is realized, transmits this organizing concept or concepts within their Gestalt rather than through any one set of meanings.

The following diagram sets out the application of this essentially Whorfian thought to the linguistic codes and their social controls discussed in this paper.

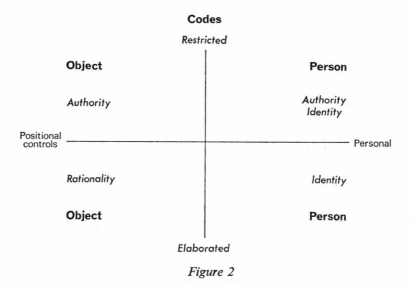

Figure 2

Positional—Restricted Code (object)
The basic organizing concept here would form around the concepts of authority or piety.

Personal—Restricted Code (person)
The basic organizing concepts here would be authority/identity in a state of unresolved tension. By 'identity' I simply mean a preoccupation with the question of 'who am I?'

Positional Elaborated Code (object)
The basic organizing concept here would centre about the concept of rationality.

Personal Elaborated Code (person)
The basic organizing concept would refer to the concept of identity.

On this view an educationally induced change of code from a restricted code (object) to an elaborated code (person) involves a shift in organizing concepts from authority/piety towards one of identity. From an organizing concept which makes irrelevant the question of personal identity to an organizing concept which places the notion of identity in the forefront of the personality. Individuals who are in the process of making such a switch of codes are involved in a basic cultural change at the level of meanings and at the sociological level of role. We need to know much more about the social and psychological consequences of radical shifts in linguistic codes.

It may be that the switch from a restricted code (object) is more likely to be towards an elaborated code (object) than towards the person mode of an elaborated code. In concrete terms, we might expect working-class children to move towards the applied sciences than towards the verbal arts. This shift from authority to rationality for working-class children may involve a less traumatic change in their role relations, systems of meanings and control, than a shift from authority to identity. Authority and rationality are both positional in the sense that the individual works *within* a framework, within a system or structure, without a critical problem of ambiguity of ends. Where the organizing concept transmitted by the code is that of identity, the individual is faced with ambiguity at the level of ends and often means. This speculation on no account should be taken to mean that it is more appropriate for individuals limited to a restricted code (object) to be guided towards the applied sciences or routine low level supervisory functions, where persons are often treated as objects. Only that it may be expected that they may well make these choices rather than choose the verbal arts. They are more likely to be concerned with object-processes than inter-personal and intra-personal processes.

One might further expect the individuals starting from restricted codes (person) will move towards elaborated codes (person) rather than towards elaborated codes (objects). Individuals in this quadrant, if they switch to elaborated codes, are likely to be restless in their search for belonging, or they might accept some belief system which creates it for them. It is thought that many may become teachers, writers, community protest leaders or perhaps become involved in drop-out movements or deviant groups. This code switch involves major problems of culture conflict.

There are relatively few individuals who are capable of managing equally both modes of an elaborated code, although one suspects that the social sciences contain many of these. The meanings, roles and controls entailed in these two modes are somewhat antithetical. At the basis of the meanings of an elaborated code (object), is the notion of one integrated system which can generate order. In an odd way it is objective idealist in character. At the basis of the meanings of an elaborated code (person) is a pluralism, a range of possibilities. It is subjective idealist or romantic in character. *Another way of seeing this might be to suggest that the major latent function of an elaborated code (object) is to remove ambiguity, whilst the major latent function of an elaborated code (person) is to create it.*

These are poorly worked out thoughts.[16] My excuse for including them is to point out the need for discussion of more general issues involved in the changing of forms of speech.

Conclusion

I have attempted within the confines of this paper to work on a broad canvas in which particular problems of language and educability may be placed within a much broader setting. The paper is really a plea for more extensive research into the social constraints upon the emergence of linguistic codes, the conditions for their maintenance and change and above all their regulative functions.

Notes

1 See Erving-Tripp, S. (1964), 'An analysis of the interaction between language, topic and listener', in *The Ethnography of Communication*, Gumperz, J. J., and Hymes, D. (eds), *American Anthropology*, special publication, Vol. 66, No. 6, part 2. Also

Erving-Tripp, S. (1967), 'Sociolinguistics', Working paper No. 3, Language-Behaviour Research Laboratory. See Gumperz, J. J. (1964), 'Linguistic and social inter-action in two communities', *American Anthropology*, Vol. 66, see above. The work of Dell Hymes should also be consulted. See Hymes, D. (1967), 'Models of the interaction of languages and social setting', *Journal of Social Issues*, 23.

2 Research carried out by the Sociological Research Unit shows that there are considerable differences between middle-class and working-class children at five years and seven years of age in their ability to switch grammar and lexes in accordance with the nature of the context. See also Hawkins, P. (1969), 'Social class, the nominal group and reference', *Language and Speech*, 12. Henderson, D., 'Social class differences in form-class usage' in *Social Class, Language and Communication*, Brandis, W. and Henderson, D., Vol. I of the Sociological Research Unit, University of London Institute of Education, Monograph Series, *Language, Primary Socialisation and Education* (ed.), Bernstein, B., London, Routledge & Kegan Paul, 1970.

3 Hymes, D. (1968), 'On communicative competence', in Diamond, S., *Anthropological Approaches to Education* (in press).

4 Bernstein, B. (1962), 'Linguistic codes, hesitation phenomena and intelligence', *Language and Speech*, 5, and in this volume.

5 In different ways Vygotsky, Sapir and Malinowski have drawn attention to the simplification of grammar and the lack of specificity in lexes where social relationships are based upon closely shared assumptions and identifications.

6 Durkheim, E. (1933), *On the Division of Labour in Society*, London, Macmillan.

7 Our research shows that the speech of middle-class children compared to working-class children at five years of age is more likely to show greater differentiation in the open set lexical choices within the nominal group, *and* that these children are more flexible in their use of the grammatical options they take up within the nominal group. The working-class children are more likely to select pronouns as heads (especially third person pronouns). Where pronouns are used as head, the possibility of both modification and qualification is considerably reduced. Further, our research shows (as does that of Loban, W. (1966), *Language Ability*, U.S. Department of Health, Education and Welfare, Office of Education) that middle-class children are more likely, in certain contexts, to use more frequently than working-class children, modal verbs of uncertainty or possibility. See Turner, G. and Pickvance, R. E., 'Social class differences in the expression of uncertainty in five-year-old children', *Language and Speech* (in press).

8 This distinction between positional and personal forms of control was set out by the author initially in an unpublished manuscript

(1962 and in a paper 'Family role systems, socialization and communication' given to the Conference on Cross-Cultural Research into Childhood and Adolescence, University of Chicago, 1963. At that time the term 'status' was used instead of positional. The terms 'positional' and 'personal' have also been used by Hanson, D. (1965), 'Personal and positional influences in informal groups', *Social Forces*, 44. However, Hanson's discussion is somewhat differently focused for he sees positional relationships as contractual, and personal relationships as non-contractual.

9   See Bernstein, B. and Henderson, D. 'Social class differences in the relevance of language to socialization', *Sociology*, Vol. 3, No. 1, Jan. 1969. Also Bernstein, B., and Brandis, W. 'Social class, communication and control' in *Social Class, Language and Communication*: Brandis, W. and Henderson, D., Vol. 1, in Sociological Research Unit Monograph Series, *Language, Primary Socialization and Education*, ed. Bernstein, B. Routledge & Kegan Paul, 1970. See also: Kohn, M. L. (1959), 'Social class and the exercise of parental authority', *American Sociological Review*, 24, 352-66; Kohn, M. L. (1959), 'Social class and parental values', *American Journal of Sociology*, 64.

10   A coding manual for social control has been developed and applied to the speech of mothers and their children. This manual gives a range of delicate sub-divisions within imperative, positional and personal forms of control. The coding manual, constructed by Bernstein, B. and Cook, J., is available from the Sociological Research Unit, University of London Institute of Education.

11   It should be clear that in this discussion I have drawn upon a range of work in the literature of sociology and social psychology. In particular, Bott, E., *Family and Social Network*, Tavistock Press, 1957; Foote, N. N. (ed.), *Household Decision-Making: Consumer Behavior*, Vol. 4, Ch. 5, New York. Univ. Press, 1961; Nye, F. I. and Berardo, F. M., *Emerging Conceptual Frameworks in Family Analysis*, New York: Macmillan, 1966; Bronfennbrenner, U., 'Socialization and social class in time and space', *Readings in Social Psychology,* eds Maccoby, E. *et al.*, New York: Holt, Rinehart & Winston, 1958.

12   Henderson's research, quoted above, as other research, indicates a marked superiority in the form-class usage of working-class girls compared to working-class boys. It is possible, however, that our very *eliciting techniques* may well create contexts for girls in which they can demonstrate a socially promoted superiority. We have reason to believe that such superiority in girls is not wholly the result of earlier biological development. The girls (five years of age) of middle-class mothers who score low on an index of reported communication, offer speech where the lexes is less differentiated than the lexes of middle-class girls whose mothers score high on an index of reported communication. The findings of Bernstein, B. and

Brandis, W. (referred to above), indicate that there is a sub-group of *middle-class* mothers (positional) who explain less and who are more coercive in the socializing of the *girl* than the socializing of the boy. Thus, different uses of language by boys and girls may partly derive from family and age group role learning. They may also be a function of the eliciting contexts constructed to obtain speech.

13 A very interesting attempt to distinguish between entrepreneurial and bureaucratic families can be found in Miller, D. and Swanson, G. E., *The Changing American Parent*, New York: Wiley, 1958.

14 A good account of this movement is given by Goldthorpe, J. and Lockwood, D. (1964), 'Affluence and the class structure', *Sociological Review*. For a general analysis of the effects of the interrelationships between the division of labour and the central value system upon the structure of socializing agencies, see Parsons, T., *Personality and Social Structure*, Ch. 8, New York: Free Press, 1964.

15 Bernstein, B. (1965), 'A socio-linguistic approach to social learning', in *Penguin Survey of the Social Sciences*, Gould, J. (ed.), Penguin Books.

16 The ideas presented in this section have been developed by Douglas, M., Reader in Social Anthropology, University College, London in her paper 'The contempt of ritual' given as the Aquinas Lecture, Blackfriars, Oxford, March 1967.

Chapter 9 Social class, language and socialization

Introduction

It may be helpful to make explicit the theoretical origins of the thesis I have been developing over the past decade. Although, initially, the thesis appeared to be concerned with the problem of educability, this problem was embedded in and was stimulated by the wider question of the relationships between symbolic orders and social structure. The basic theoretical question, which dictated the approach to the initially narrow but important empirical problem, was concerned with the fundamental structure and changes in the structure of cultural transmission. Indeed, any detailed examination of what superficially may seem to be a string of somewhat repetitive papers, I think would show three things.

(1) The gradual emergence of the dominance of the major theoretical problem from the local, empirical problem of the social antecedents of the educability of different groups of children.

(2) Attempts to develop both the generality of the thesis and to develop increasing specificity at the contextual level.

(3) Entailed in (2) were attempts to clarify both the logical and empirical status of the basic organizing concept, code. Unfortunately, until recently these attempts were more readily seen in the *planning* and *analysis* of the empirical research than available as formal statements.

Looking back, however, I think I would have created less misunderstanding if I had written about socio-linguistic codes rather than linguistic codes. Through using only the latter concept it gave the impression that I was reifying syntax and at the cost of semantics; or worse, suggesting that there was a one-to-one relation between meaning and a given syntax. Also, by defining the codes in a context free fashion, I robbed myself of properly understanding, at a theoretical level, their significance. *I should point out that nearly all the empirical planning was directed to trying to find out the code realizations in different contexts.*

The concept of socio-linguistic code points to the social structuring of meanings *and* to their diverse but *related* contextual linguistic realizations. A careful reading of the papers always shows the emphasis given to the form of the social relationship, that is to the structuring of relevant meanings. Indeed, role is defined as a complex coding activity controlling the creation and organization of specific meanings and the conditions for their transmission and reception. The general socio-linguistic thesis attempts to explore how symbolic systems are both realizations and regulators of the structure of social relationships. The particular symbolic system is that of speech *not* language.

It is pertinent, at this point, to make explicit earlier work in the social sciences which formed the implicit starting point of the thesis. It will then be seen, I hope, that the thesis is an integration of different streams of thought. The major starting points are Durkheim and Marx, and a small number of other thinkers have been drawn into the basic matrix. I shall very briefly, and so selectively, outline this matrix and some of the problems to which it gave rise.

Durkheim's work is a truly magnificent insight into the relationships between symbolic orders, social relationships and the structuring of experience. In a sense, if Marx turned Hegel on his head, then Durkheim attempted to turn Kant on his head. For in *Primitive Classification* and in *The Elementary Forms of the Religious Life,* Durkheim attempted to derive the basic categories of thought from the structuring of the social relation. It is beside the point as to his success. He raised the whole question of the relation between the classifications and frames of the symbolic order *and* the structuring of experience. In his study of different forms of social integration he pointed to the implicit, condensed, symbolic structure of mechanical solidarity and the more explicit and differentiated symbolic structures of organic solidarity. Cassirer, the early cultural anthropologists, and, in particular, Sapir (I was not aware of Von Humboldt until much later), sensitized me to the cultural properties of speech. Whorf, particularly where he refers to the fashions of speaking, frames of consistency, alerted me to the selective effect of the culture (acting through its patterning of social relationships) upon the *patterning* of grammar *together* with the pattern's semantic and thus cognitive significance. Whorf more than anyone, I think, opened up, at least for me, the question of the deep structure of linguistically regulated communication.

In all the above work I found two difficulties. If we grant the fundamental linkage of symbolic systems, social structure and the shaping of experience it is still unclear *how* such shaping takes place. The *processes* underlying the social structuring of experience are not explicit. The second difficulty is in dealing with the question of change of symbolic systems. Mead is of central importance in the solution of the first difficulty, the HOW. Mead outlined in general terms the relationships between role, reflexiveness and speech and in so doing provided the basis of the solution to the HOW. It is still the case that the Meadian solution does not allow us to deal with the problem of change. For the concept, which enables role to be related to a higher order concept, 'the generalized other', is, itself, not subject to systematic enquiry. Even if 'the generalized other' is placed within a Durkheimian framework, we are still left with the problem of change. Indeed, in Mead change is introduced only at the cost of the re-emergence of a traditional Western dichotomy in the concepts of the 'I' and the 'me'. The 'I' is both the indeterminate response to the 'me' and yet, at the same time, shapes it. The Meadian 'I' points to the voluntarism in the affairs of men, to the fundamental creativity of man, made possible by speech; a little before Chomsky.

Thus Meadian thought helps to solve the puzzle of the HOW but it does not help with the question of change in the structuring of experience; although both Mead implicitly and Durkheim explicitly pointed to the conditions which bring about pathological structuring of experience.

One major theory of the development of and change in symbolic structures is, of course, that of Marx. Although Marx is less concerned with the internal structure and the process of transmission of symbolic systems, he does give us a key to their institutionalization and change. The key is given in terms of the social significance of society's productive system and the power relationships to which the productive system gives rise. Further, access to, control over, orientation of and *change* in critical symbolic systems, according to the theory, is governed by power relationships as these are embodied in the class structure. It is not only capital, in the strict economic sense, which is subject to appropriation, manipulation and exploitation, but also *cultural* capital in the form of the symbolic systems through which man can extend and change the boundaries of his experience.

I am not putting forward a matrix of thought necessary for the study of the basic structure and change in the structure of cultural transmission, *only* the specific matrix which underlies my own approach. Essentially and briefly I have used Durkheim and Marx at the macro-level and Mead at the micro-level to realize a socio-

linguistic thesis which could meet with a range of work in anthropology, linguistics, sociology and psychology.

I want first of all to make clear what I am not concerned with.
Chomsky, in *Aspects of the Theory of Syntax,* neatly severs the study
of the rule system of language from the study of the social rules
which determine their contextual use. He does this by making a distinction between competence and performance. Competence refers
to the child's tacit understanding of the rule system, performance
relates to the essentially social use to which the rule system is put.
Competence refers to man abstracted from contextual constraints.
Performance refers to man in the grip of the contextual constraints
which determine his speech acts. Competence refers to the Ideal,
performance, refers to the Fall. In this sense Chomsky's notion of
competence is Platonic. Competence has its source in the very biology of man. There is no difference between men in terms of their
access to the linguistic rule system. Here Chomsky like many other
linguists before him, announces the communality of man; all men
have equal access to the creative act which is language. On the other
hand, performance is under the control of the social—performances
are culturally specific acts, they refer to the choices which are made
in specific speech encounters. Thus, according to Hymes, Chomsky
indicates the tragedy of man, the potentiality of competence and
the degeneration of performance.

Clearly, much is to be gained in rigour and explanatory power
through the severing of the relationship between the formal properties of the grammar and the meanings which are realized in its
use. But if we are to study speech, *la parole,* we are inevitably involved in a study of a rather different rule system; we are involved in
a study of rules, formal and informal, which regulate the options we
take up in various contexts in which we find ourselves. This second
rule system is the cultural system. This raises immediately the question of the relationship between the linguistic rule system and the
cultural system. Clearly, specific linguistic rule systems are part of
the cultural system, but it has been argued that the linguistic rule
system in various ways shapes the cultural system. This very briefly is
the view of those who hold a narrow form of the linguistic relativity
hypothesis. I do not intend to get involved in that particular quag-
mire. Instead, I shall take the view that the code which the linguist
invents to explain the formal properties of the grammar is capable
of generating any number of speech codes, and there is no reason for
believing that any one language code is better than another in this
respect. On this argument, language is a set of rules to which all
speech codes must comply, but which speech codes are realized is
a function of the culture acting through social relationships in

specific contexts. Different speech forms or codes symbolize the form of the social relationship, regulate the nature of the speech encounters, and create for the speakers different orders of relevance and relation. The experience of the speakers is then transformed by what is made significant or relevant by the speech form. This is a sociological argument because the speech form is taken as a consequence of the form of the social relation or, put more generally, is a quality of a social structure. Let me qualify this immediately. Because the speech form is initially a function of a given social arrangement, it does not mean that the speech form does not in turn modify or even change that social structure which initially evolved the speech form. This formulation, indeed, invites the question: Under what conditions does a given speech form free itself sufficiently from its embodiment in the social structure so that the system of meanings it realizes points to alternative realities, alternative arrangements in the affairs of men? Here we become concerned immediately with the antecedents and consequences of the boundary maintaining principles of a culture or sub-culture. I am here suggesting a relationship between forms of boundary maintenance at the cultural level and forms of speech.

I am required to consider the relationship between language and socialization. It should be clear from these opening remarks that I am not concerned with language, but with speech, and concerned more specifically with the contextual constraints upon speech. Now what about socialization? I shall take the term to refer to the process whereby a child acquires a specific cultural identity, *and* to his responses to such an identity. Socialization refers to the process whereby the biological is transformed into a specific cultural being. It follows from this that the process of socialization is a complex process of control, whereby a particular moral, cognitive and affective awareness is evoked in the child and given a specific form and content. Socialization sensitizes the child to the various orderings of society as these are made substantive in the various roles he is expected to play. In a sense, then, socialization is a process for making people safe. The process acts selectively on the possibilities of man by creating through time a sense of the inevitability of a given social arrangement, and through limiting the areas of permitted change. The basic agencies of socialization in contemporary societies are the family, the peer group, school and work. It is through these agencies, and in particular through their relationship to each other, that the various orderings of society are made manifest.

Now it is quite clear that given this view of socialization it is necessary to limit the discussion. I shall limit our discussion to socialization within the family, but it should be obvious that the focusing and filtering of the child's experience within the family in a large measure is a microcosm of the macroscopic orderings of society. Our question now becomes: What are the sociological factors which affect linguistic performances within the family critical to the process of socialization?

Without a shadow of doubt the most formative influence upon the procedures of socialization, from a sociological viewpoint, is social class. The class structure influences work and educational roles and brings families into a special relationship with each other and deeply penetrates the structure of life experiences within the family. The class system has deeply marked the distribution of knowledge within society. It has given differential access to the sense that the world is permeable. It has sealed off communities from each other and has ranked these communities on a scale of invidious worth. We have three components, knowledge, possibility and invidious insulation. It would be a little naïve to believe that differences in knowledge, differences in the sense of the possible, combined with invidious insulation, rooted in differential *material* well-being, would not affect the forms of control and innovation in the socializing procedures of different social classes. I shall go on to argue that the deep structure of communication itself is affected, but not in any final or irrevocable way.

As an approach to my argument, let me glance at the social distribution of knowledge. We can see that the class system has affected the distribution of knowledge. Historically, and now, only a tiny percentage of the population has been socialized into knowledge at the level of the meta-languages of control and innovation, whereas the mass of the population has been socialized into knowledge at the level of context-tied operations.

A tiny percentage of the population has been given access to the principles of intellectual change, whereas the rest have been denied such access. This suggests that we might be able to distinguish between two orders of meaning. One we could call universalistic, the other particularistic. Universalistic meanings are those in which principles and operations are made linguistically explicit, whereas particularistic orders of meaning are meanings in which principles and operation are relatively linguistically implicit. If orders of meaning are universalistic, then the meanings are less tied to a given context. The meta-languages of public forms of thought as these apply to objects and persons realize meanings of a universalistic type. Where meanings have this characteristic then individuals have access to the grounds of their experience and can change the grounds. Where orders of meaning are particularistic, where principles are linguistically implicit, then such meanings are less context independent and *more* context bound, that is, tied to a local relationship and to a local social structure. Where the meaning system is particularistic, much of the meaning is embedded in the context and may be restricted to those who share a similar contextual history. Where meanings are universalistic, they are in principle available to all because the principles and operations have been made explicit, and so public.

I shall argue that forms of socialization orient the child towards speech codes which control access to relatively context-tied or relatively context-independent meanings. Thus I shall argue that elaborated codes orient their users towards universalistic meanings, whereas restricted codes orient, sensitize, their users to particularistic meanings: that the linguistic realization of the two orders are different, and so are the social relationships which realize them. Elaborated codes are less tied to a given or local structure and thus contain the potentiality of change in principles. In the case of elaborated codes the speech may be freed from its evoking social structure and it can take on an autonomy. A university is a place organized around talk. Restricted codes are more tied to a local social structure and have a reduced potential for change in principles. Where codes are elaborated, the socialized has more access to the grounds of his own socialization, and so can enter into a reflexive relationship to the social order he has taken over. Where codes are restricted, the socialized has less access to the grounds of his socialization, and thus reflexiveness may be limited in range. *One of the effects of the class system is to limit access to elaborated codes.*

I shall go on to suggest that restricted codes have their basis in condensed symbols, whereas elaborated codes have their basis in articulated symbols; that restricted codes draw upon metaphor, whereas elaborated codes draw upon rationality; that these codes constrain the contextual use of language in critical socializing contexts and in this way regulate the orders of relevance and relation which the socialized takes over. From this point of view, change in habitual speech codes involves changes in the means by which object and person relationships are realized.

I want first to start with the notions of elaborated and restricted speech variants. A variant can be considered as the contextual constraints upon grammatical-lexical choices.

Sapir, Malinowski, Firth, Vygotsky and Luria have all pointed out from different points of view that the closer the identifications of speakers the greater the range of shared interests, the more probable that the speech will take a specific form. The range of syntactic alternatives is likely to be reduced and the lexis to be drawn from a narrow range. Thus, the form of these social relations is acting selectively on the meanings to be verbally realized. In these relationships the intent of the other person can be taken for granted as the speech is played out against a back-drop of common assumptions, common history, common interests. As a result, there is less need to raise meanings to the level of explicitness or elaboration. There is a reduced need to make explicit through syntactic choices the logical structure of the communication. Further, if the speaker wishes to individualize his communication, he is likely to do this by varying the expressive associates of the speech. Under these conditions, the speech is likely to have a strong metaphoric element. In these situations the speaker may be more concerned with how something is said, when it is said; silence takes on a variety of meanings. Often in these encounters the speech cannot be understood apart from the context, and the context cannot be read by those who do not share the history of the relationships. Thus the form of the social relationship acts selectively in the meanings to be verbalized, which in turn affect the syntactic and lexical choices. The unspoken assumptions underlying the relationship are not available to those who are outside the relationship. For these are limited, and restricted to the speakers. The symbolic form of the communication is condensed, yet the specific cultural history of the relationship is alive in its form. We can say that the roles of the speakers are communalized roles. Thus, we can make a relationship between restricted social relationships based upon communalized roles and the verbal realization of their meaning. In the language of the earlier part of this paper, restricted social relationships based upon communalized roles evoke particularistic, that is, context-tied, meanings, realized through a restricted speech variant.

Imagine a husband and wife have just come out of the cinema, and are talking about the film: 'What do you think?' 'It had a lot to say' 'Yes, I thought so too—let's go to the Millers, there may be something going there'. They arrive at the Millers, who ask about the film. An hour is spent in the complex, moral, political, aesthetic subtleties of the film and its place in the contemporary scene. Here we have an elaborated variant; the meanings now have to be made public to others who have not seen the film. The speech shows careful editing, at both the grammatical and lexical levels, It is no longer context-tied. The meanings are explicit, elaborated and individualized. Whilst expressive channels are clearly relevant, the burden of meaning inheres predominantly in the verbal channel. The experience of the listeners cannot be taken for granted. Thus each member of the group is on his own as he offers his interpretation. Elaborated variants of this kind involve the speakers in particular role relationships, and *if you cannot manage the role, you can't produce the appropriate speech.* For as the speaker proceeds to individualize his meanings, he is differentiated from others like a figure from its ground.

The roles receive less support from each other. There is a measure of isolation. *Difference* lies at the basis of the social relationship, and is made verbally active, whereas in the other context it is *consensus*. The insides of the speaker have become psychologically active through the verbal aspect of the communication. Various defensive strategies may be used to decrease potential vulnerability of self and to increase the vulnerability of others. The verbal aspect of the communication becomes a vehicle for the transmission of individuated symbols. The 'I' stands over the 'we'. Meanings which are discrete to the speaker must be offered so that they are intelligible to the listener. Communalized roles have given way to individualized roles, condensed symbols to articulated symbols. Elaborated speech variants of this type realize universalistic meanings in the sense that they are less context-tied. Thus individualized roles are realized through elaborated speech variants which involve complex editing at the grammatical and lexical levels and which point to universalistic meanings.

Let me give another example. Consider the two following stories which Peter Hawkins, Assistant Research Officer in the Sociological Research Unit, University of London Institute of Education, constructed as a result of his analysis of the speech of middle-class and working-class five-year-old children. The children were given a series of four pictures which told a story and they were invited to tell the story. The first picture showed some boys playing football; in the second the ball goes through the window of a house; the third shows a woman looking out of the window and a man making an ominous gesture, and in the fourth the children are moving away.

Here are the two stories:

(1) Three boys are playing football and one boy kicks the ball and it goes through the window the ball breaks the window and the boys are looking at it and a man comes out and shouts at them because they've broken the window so they run away and then that lady looks out of her window and she tells the boys off.

(2) They're playing football and he kicks it and it goes through there it breaks the window and they're looking at it and he comes out and shouts at them because they've broken it so they run away and then she looks out and she tells them off.

With the first story the reader does not have to have the four pictures which were used as the basis for the story, whereas in the case of the second story the reader would require the initial pictures in order to make sense of the story. The first story is free of the context which generated it, whereas the second story is much more closely tied to its context. As a result the meanings of the second story are implicit, whereas the meanings of the first story are explicit. It is not that the working-class children do not have in their passive vocabulary the vocabulary used by the middle-class children. Nor is it the case that the children differ in their tacit understanding of the linguistic rule system. Rather, what we have here are differences in the use of language arising out of a specific context. One child makes explicit the meanings which he is realizing through language for the person he is telling the story to, whereas the second child does not to the same extent. The first child takes very little for granted, whereas the second child takes a great deal for granted. Thus for the first child the task was seen as a context in which his meanings were required to be made explicit, whereas the task for the second child was not seen as a task which required such explication of meaning. It would not be difficult to imagine a context where the first child would produce speech rather like the second. What we are dealing with here are differences between the children in the way they realize in language-use apparently the same context. We could say that the speech of the first child generated universalistic meanings in the sense that the meanings are freed from the context and so understandable by all, whereas the speech of the second child generated particularistic meanings, in the sense that the meanings are closely tied to the context and would be fully understood by others only if they had access to the context which originally generated the speech.

It is again important to stress that the second child has access to a more differentiated noun phrase, but there is a restriction on its *use*. Geoffrey Turner, Linguist in the Sociological Research Unit, shows that working-class, five-year-old children in the same contexts examined by Hawkins, use fewer linguistic expressions of uncertainty when compared with the middle-class children. This does not mean that working-class children do *not* have access to such expressions, but that the eliciting speech context did not provoke them. Telling a story from pictures, talking about scenes on cards, *formally framed* contexts, do not encourage working-class children to consider the possibilities of alternate meanings and so there is a reduction in the linguistic expressions of uncertainty. Again, working-class children have access to a wide range of syntactic choices which involve the use of logical operators, 'because', 'but', 'either', 'or', 'only'. The constraints exist on the conditions for their *use*. Formally framed contexts used for eliciting context-independent universalistic meanings may evoke in the working-class child, relative to the middle-class child, restricted speech variants, because the working-class child has difficulty in managing the role relationships which such contexts require. This problem is further complicated when such contexts carry meanings very much removed from the child's cultural experience. In the same way we can show that there are constraints upon the middle-class child's use of language. Turner found that when middle-class children were asked to role-play in the picture story series, a higher percentage of these children, when compared with working-class children, initially refused. When the middle-class children were asked 'What is the man saying?' or linguistically equivalent questions, a relatively higher percentage said 'I don't know'. When this question was followed by the hypothetical question 'What do you think the man might be saying?' they offered their interpretations. The working-class children role-played without difficulty. It seems then that middle-class children at five need to have a very precise instruction to *hypothesize in that particular* context. This may be because they are more concerned here with getting their answers right or correct. When the children were invited to tell a story about some doll-like figures (a little boy, a little girl, a sailor and a dog) the working-class children's stories were freer, longer and more imaginative than the stories of the middle-class children. The latter children's stories were tighter, constrained within a strong narrative frame. It was as if these children were dominated by what they took to be the *form* of a narrative and the content was secondary. This is an example of the concern of the middle-class child with the structure of the contextual frame. It may be worthwhile to amplify this further. A number of studies have shown that when working-class black children are asked to associate to a series of words, their responses show considerable diversity, both from the meaning and form-class of the stimulus word. Our analysis suggests this may be because the children for the following reasons are less constrained. The form-class of the stimulus word may have reduced associative significance and this would less constrain the selection of potential words *or* phrases. With such a weakening of the grammatical frame there is a greater range of alternatives as possible candidates for selection. Further, the closely controlled, middle-class, linguistic socialization of the young child may point the child towards both the grammatical significance of the stimulus word and towards a tight logical ordering of semantic space. Middle-class children may well have access to deep interpretative rules which regulate their linguistic responses in certain formalized contexts. The consequences may limit their imagination through the tightness of the frame which these interpretative rules create. It may even be that with *five*-year-old children, the middle-class child will innovate *more* with the arrangements of objects (i.e. bricks) than in his linguistic usage. His linguistic usage is under close supervision by adults. He has more *autonomy* in his play.

To return to our previous discussion, we can say, briefly, that as we move from communalized to individualized roles, so speech takes on an increasingly reflexive function. The unique selves of others become palpable through speech and enter into our own self; the grounds of our experience are made verbally explicit; the security of the condensed symbol is gone. It has been replaced by rationality. There is a change in the basis of our vulnerability.

So far, then, I have discussed certain types of speech variants and the role relationships which occasion them. I am now going to raise the generality of the discussion and focus upon the title of the paper. The socialization of the young in the family proceeds within a critical set of interrelated contexts. Analytically, we may distinguish four contexts.

(1) The regulative context—these are authority relationships where the child is made aware of the rules of the moral order and their various backings.

(2) The instructional context, where the child learns about the objective nature of objects and persons, and acquires skills of various kinds.

(3) The imaginative or innovating contexts, where the child is encouraged to experiment and re-create his world on his own terms, and in his own way.

(4) The interpersonal context, where the child is made aware of affective states—his own, and others.

I am suggesting that the critical orderings of a culture or sub-culture are made substantive—are made palpable—through the forms of its linguistic realizations of these four contexts—initially in the family and kin.

Now if the linguistic realization of these four contexts involves the predominant use of restricted speech variants, I shall postulate that the deep structure of the communication is a restricted code having its basis in communalized roles, realizing context-dependent meanings, i.e. particularistic meaning orders. Clearly the specific grammatical and lexical choices will vary from one to another.

If the linguistic realization of these four contexts involves the predominant usage of elaborated speech variants, I shall postulate that the deep structure of the communication is an elaborated code having its basis in individualized roles realizing context-independent universalistic meanings.

In order to prevent misunderstanding an expansion of the text is here necessary. It is likely that where the code is restricted, the speech in the regulative context may well be limited to command and simple rule-announcing statements. The latter statements are not context-dependent in the sense previously given, for they announce general rules. We need to supplement the context-independent (universalistic) and context-dependent (particularistic) criteria with criteria which refer to the extent to which the speech in the regulative context varies in terms of its *contextual specificity*. If the speech is context-specific then the socializer cuts his meanings to the *specific* attributes/intentions of the socialized, the specific characteristics of the problem, the specific requirements of the context. Thus the general rule may be transmitted with degrees of *contextual specificity*. When this occurs the rule is individualized (fitted to the local circumstances) in the process of its transmission. Thus with code elaboration we should expect:

(1) Some developed grounds for the rule
(2) Some qualification of it in the light of the particular issue
(3) Considerable *specificity* in terms of the socialized, the context and the issue

This does *not* mean that there would be an *absence* of command statements. It is also likely that with code elaboration the socialized would be *given* opportunities (role options) to question.

Bernstein and Cook (1965) and Cook (1971) have developed a semantic coding grid which sets out with considerable delicacy a general category system which has been applied to a limited regulative

Realization of the regulative context

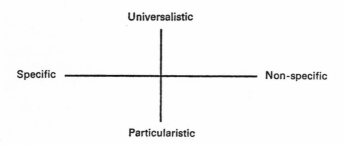

context. G. Turner, linguist to the Sociological Research Unit, is attempting a linguistic realization of the same grid.

We can express the two sets of criteria diagrammatically. A limited application is given by Henderson (1970).

It may be necessary to utilize the two sets of criteria for *all* four socializing contexts.

If we look at the linguistic realization of the regulative context in greater detail we may be able to clear up another source of possible misunderstanding. In this context it is very likely that syntactic markers of the logical distribution of meaning will be extensively used.

'If you do that, then. . . .'
'Either you . . . or. . . .'
'You can do that, but if. . . .'
'You do that and you'll pay for it.'

Thus it is very likely that all young children may well in the *regulative* context have access to a range of syntactic markers which express the logical/hypothetical, irrespective of code restriction or elaboration. However, where the code is restricted it is expected that there will be reduced specificity in the sense outlined earlier. Further, the speech in the control situation is likely to be well organized in the sense that the sentences come as wholes. The child responds to the total *frame*. However, I would suggest that the informal *instructional* contexts within the family may well be limited in range and frequency. Thus the child, of course, would have access to, and so have *available*, the hypotheticals, conditionals, disjunctives etc., but these might be rarely used in *instructional* contexts. In the same way, as we have suggested earlier, all children have access to linguistic expressions of uncertainty but they may differ in the context in which they receive and realize such expressions.

I must emphasize that because the code is restricted it does not mean that speakers at no time will not use elaborated speech variants; only that the use of such variants will be infrequent in the socialization of the child in his family.

Now, all children have access to restricted codes and their various systems of condensed meaning, because the roles the code presupposes are universal. But there may well be selective access to elaborated codes because there is selective access to the role system which evokes its use. Society is likely to evaluate differently the experiences realized through these two codes. I cannot here go into details, but the different focusing of experience through a restricted code creates a major problem of educability only where the school produces discontinuity between its symbolic orders and those of the child. Our schools are not made for these children; why should the children respond? To ask the child to switch to an elaborated code which presupposes different role relationships and systems of meaning without a sensitive understanding of the required contexts may create for the child a bewildering and potentially damaging experience.

So far, then, I have sketched out a relationship between speech codes and socialization through the organization of roles through which the culture is made psychologically active in persons. I have indicated that access to the roles and thus to the codes is broadly related to social class. However, it is clearly the case that social class groups today are by no means homogeneous groups. Further, the division between elaborated and restricted codes is too simple. Finally, I have not indicated in any detail how these codes are evoked by families, and how the family types may shape their focus.

What I shall do now is to introduce a distinction between family types and their communication structures. These family types can be found empirically within each social class, although any one type may be rather more modal at any given historical period.

I shall distinguish between families according to the strength of their boundary maintaining procedures. Let me first give some idea of what I mean by boundary maintaining procedures. I shall first look at boundary maintenance as it is revealed in the symbolic ordering of space. Consider the lavatory. In one house, the room is pristine, bare and sharp, containing only the necessities for which the room is dedicated. In another there is a picture on the wall, in the third there are books, in the fourth all surfaces are covered with curious postcards. We have a continuum from a room celebrating the purity of categories to one celebrating the mixture of categories, from strong to weak boundary maintenance. Consider the kitchen. In one kitchen, shoes may not be placed on the table, nor the child's chamber pot—all objects and utensils have an assigned place. In another kitchen the boundaries separating the different classes of objects are weak. The symbolic ordering of space can give us indications of the relative strength of boundary maintaining procedures. Let us now look at the relationship between family members. Where boundary procedures are strong, the differentiation of members and the authority structure is based upon clear-cut, unambiguous definitions of the status of the member of the family. The boundaries between the statuses are strong and the social identities of the members very much a function of their age, sex and age-relation status. As a short-hand, we can characterize the family as *positional*.

On the other hand, where boundary procedures are weak or flexible, the differentiation between members and the authority relationships are less on the basis of position, because here the status boundaries are blurred. Where boundary procedures are weak, the differentiation between members is based more upon *differences between persons*. In such families the relationships become more egocentric and the unique attributes of family members are made more and more substantive in the communication structure. We will call these *person-centred* families. Such families do not reduce but increase the substantive expression of ambiguity and ambivalence. In person-centred families, the role system would be continuously evoking, accommodating and assimilating the different interests and attributes of its members. In such families, unlike positional families, the members would be making their roles rather than stepping into them. In a person-centred family, the child's developing self is differentiated by continuous adjustment to the verbally realized and elaborated intentions, qualifications and motives of others. The boundary between self and other is blurred. In positional families, the child takes over and responds to the formal pattern of obligation and privilege. It should be possible to see, without going into details, that the communication structures within these two types of family are somewhat differently focused. We might then expect that the reflexiveness induced by positional families is sensitized to the general attributes of persons, whereas the reflexiveness produced by person-centred families is more sensitive towards the particular aspects of persons. Think of the difference between Dartington Hall or Gordonstoun public schools in England, or the difference between West Point and a progressive school in the USA. Thus, in person-centred families, the insides of the members are made public through the communication structure, and thus more of the person has been invaded and subject to control. Speech in such families is a major medium of control. In positional families, of course, speech is relevant but it symbolizes the boundaries given by the formal structure of the relationships. So far as the child is concerned, in positional families he attains a strong sense of social identity at the cost of autonomy; in person-centred families, the child attains a strong sense of autonomy but his social identity may be weak. Such ambiguity in the sense of identity, the lack of boundary, may move such children towards a radically closed value system.

If we now place these family types in the framework of the previous discussion, we can see that although the code may be elaborated, it may be differently focused according to the family type. Thus, we can have an elaborate code focusing upon persons or an elaborated code in a positional family may focus more upon objects. We can expect the same with a restricted code. Normally, with code restriction we should expect a positional family; however, if it showed signs of being person-centred, then we might expect the children to be in a situation of potential code switch.

Where the code is elaborated, and focused by a person-centred family, then these children may well develop acute identity problems concerned with authenticity, with limiting responsibility—they may come to see language as phony, a system of counterfeit masking the absence of belief. They may move towards the restricted codes of the various peer group sub-cultures, or seek the condensed symbols of affective experience, or both.

One of the difficulties of this approach is to avoid implicit value judgments about the relative worth of speech systems and the cultures which they symbolize. Let it be said immediately that a restricted code gives access to a vast potential of meanings, of delicacy, subtlety and diversity of cultural forms, to a unique aesthetic the basis of which in condensed symbols may influence the form of the imagining. Yet, in complex industrialized societies its differently-focused experience may be disvalued and humiliated within schools, or seen, at best, to be irrelevant to the educational endeavour. For the schools are predicated upon elaborated code and its system of social relationships. Although an elaborated code does not entail any specific value system, the value system of the middle class penetrates the texture of the very learning context itself.

Elaborated codes give access to alternative realities, yet they carry the potential of alienation, of feeling from thought, of self from other, of private belief *from role obligation*.

Finally I should like to consider briefly the sources of change of linguistic codes. The first major source of change I suggest is to be located in the division of labour. As the division of labour changes from simple to complex, then this changes the social and knowledge characteristics of occupational roles. In this process there is an extension of access, through education, to elaborated codes, but access is controlled by the class system. The focusing of the codes I have suggested is brought about by the boundary maintaining procedures within the family. However, we can generalize and say that the focusing of the codes is related to the boundary maintaining procedures as these affect the major socializing agencies—family, age group, education and work. We need, therefore, to consider together with the question of the degree and type of complexity of the division of labour, the value orientations of society which, it is hypothesized, affect the boundary maintaining procedures. It is the case that we can have societies with a similar complexity in their division of labour but which differ in their boundary maintaining procedures.

I suggest then that it is important to make a distinction between societies in terms of their boundary maintaining procedures if we are to deal with this question of the focusing of codes. One possible way of examining the relative strength of boundary maintenance is to consider the strength of the *constraints* upon the choice of values which legitimize authority/power relationships. Thus in societies where there is weak constraint upon such legitimizing values, that is, where there is a variety of formally permitted legitimizing values, we might expect a marked shift towards person type control; whereas in societies with strong constraints upon legitimizing values, where there is a severe *restriction* upon the choice, we might expect a marked shift towards positional control.

I shall illustrate these relationships with reference to the family:

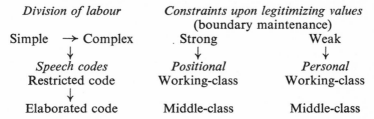

Division of labour	*Constraints upon legitimizing values* (boundary maintenance)	
Simple → Complex	Strong	Weak
↓	↓	↓
Speech codes	*Positional*	*Personal*
Restricted code	Working-class	Working-class
↓		
Elaborated code	Middle-class	Middle-class

Thus the division of labour influences the availability of elaborated codes; the class system affects their distribution; the focusing of codes can be related to the boundary maintaining procedures, i.e. the value system. I must point out that this is only a coarse interpretative framework.

Conclusion

I have tried to show how the class system acts upon the deep structure of communication in the process of socialization. I refined the crudity of this analysis by showing how speech codes may be differently focused through family types. Finally, it is conceivable that there are general aspects of the analysis which might provide a starting point for the consideration of symbolic orders other than languages. I must point out that there is more to socialization than the forms of its linguistic realization.

References

BERNSTEIN, B. (1970), 'Education cannot compensate for society', *New Society* No. 387, February.

BERNSTEIN, B. (1962), 'Family role systems, socialisation and communication', manuscript, Sociological Research Unit, University of London Institute of Education; also in 'A socio-linguistic approach to socialisation', *Directions in Sociolinguistics*, Gumperz, J. J. and Hymes, D. (eds), New York: Holt, Rinehart & Winston.

BERNSTEIN, B. and COOK, J. (1965), 'Coding grid for maternal control', available from Department of Sociology, University of London Institute of Education.

BERNSTEIN, B. and HENDERSON, D. (1969), 'Social class differences in the relevance of language to socialisation', *Sociology* 3, No. 1.

BRIGHT, N. (ed.) (1966), *Sociolinguistics*, Mouton Press.

CARROLL, J. B. (ed.) (1956), *Language, Thought and Reality: selected writings of Benjamin Lee Whorf*, New York: Wiley.

CAZDEN, C. B. (1969), 'Sub-cultural differences in child language: an interdisciplinary review', *Merrill-Palmer Quarterly* 12.

CHOMSKY, N. (1965), *Aspects of Linguistic Theory*, Cambridge M.I.T.

COOK, J. (1971), 'An enquiry into patterns of communication and control between mothers and their children in different social classes', Ph.D. Thesis, University of London.

COULTHARD, M. (1969), 'A discussion of restricted and elaborated codes', *Educ. Rev.* 22, No. 1.

DOUGLAS, M. (1970), *Natural Symbols*, Barrie & Rockliff, The Cresset Press.

FISHMAN, J. A. (1960), 'A systematization of the Whorfian hypothesis', *Behavioral Science* 5.

GUMPERZ, J. J. and HYMES, D. (eds.) (1971), *Directions in Sociolinguistics*, New York: Holt, Reinhart & Winston. (In press.)

HALLIDAY, M. A. K. (1969), 'Relevant models of language', *Educ. Rev.* 22, No. 1.

HAWKINS, P. R. (1969), 'Social class, the nominal group and reference', *Language and Speech* 12, No. 2.

HENDERSON, D. (1970), 'Contextual specificity, discretion and cognitive socialisation: with special reference to language', *Sociology* 4, No. 3.

HOIJER, H. (ed.) (1954), 'Language in Culture', *American Anthropological Association Memoir* No. 79; also published by Univ. of Chicago Press.

HYMES, D. (1966), 'On communicative competence', Research Planning Conference on Language Development among Disadvantaged Children, Ferkauf Graduate School, Yeshiva University.

HYMES, D. (1967), 'Models of the interaction of language and social setting', *Journal of Social Issues* 23.

LABOV, W. (1965), 'Stages in the acquisition of standard English', in Shuy, W. (ed.), *Social Dialects and Language Learning*, Champaign, Illinois: National Council of Teachers of English.

LABOV, W. (1966), 'The social stratification of English in New York City', Washington D.C. Centre for Applied Linguistics.

MANDELBAUM, D. (ed.) (1949), *Selected Writings of Edward Sapir*, Univ. of California Press.

PARSONS, T. and SHILS, E. A. (eds.) (1962), *Toward a General Theory of Action*, Harper Torchbooks (Chapter 1, especially).

SCHATZMAN, L. and STRAUSS, A. L. (1955), 'Social class and modes of communication', *Am.J.Soc.* 60.

TURNER, G. and PICKVANCE, R. E. (1971), 'Social class differences in the expression of uncertainty in five-year-old children', *Language and Speech* (in press).

WILLIAMS, F. and NAREMORE, R. C. (1969), 'On the functional analysis of social class differences in modes of speech, *Speech Monographs* 36, No. 2.

Chapter 10   A critique of the concept of compensatory education

Since the late 1950s there has been a steady outpouring of papers and books in the USA which are concerned with the education of children of low social class whose *material* circumstances are inadequate, or with the education of black children of low social class whose *material* circumstances are chronically inadequate. An enormous research and educational bureaucracy developed in the USA financed by funds obtained from Federal, State or private foundations. New educational categories were developed (the culturally deprived, the linguistically deprived, the socially disadvantaged) and the notion of compensatory education was introduced as a means of changing the status of those children in the above categories. Compensatory education issued in the form of massive pre-school introductory programmes, large-scale research programmes such as those of Deutch in the early 1960s, and a plethora of small scale 'intervention' or 'enrichment' programmes for pre-school children or children in the first years of compulsory education. Very few sociologists were involved in these studies as, until recently, education was a low status area. On the whole, they were carried out by psychologists.

The focus of these studies was on the child in the family and on the local classroom relationships between teacher and child. In the last two years one can detect a change in this focus. As a result of the movements towards integration and the opposed movement towards segregation (the latter a response to the wishes of the various Black Power groups), more studies are being made in the USA of the *school*. Work in England has been almost limited to the effects of streaming. Rosenthal and Jacobson's study *Pygmalion in the Classroom* drew attention to the critical importance of the teacher's expectations of the child. Here we have been aware of the educational problem since the pre-war writings of Sir Cyril Burt. His book *The Backward Child* is probably still the best descriptive study we have. After the war a series of sociological surveys and public enquiries into education brought this educational problem into the arena of national debate, and so of social policy. Now in Wales there is a large research unit, financed by the Schools Council, concerned with compensatory education. Important research of a most significant kind is taking place in the University of Birmingham into the problems of the education of Commonwealth children. The Social Science Research Council and the Department of Education and Science have given £175,000, in part for the development of special pre-school programmes concerned to introduce children to compensatory education.

One University Department of Education offers an advanced diploma in compensatory education. Colleges of Education also offer special courses under the same title. It might be worth a few lines to consider the assumptions underlying this work and the concepts which describe it, particularly as my own writings have sometimes been used (and more often abused) to highlight aspects of the general problems and dilemmas.

To begin with I find the term 'compensatory education' a curious one for a number of reasons. I do not understand how we can talk about offering compensatory education to children who, in the first place, have as yet not been offered an adequate educational environment. The Newsom Report showed that 79 per cent of all secondary modern schools in slum and problem areas were materially grossly inadequate, and that the holding power of these schools over the teachers was horrifyingly low. The same Report also showed very clearly how the depression in the reading scores of these children compared with the reading scores of children who were at school in areas which were neither problem nor slum. This does not conflict with the findings that, on average for the country as a whole, there has been an improvement in children's reading ability. The Plowden Report was rather more coy about all the above points, but we have little reason to believe that the situation is very much better for primary schools in similar areas. Thus we offer a large number of children, both at the primary and secondary level, materially inadequate schools and unstable teaching staff, and we further expect a small group of dedicated teachers to cope. The strain on these teachers inevitably produces fatigue and illness and it is not uncommon to find, in any week, teachers having to deal with doubled-up classes of eighty children. And we wonder why the children display very early in their educational life a range of learning difficulties. At the same time, the organization of schools creates delicate overt and covert streaming arrangements which neatly lower the expectations and motivations of teachers and taught. A vicious spiral is set up with an all too determinate outcome. It would seem then that we have as yet failed to provide on the scale required an *initial* satisfactory educational environment.

The concept 'compensatory education' serves to direct attention away from the internal organization and the educational context of the school, and focus our attention upon the families and children. The concept 'compensatory education' implies that something is lacking in the family, and so in the child. As a result the children are unable to benefit from schools. It follows then that the school has to 'compensate' for the something which is missing in the family and the children become little deficit systems. If only the parents were interested in the goodies we offer; if only they were like middle-class parents, then we could do our job. Once the problem is seen even implicitly in this way, then it becomes appropriate to coin the terms 'cultural deprivation', 'linguistic deprivation', etc. And then these labels do their own sad work.

If children are labelled 'culturally deprived' then it follows that the parents are inadequate, the spontaneous realizations of their culture, its images and symbolic representations are of reduced value and significance. Teachers will have lower expectations of the children, which the children will undoubtedly fulfil. All that informs the child, that gives meaning and purpose to him outside the school, ceases to be valid and accorded significance and opportunity for enhancement within the school. He has to orient towards a different structure of meaning, whether it is in the form of reading books (Janet and John), in the form of language-use and dialect, or in the patterns of social relationships. Alternatively, the meaning structure of the school is explained to the parents and imposed upon, rather than integrated within, the form and content of their world. A wedge is progressively driven between the child as a member of a family and community, and the child as a member of a school. Either way the child is expected, and his parents as well, to drop their social identity, their way of life and its symbolic representation, at the school gate. For, by definition, their culture is deprived, the parents inadequate in both the moral and skill orders they transmit. I do not mean by this that no satisfactory home-school relations can take place or do not take place; I mean rather that the parents must be brought *within* the educational experience of the school child by doing what they *can* do, and can do with *confidence*. There are many ways in which parents can help the child in his *learning* which are *within* the parents' sphere of competence. If this happens, then the parents can feel adequate and confident both in relation to the child *and* the school. This may mean that the *contents* of the learning in school should be drawn much more from the child's experience in his family and community.

So far then I have criticized the use of the concept of 'compensatory education' because it distracts attention from the deficiencies in the school itself and focuses upon deficiencies within the community, family and child. We can add to these criticisms a third. The concept of 'compensatory education' points to the overwhelming significance of the early years of the child's life in the shaping of his later development. Clearly, there is much evidence to support this view and to its implication that we should create an extensive nursery school system. However, it would be foolhardy indeed to write off the post-seven-years-of-age educational experience as having little influence. Minimally, what is required *initially* is to consider the whole age period up to the conclusion of the primary stages as a unity. This would require considering our approach at any *one* age in the context of the *whole* of the primary stage. This implies a *systematic,* rather than a piecemeal, approach. I am arguing here for taking as the unit, *not* a particular period in the life of the child (for example three to five years, or five to seven years), but taking as the unit a *stage of education;* the primary stage. We should see all we do in terms of the sequencing of learning, the development of sensitivities within the context of the primary stage. In order to accomplish this the present social and educational division between infant and junior stages must be weakened, as well as the insulation between primary and secondary stages, otherwise gains at any one age in the child may well be vitiated by losses at a later age.

I suggest that we should stop thinking in terms of 'compensatory education' but consider instead most seriously and systematically the conditions and contexts of the educational environment.

The very form our research takes tends to confirm the beliefs underlying the organization, transmission and evaluation of knowledge by the school. The research proceeds by assessing criteria of attainment that schools hold, and then measures the competence of different social groups in reaching these criteria. We take one group of children whom we know beforehand possess attributes favourable to school achievement, and a second group of children whom we know beforehand lack these attributes. Then we evaluate one group in terms of what it *lacks* when compared with another. In this way research, unwittingly, underscores the notion of *deficit* and confirms the *status quo* of a given organization, transmission and, in particular, *evaluation* of knowledge. Research very rarely challenges or exposes the social assumptions underlying what counts as valid knowledge, or what counts as a valid realization of that knowledge. There are exceptions in the area of curriculum development, but even here, the work often has no built-in attempt to *evaluate* the changes. This holds particularly for the EPA 'feasibility' projects.

Finally we do not face up to the basic question: *What is the potential for change within educational institutions as they are presently constituted?* A lot of activity does not necessarily mean *action.*

I have taken so much space discussing the new educational concepts and categories because, in a small way, the work I have been doing has inadvertently contributed towards their formulation. It might be, and has been, said that my research, through focusing upon the sub-culture and forms of familial socialization, has also distracted attention from the conditions and contexts of learning in school. The focus upon usage of language sometimes led people to divorce the use of language from the sub-stratum of cultural meanings which are initially responsible for the language-use. The concept 'restricted code' has been equated with 'linguistic deprivation', or even with the non-verbal child.

We can distinguish between uses of language which can be called 'context bound' and uses of language which are less context bound. Consider, for example, the two following stories which Peter Hawkins, A.R.O. in the S.R.U., constructed as a result of his analysis of the speech of middle-class and working-class five-year-old children. The children were given a series of four pictures which told a story and they were invited to tell the story. The first picture showed some boys playing football; in the second the ball goes through the window of a house; the third shows a woman looking out of the window and a man making an ominous gesture, and in the fourth the children are moving away.
Here are the two stories:

(1)   Three boys are playing football and one boy kicks the ball and it goes through the window the ball breaks the window and the boys are looking at it and a man comes out and shouts at them because they've broken the window so they run away and then that lady looks out of her window and she tells the boys off.

(2)   They're playing football and he kicks it and it goes through there it breaks the window and they're looking at it and he comes out and shouts at them because they've broken it so they run away and then she looks out and she tells them off.

With the first story the reader does not have to have the four pictures which were used as the basis for the story, whereas in the case of the second story the reader would require the initial pictures in order to make sense of the story. The first story is free of the context which generated it, whereas the second story is much more closely tied to its context. As a result the meanings of the second story are implicit, whereas the meanings of the first story are explicit. It is not that the working-class children do not have in their passive vocabulary the vocabulary used by the middle-class children. Nor is it the case that the children differ in their tacit understanding of the linguistic rule system. Rather, what we have here are differences in the use of language arising out of a specific context. One child makes explicit the meanings which he is realizing through language for the person he is telling the story to, whereas the second child does not to the same extent. The first child takes very little for granted, whereas the second child takes a great deal for granted. Thus for the first child the task was seen as a context in which his meanings were required to be made explicit, whereas the task for the second child was not seen as a task which required such explication of meaning. It would not be difficult to imagine a context where the first child would produce speech rather like the second. What we are dealing with here are differences between the children in the way they realize in language-use apparently the same context. We could say that the speech of the first child generated universalistic meanings in the sense that the meanings are freed from the context and so understandable by all, whereas the speech of the second child generated particularistic meanings, in the sense that the meanings are closely tied to the context and would be fully understood by others only if they had access to the context which originally generated the speech. Thus universalistic meanings are less bound to a given context, whereas particularistic meanings are severely context bound.

Let us take another example. One mother when she controls her child places a great emphasis upon language because she wishes to make explicit, and to elaborate for the child, certain rules and the reasons for the rules and their consequences. In this way the child has access through language to the relationships between his particular act which evoked the mother's control, and certain general principles, reasons and consequences which serve to universalize the particular act. Another mother places less emphasis upon language when she controls her child and deals with only the particular act and does not relate this to general principles and their reasoned basis and consequences. Both children learn that there is something they are supposed, or not supposed, to do, but the first child has learned rather more than this. The grounds of the mother's acts have been made explicit and elaborated, whereas the grounds of the second mother's acts are implicit: they are unspoken. Our research shows just this: That the social classes differ in terms of the *contexts* which evoke certain linguistic realizations. Mothers in the middle class, and it is important to add not all, relative to the working class (and again it is important to add not all, by any means) place greater emphasis upon the use of language in socializing the child into the moral order, in disciplining the child, in the communication and recognition of feeling. Again we can say that the child here is oriented towards universalistic meanings which transcend a given context, whereas the second child is oriented towards particularistic meanings which are closely tied to a given context and so do not transcend it. This does not mean that working-class mothers are non-verbal, only that they differ from the middle-class mothers in the *contexts* which evoke universalistic meanings. They are *not* linguistically deprived, neither are their children.

We can generalize from these two examples and say that certain groups of children, through the forms of their socialization, are oriented towards receiving and offering universalistic meanings in *certain contexts*, whereas other groups of children are oriented towards particularistic meanings. The linguistic realization of universalistic orders of meaning are very different from the linguistic realization of particularistic orders of meaning, and so are the forms of the social relation (e.g. between mother and child) which generate these. We can say then that what is made available for learning, how it is made available and the patterns of social relation are also very different.

Now when we consider the children in school we can see that there is likely to be difficulty. For the school is necessarily concerned with the transmission and development of universalistic orders of meaning. The school is concerned with the making explicit and elaborating through language, principles and operations, as these apply to objects (science subjects) and persons (arts subjects). One child, through his socialization, is already sensitive to the symbolic orders of the school, whereas the second child is much less sensitive to the universalistic orders of the school. The second child is oriented towards particularistic orders of meaning which are context bound, in which principles and operations are implicit, and towards a form of language-use through which such meanings are realized. The school is necessarily trying to develop in the child orders of relevance and relation as these apply to persons and objects, which are not initially the ones he spontaneously moves towards. The problem of educability at one level, whether it is in Europe, the USA or newly developing societies, can be understood in terms of a confrontation between the universalistic orders of meaning and the social relationships which generate them, of the school, and the particularistic orders of meanings and the social relationships which generate them, which the child brings with him to the school. *Orientations towards meta-languages of control and innovation are not made available to these children as part of their initial socialization.*

I have stressed that the school is attempting to transmit un-commonsense knowledge, that is, public knowledge realized through various meta-languages. Such knowledge I have called universalistic. However, it is also the case that the school is both implicitly and explicitly transmitting values and their attendant morality which affect educational contents and contexts of education. They do this by establishing criteria for acceptable pupil and staff conduct. Further, these values and morals affect the *content* of educational knowledge through the selection of books, texts, films *and* through examples and analogies used to assist access to public knowledge (universalistic meanings). Thus the working-class child may be placed at a considerable disadvantage in relation to the *total* culture of the school. It is not made for him; he may not answer to it.

Now I have suggested that the forms of an elaborated code give access to universalistic orders of meaning in the sense that the principles and operations controlling object and person relationships are made explicit through the use of language, whereas restricted codes give access to particularistic orders of meaning in which the principles and operations controlling object and person relationships are rendered implicit through the use of language (Bernstein, 1962). I have also tried to explain the cultural origins of these codes and their change (the most developed version is in Bernstein, 1971). If we now go back to our earlier formulation we can say that elaborated codes give access to universalistic orders of meaning, which are less context bound, whereas restricted codes give access to particularistic orders of meaning, which are far more context bound, that is, tied to a particular context.

Because a code is restricted it does not mean that a child is non-verbal, nor is he in the technical sense linguistically deprived, for he possesses the same tacit understanding of the linguistic rule system as any child. It simply means that there is a restriction on the *contexts* and on the *conditions* which will orient the child to universalistic orders of meaning, and to making those linguistic choices through which such meanings are realized and so made public. It does not mean that the children cannot produce at any time elaborated speech in particular contexts. It is critically important to distinguish between speech variants and a restricted code. A speech variant is a pattern of linguistic choices which is specific to a particular context; for example, when one talks to children, a policeman giving evidence in court, talking to friends whom one knows well, the rituals of cocktail parties, or train encounters. Because a code is restricted it does not mean that a speaker will not in *some* contexts, and under *specific* conditions, not use a range of modifiers or subordinations etc., but it does mean that where such choices are made they will be *highly context specific*. Because a code is elaborated it does not mean that in some contexts, under specific conditions, a speaker will not use a limited range of modifiers, subordinations etc., but it does mean that such choices will be *highly context specific*. For example, if an individual has to produce a summary (consider a précis), then it is likely that this will affect his linguistic choices.

The concept code refers to the transmission of the deep meaning structure of a culture or sub-culture: the basic interpretative rules.

Codes on this view make substantive the culture or sub-culture through their control over the linguistic realizations of contexts *critical* to the process of *socialization*. Building on the work of Professor Michael Halliday we can distinguish analytically four critical contexts:

(1) The regulative contexts: these are the authority relations where the child is made aware of the moral order and its various backings.

(2) The instructional contexts: here the child learns about the objective nature of objects and acquires various skills.

(3) The imaginative or innovating contexts: here the child is encouraged to experiment and re-create his world on his own terms and in his own way.

(4) The interpersonal contexts: here the child is made aware of affective states—his own and others.

In practice these are inter-dependent, but the emphasis and contents will vary from one group to another. I am suggesting that the critical orderings of a culture or sub-culture are made substantive, are made palpable through the form of its linguistic realizations of these four contexts—initially in the family. If these four contexts are realized through the predominant use of restricted speech variants pointing to particularistic, that is relatively context-tied, meanings, then I infer that the deep structure of the communication is controlled by a restricted code. [See for more detailed definition in the previous paper.] If these four contexts are realized predominantly through elaborated speech variants, which point towards relatively context independent, that is, universalistic, meanings, then I infer that the deep structure of the communication is controlled by an elaborated code. Because the code is restricted it does not mean that the users do not realize, at any time, elaborated speech variants, *only that such variants will be used infrequently in the process of the socialization of the child in his family.*

The concept code involves a distinction similar to the distinction which linguists make between surface and deep structure of the grammar. Thus sentences which look superficially different can be shown to be generated from the same rules. In the same way, although the linguistic choices involved in a summary will be markedly different from the linguistic choices involved in a self-conscious poem, which in turn will be markedly different from the linguistic choices involved in an analysis of physical or moral principles, or different again from the linguistic realization of forms of control, they may all, under certain conditions, point to the underlying regulation of restricted or elaborated codes.

Now because the sub-culture or culture through its forms of social integration generates a restricted code, it does not mean that the resultant speech and meaning system is linguistically or culturally deprived, that the children have nothing to offer the school, that their imaginings are not significant. Nor does it mean that we have to teach the children formal grammar. Nor does it mean that we have to interfere with their dialect. There is nothing, but nothing, in the dialect as such, which prevents a child from internalizing and learning to use universalistic meanings. But if the contexts of learning, the examples, the reading books, are not contexts which are triggers for the children's imaginings, are not triggers on the children's curiosity and explorations in his family and community, then the child is not at home in the educational world. If the teacher has to say continuously, 'Say it again darling, I didn't understand you', then in the end the child may say nothing. *If the culture of the teacher is to become part of the consciousness of the child, then the culture of the child must first be in the consciousness of the teacher.* This may mean that the teacher must be able to understand the child's dialect, rather than deliberately attempt to change it. Much of the contexts of our schools are unwittingly drawn from aspects of the symbolic world of the middle class, and so when the child steps into school he is stepping into a symbolic system which does not provide for him a linkage with his life outside.

It is an accepted educational principle that we should work with what the child can offer: why don't we practise it? The introduction of the child to the universalistic meanings of public forms of thought is not compensatory education—*it is education*. It is in itself not making children middle class. The implicit values underlying the form and contents of the educational environment might. We need to distinguish between the principles and operations, that is our task as teachers to transmit and develop in the children, *and* the contexts we create in order to do this. We should start knowing that the social experience the child already possesses is valid and significant, and that this social experience should be reflected back to him as being valid and significant. It can be reflected back to him only if it is a part of the texture of the learning experience we create. If we spent as much time thinking through the implications of this as we do thinking about the implications of the Piagetian developmental sequences, then possibly schools might become exciting and challenging environments for parents, children and teachers.

Over and beyond the issues raised so far stand much larger questions: the question of what counts as having knowledge, the question of what counts as a valid realization of that knowledge, the question of the organizational contexts we create for educational purposes. And for each of these questions we can add, 'in relation to what age?' I have deliberately avoided extending these questions to include 'in relation to what ability group?' because even if such a question at some point becomes relevant, the answer to it depends upon the answers to the earlier questions.

We need to examine the social assumptions underlying the organization, distribution and evaluation of knowledge, for it is not the case that there is one and only one answer to the above questions. The power relationships created outside the school penetrate the organization, distribution and evaluation of knowledge through the social context of their transmission. The definition of educability is itself at any one time an attenuated consequence of these power relationships. To ask these questions is not to eschew the past, is not to foreshorten one's perspective to the strictly contemporary; it is rather to invite us to consider R. Lynd's question: knowledge for what?

Finally, we do not know what a child is capable of, as we have as yet no theory which enables us to create sets of optimal learning environments, and even if such a theory existed it is most unlikely that resources would be made available to make it substantive on the scale required.

References

BERNSTEIN, B. (1962), 'Linguistic codes, hesitation phenomena and intelligence', *Language and Speech* 5, 31.
BERNSTEIN, B. (1965), 'A socio-linguistic approach to social learning', *Social Science Survey*, (ed.) Gould, J., Penguin.
BERNSTEIN, B. (1971), 'A socio-linguistic approach to socialization: with some reference to educability', *Directions in Sociolinguistics*, Gumperz, J. and Hymes, Dell (eds), New York: Holt, Reinhart & Winston. (In press.)
BERNSTEIN, B. and HENDERSON, D. (1969), 'Social class differences in the relevance of language to socialisation', *Sociology* 3, No. 1.

FANTINI, M. D. and WEINSTEIN, G. (1968), *The Disadvantaged: Challenge to Education*, Harper & Row.

HALLIDAY, M. A. K. (1969), 'Relevant models of language', *Educ. Rev.* 22, No. 1.

HAWKINS, P. R. (1969), 'Social class, the nominal group and reference', *Language and Speech* 12, No. 2.

Chapter 11   On the classification and framing of educational knowledge

Foreword

The reader may consider that this paper is out of place in a book concerned with language and socialization. I have included it for a number of reasons. It is an attempt to understand the inter-relationships between symbolic orders, form of social organization and the shaping of experience in terms of codes; here in terms of educational knowledge codes. It is concerned with the problems of change and, like the earlier work, draws on Durkheim explicitly and Marx and Mead implicitly. From another point of view, it considers different forms of the institutionalizing of elaborated codes and their consequences.

Introduction

How a society selects, classifies, distributes, transmits and evaluates the educational knowledge it considers to be public, reflects both the distribution of power and the principles of social control. From this point of view, differences within and change in the organization, transmission and evaluation of educational knowledge should be a major area of sociological interest (Bernstein, B., 1966, 1967; Davies, D. I., 1970a, 1970b; Musgrove, 1968; Hoyle, 1969; Young, M., 1970). Indeed, such a study is a part of the larger question of the structure and changes in the structure of cultural transmission. For various reasons, British sociologists have fought shy of this question. As a result, the sociology of education has been reduced to a series of input-output problems; the school has been transformed into a complex organization or people-processing institution; the study of socialization has been trivialized.

Educational knowledge is a major regulator of the structure of experience. From this point of view, one can ask 'How are forms of experience, identity and relation evoked, maintained and changed by the formal transmission of educational knowledge and sensitivities?'

Formal educational knowledge can be considered to be realized through three message systems: curriculum, pedagogy and evaluation. Curriculum defines what counts as valid knowledge, pedagogy defines what counts as a valid transmission of knowledge, and evaluation defines what counts as a valid realization of this knowledge on the part of the taught. The term 'educational knowledge code', which will be introduced later, refers to the underlying principles which shape curriculum, pedagogy and evaluation. It will be argued that the form this code takes depends upon social principles which regulate the classification and framing of knowledge made public in educational institutions. Both Durkheim and Marx have shown us that the structure of society's classifications and frames reveals both the distribution of power and the principles of social control. I hope to show, *theoretically*, that educational codes provide excellent opportunities for the study of classification and frames through which experience is given a distinctive form. The paper is organized as follows:

(1) I shall first distinguish between two types of curricula: collection and integrated.
(2) I shall build upon the basis of this distinction in order to establish a more general set of concepts: classification and frame.
(3) A typology of educational codes will then be derived.
(4) Sociological aspects of two very different educational codes will then be explored.
(5) This will lead on to a discussion of educational codes and problems of social control.
(6) Finally there will be a brief discussion of the reasons for a weakening of one code and a strengthening of the movement of the other.

Two types of curricula

Initially, I am going to talk about the curriculum in a very general way. In all educational institutions there is a formal punctuation of time into periods. These may vary from ten minutes to three hours or more. I am going to call each such formal period of time a 'unit'. I shall use the word 'content' to describe how the period of time is used. I shall define a curriculum initially in terms of the principle by which units of time and their contents are brought into a special relationship with each other. I now want to look more closely at the phrase 'special relationship'.

Firstly, we can examine relationships between contents in terms of the amount of time accorded to a given content. Immediately, we can see that more time is devoted to some contents rather than others. Secondly, some of the contents may, from the point of view of the pupils, be compulsory or optional. We can now take a very crude measure of the relative status of a content in terms of the number of units given over to it, and whether it is compulsory or optional. This raises immediately the question of the relative status of a given content and its significance in a given educational career.

We can, however, consider the relationship between contents from another, perhaps more important, perspective. We can ask about any given content whether the boundary between it and another content is clear cut or blurred. To what extent are the various contents well insulated from each other? If the various contents are well insulated from each other, I shall say that the contents stand in a *closed* relation to each other. If there is reduced insulation between contents, I shall say that the contents stand in an *open* relationship to each other. So far, then, I am suggesting that we can go into any educational institution and examine the organization of time in terms of the relative status of contents, and whether the contents stand in an open/closed relationship to each other. I am deliberately using this very abstract language in order to emphasize that there is nothing intrinsic to the relative status of various contents, there is nothing intrinsic to the relationships between contents. Irrespective of the question of the intrinsic logic of the various forms of public thought, the *forms* of their transmission, that is, their classification and framing, are social facts. There are a number of alternative means of access to the public forms of thought, and so to the various realities which they make possible. I am therefore emphasizing the social nature of the system of alternatives from which emerges a constellation called a curriculum. From this point of view, any curriculum entails a principle or principles whereby of all the possible contents of time, some contents are accorded differential status and enter into open or closed relation to each other.

I shall now distinguish between two broad types of curriculum. If contents stand in a closed relation to each other, that is, if the contents are clearly bounded and insulated from each other, I shall call such a curriculum a *collection* type. Here, the learner has to collect a group of favoured contents in order to satisfy some criteria of evaluation. There may of course be some underlying concept to a collection: the gentleman, the educated man, the skilled man, the non-vocational man.

Now I want to juxtapose against the collection type a curriculum where the various contents do not go their own separate ways, but where the contents stand in an open relation to each other. I shall call such a curriculum an integrated type. Now we can have various types of collection, and various degrees and types of integration.

Classification and frame

I shall now introduce the concepts, classification and frame, which will be used to analyse the underlying structure of the three message systems, curriculum, pedagogy and evaluation, which are realizations of the educational knowledge code. The basic idea is embodied in the principle used to distinguish the two types of curricula: collection and integrated. Strong insulation between contents pointed to a collection type, whereas reduced insulation pointed to an integrated type. The principle here is the strength of the *boundary* between contents. This notion of boundary strength underlies the concepts of classification and frame.

Classification, here, does not refer to *what* is classified, but to the *relationships* between contents. Classification refers to the nature of the differentiation between contents. Where classification is strong, contents are well insulated from each other by strong boundaries. Where classification is weak, there is reduced insulation between contents, for the boundaries between contents are weak or blurred. *Classification thus refers to the degree of boundary maintenance between contents.* Classification focuses our attention upon boundary strength as the critical distinguishing feature of the division of labour of educational knowledge. It gives us, as I hope to show, the basic structure of the message system, curriculum.

The concept 'frame' is used to determine the structure of the message system, pedagogy. Frame refers to the form of the *context* in which knowledge is transmitted and received. Frame refers to the specific pedagogical relationship of teacher and taught. In the same way as classification does not refer to contents, so frame does not refer to the contents of the pedagogy. Frame refers to the strength of the boundary between what may be transmitted and what may not be transmitted, in the pedagogical relationship. Where framing is strong, there is a sharp boundary, where framing is weak, a blurred boundary, between what may and may not be transmitted. Frame refers us to the range of options available to teacher and taught in the *control* of what is transmitted and received in the context of the pedagogical relationship. Strong framing entails reduced options; weak framing entails a range of options. *Thus frame refers to the degree of control teacher and pupil possess over the selection, organization, and pacing of the knowledge transmitted and received in the pedagogical relationship.*[1]

There is another aspect of the boundary relationship between what may be taught and what may not be taught and, consequently, another aspect to framing. We can consider the relationship between the non-school everyday knowledge of the teacher or taught, *and* the educational knowledge transmitted in the pedagogical relationship. We can raise the question of the strength of the boundary, the degree of insulation, between the everyday knowledge of teacher and taught and educational knowledge. Thus, we can consider variations in the strength of frames as these refer to the strength of the boundary between educational knowledge and everyday non-school knowledge of teacher and taught.

From the perspective of this analysis, the basic structure of the message system curriculum is given by variations in the strength of classification and the basic structure of the message system pedagogy is given by variations in the strength of frames. It will be shown later that the structure of the message system, evaluation, is a function of the strength of classification and frames. It is important to realize that the strength of classification and the strength of frames can vary independently of each other. For example, it is possible to have weak classification and exceptionally strong framing. Consider programmed learning. Here the boundary between educational contents may be blurred (weak classification) but there is little control by the pupil (except for pacing) over *what* is learned (strong framing). This example also shows that frames may be examined at a number of levels and the strength can vary as between the levels of selection, organization, and pacing of the knowledge transmitted in the pedagogical relationship.

I should also like to bring out (this will be developed more fully later in the analysis) the power component of this analysis and what can be called the 'identity' component. Where classification is strong, the boundaries between the different contents are sharply drawn. If this is the case then it presupposes strong boundary maintainers. Strong classification also creates a strong sense of membership in a particular class and so a specific identity. Strong frames reduce the power of the pupil over what, when and how he receives knowledge and increases the teacher's power in the pedagogical relationship. However, strong *classification* reduces the power of the *teacher* over what he transmits as he may not overstep the boundary between contents *and* strong classification reduces the power of the teacher *vis-à-vis* the boundary maintainers.

It is now possible to make explicit the concept of educational knowledge codes. The code is fully given *at the most general level* by the relationship between classification and frame.

A typology of educational knowledge codes

In the light of the conceptual framework we have developed, I shall use the distinction between collection and integrated curricula in order to realize a typology of types and sub-types of educational codes. The *formal* basis of the typology is the strength of classification and frames. However, the sub-types will be distinguished, initially, in terms of substantive differences.

Any organization of educational knowledge which involves strong classification gives rise to what is here called a collection code. Any organization of educational knowledge which involves a marked attempt to reduce the strength of classification is here called an integrated code. Collection codes may give rise to a series of sub-types, each varying in the relative strength of their classification and frames. Integrated codes can also vary in terms of the strength of frames, as these refer to the *teacher/pupil/student* control over the knowledge that is transmitted.

Figure 1 sets out general features of the typology.

Collection codes

The first major distinction *within* collection codes is between specialized and non-specialized types. The extent of specialization can be measured in terms of the number of closed contents publicly examined at the end of the secondary educational stage. Thus in England, *although there is no formal limit*, the student usually sits for three 'A' level subjects, compared with the much greater range of subjects which make up the Abitur in Germany, the Baccalauréat in France, or the Studente Exam in Sweden.

Within the English specialized type, we can distinguish two varieties: a pure and an impure variety. The pure variety exists where 'A' level subjects are drawn from a common universe of knowledge, e.g. chemistry, physics, mathematics. The impure variety exists where 'A' level subjects are drawn from different universes of knowledge, e.g. religion, physics, economics. The latter combination, although formally possible, very rarely substantively exists, for pupils are not encouraged to offer—neither does timetabling usually permit—such a combination. It is a matter of interest that until very recently the pure variety at the university level received the higher status of an honours degree, whereas the impure variety tended to lead to the lower status of the general degree.[2] One can detect the beginnings of a shift in England from the pure to the impure variety, which appears to be trying to work towards the non-specialized type of collection.

Within the non-specialized collection code, we can distinguish two varieties, according to whether a subject or course is the basic knowledge unit. Thus the standard European form of the collection code is non-specialized, *subject*-based. The USA form of the collection code is non-specialized, course-based.

I have so far described sub-types and varieties of the collection code in simple descriptive terms; as a consequence it is not easy to see how their distinctive features can be translated into sociological concepts in order to realize a specific sociological problem. Clearly, the conceptual language here developed has built into it a specific perspective; that of power and social control. In the process of translating the descriptive features into the language of classification and frames, the question must arise as to whether the hypotheses about their relative strength fits a particular case.

Here are the hypotheses, given for purposes of illustration:

(1) I suggest that the European, non-specialized, subject-based form of collection involves strong classification but *exceptionally* strong framing; that is, at levels *below* higher education, there are relatively few options available to teacher, and especially taught, over the transmission of knowledge. Curricula and syllabus are very explicit.

(2) The English version, I suggest, involves *exceptionally* strong classification, but relatively weaker framing than the European type. The fact that it is specialized determines what contents (subjects) may be put together. There is very strong insulation between the 'pure' and the 'applied' knowledge. Curricula are graded for particular ability groups. There can be high insulation between a subject and a class of pupils. 'D' stream secondary pupils will not have access to certain subjects, and 'A' stream students will also not have access to certain subjects. However, I suggest that framing, relative to Europe, is weaker. This can be seen particularly at the primary level. There is also, *relative* to Europe, less *central* control over what is transmitted, although, clearly, the various requirements of the university level exert a strong control over the secondary level.[3] I suggest that, although again this is *relative*, there is a weaker frame in England between educational knowledge and the everyday community knowledge for certain classes of students: the so-called 'less able'. Finally, relative to Europe, I suggest that there are more options available to the pupil within the pedagogical relationships. The frame as it refers to pupils is weaker. Thus I suggest that framing

as it relates to teachers and pupils is relatively weaker, but that classification is relatively much stronger in the English than the European system. Scotland is nearer to the European version of the collection.

(3) The course-based, non-specialized USA form of the collection, I suggest, has the weakest classification *and* framing of the collection code, especially at the secondary and university level. A far greater range of subjects can be taken at the secondary and university level, and these are capable of combination; this indicates weak classification. The insulation between educational knowledge and everyday community knowledge is weaker, as can be evidenced by community control over school; this indicates weak frames. The range of options available to pupils within the pedagogical relationship is, I suggest, greater. I would guess, then, that classification and framing in the USA is the weakest of the collection codes.

Integrated codes

It is important to be clear about the term 'integrated'. Because one subject uses the theories of another subject, this type of intellectual inter-relationship does not constitute integration. Such intellectual inter-relation may well be part of a collection code at some point in the history of the development of knowledge. Integration, as it is used here, refers minimally to the *subordination* of previously insulated subjects *or* courses to some *relational* idea, which blurs the boundaries between the subjects. We can distinguish two types. The first type is *teacher* based. Here the teacher, as in the infant school, has an extended block of time with often the same group of children. The teacher may operate with a collection code and keep the various subjects distinct and insulated, or he can blur the boundaries between the different subjects. This type of integrated code is easier to introduce than the second type, which is *teachers*-based. Here, integration involves relationships with other teachers. In this way, we can have degrees of integration in terms of the number of teachers involved.

We can further distinguish two varieties according to whether the integration refers to a group of teachers *within* a common subject, or the *extent* to which integration involves teachers of different subjects. Whilst integrated codes, by definition, have the weakest classification, they may vary as to framing. During the initiating period, the frames the teachers enter will be weak, but other factors will affect the final frame strength. It is also possible that the frames the *pupils* enter can vary in strength.

Thus integrated codes may be confined to one subject or they can cross subjects. We can talk of code strength in terms of the range of different subjects co-ordinated by the code, or if this criterion cannot be applied, it can be measured in terms of the *number* of teachers co-ordinated through the code. Integrated codes can also vary as to frame strength as this applies to teachers or pupils, or both.

Differences within, and between, educational knowledge codes from the perspective developed here lie in variations in the strength and nature of the boundary maintaining procedures, as these are given by the classification and framing of the knowledge. It can be seen that the nature of classification and framing affects the authority/ power structure which controls the dissemination of educational knowledge, and the *form* of the knowledge transmitted. In this way, principles of power and social control are realized through educational knowledge codes and through the codes enter into, and shape, consciousness. Thus variations within and change of knowledge codes should be of critical concern to sociologists. The following problems arise out of this analysis:

(1)   What are the antecedents of variations in the strength of classification and frames?*

(2)   How does a given classification and framing structure perpetuate itself? What are the conditions of, and resistance to, change?

(3)   What are the different socializing experiences realized through variations in the strength of classifications and frames?

I shall limit the application of this analysis to the consideration of aspects of the last two questions. I feel I ought to apologize to the reader for this rather long and perhaps tedious conceptual journey, before he has been given any notion of the view to which it leads.

Application

I shall examine the patterns of social relationship and their socializing consequences which are realized through the European, particularly English, version of the collection code and those which are *expected* to arise out of integrated codes, *particularly those which develop weak framing*. I shall suggest that there is some movement towards forms of the integrated code, examine the nature of the resistance towards such a change and suggest some reasons for this movement.

* Such variations may well be linked to variations in the development of class structures. *See* 'Class and pedagogies: visible and invisible', Basil Bernstein (1973), available from O.E.C.D. (C.E.R.I.) Paris, or Sociological Research Unit, Department of the Sociology of Education, University of London Institute of Education.

Classification and framing of the European form of the collection code

There will be some difficulty in this analysis, as I shall at times switch from secondary to university level. Although the English system has the distinguishing feature of specialization, it does share certain features of the European system. This may lead to some blurring in the analysis. As this is the beginnings of a limited sociological theory which explores the social organization and structuring of educational knowledge, it follows that all statements, including those which have the character of descriptive statements, are hypothetical. The descriptive statements have been selectively patterned according to their significance for the theory.

One of the major differences between the European and English versions of the collection code is that, with the specialized English type, a membership category is established early in an educational career, in terms of an early choice between the pure and the applied, between the sciences and the arts, between having and not having a specific educational identity. A particular status in a given collection is made clear by streaming and/or a delicate system of grading. One nearly always knows the social significance of where one is, and, in particular, *who* one is, with each advance in the educational career. (Initially, I am doing science, or arts, pure or applied; or I am not doing anything; later I am becoming a physicist, economist, chemist, etc.) *Subject loyalty* is then systematically developed in

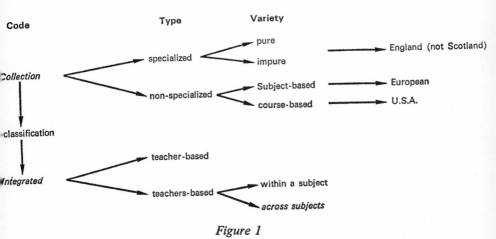

Figure 1

pupils and finally students, with each increase in the educational life and then transmitted by them as teachers and lecturers. The system is self-perpetuating through this form of socialization. With the specialized form of the collection it is banal to say as you get older you learn more and more about less and less. Another, more socio-logical, way of putting this is to say as you get older, you become increasingly *different* from others. Clearly, this will happen at some point in any educational career, but with specialization this happens much earlier. Therefore, specialization very soon reveals *difference from* rather than communality with. It creates relatively quickly an educational identity which is clear-cut and bounded. The educational category or identity is *pure*. Specialized versions of the collection code tend to abhor mixed categories and blurred identities, for they represent a potential openness, an ambiguity, which makes the con-sequences of previous socialization problematic. Mixed categories such as bio-physicist, psycho-linguist, are permitted to develop only after long socialization into a subject loyalty. Indeed, in order to change an identity, a previous one has to be weakened and a new one created. For example in England, if a student has a first degree in psychology and he wishes to read for a higher degree in sociology, either he is not permitted to make the switch or he is expected to take a number of papers at first degree level in sociology. In the process of taking the papers, he usually enters into social relation-ships with accredited sociologists and students through whom he acquires the cognitive and social style particular to the sociological identity. Change of an educational identity is accomplished through a process of resocialization into a *new* subject loyalty. A sense of the sacred, the 'otherness' of educational knowledge, I submit does not arise so much out of an ethic of knowledge for its own sake, but is more a function of socialization into subject loyalty: for it is the subject which becomes the lynch pin of the identity. Any attempt to weaken or *change* classification strength (or even frame strength) may be felt as a threat to one's identity and may be experienced as a pollution endangering the sacred. Here we have one source of the resistance to change of educational code.

The specialized version of the collection code will develop care-ful screening procedures to see who belongs and who does not be-long, and once such screening has taken place, it is very difficult to change an educational identity. The various classes of knowledge are well insulated from each other. Selection and differentiation are early features of this particular code. Thus, the deep structure of the specialized type of collection code is *strong boundary maintenance creating control from within through the formation of specific iden-tities;* an interesting aspect of the protestant spirit.

Strong boundary maintenance can be illustrated with reference to attempts to institutionalize new forms, or attempts to change the strength, of classification, within either the European or English type of collection. Because of the exceptional strength of classification in England, such difficulties may be greater here. Changes in classification strength and the institutionalizing of new forms of knowledge may become a matter of importance when there are changes in the structure of knowledge at the higher levels and/or changes in the economy. Critical problems arise with the question of new forms, as to their legitimacy, at what point they belong, when, where and by whom the form should be taught. I have referred to the 'sacred' in terms of an educational identity, but clearly there is the 'profane' aspect to knowledge. We can consider as the 'profane' the property aspect of knowledge. Any new form or weakening of classification clearly derives from past classifications. Such new forms or weakened classifications can be regarded as attempts to break or weaken existing monopolies. Knowledge under collection is private property with its own power structure and market situation. This affects the whole ambience surrounding the development and marketing of new knowledge. Children and pupils are early socialized into this concept of knowledge as *private* property. They are encouraged to work as isolated individuals with their arms around their work. This phenomenon, until recently, could be observed in any grammar school. It can be most clearly observed in examination halls. Pupils and students, particularly in the arts, appear, from this point of view, to be a type of entrepreneur.

There are, then, strong inbuilt controls on the institutionalizing of new knowledge forms, on the changing of strength of classification, on the production of new knowledge which derive from both 'sacred' and 'profane' sources.

So far, I have been considering the relationship between strong classification of knowledge, the concept of property and the creation of specific identities with particular reference to the specialized form of the collection code. I shall now move away from the classification of knowledge to its *framing* in the process of transmission.

Any collection code involves a hierarchical organization of knowledge, such that the ultimate mystery of the subject is revealed very late in the educational life. By the ultimate mystery of the subject I mean its potential for creating new realities. It is also the case, and this is important, that the ultimate mystery of the subject is not coherence, but incoherence: not order, but disorder, not the known but the unknown. As this mystery, under collection codes, is revealed very late in the educational life—and then only to a select few who have shown the signs of successful socialization—then only the few *experience* in their bones the notion that knowledge is permeable, that its orderings are provisional, that the dialectic of knowledge is closure and openness. For the many, socialization into knowledge is socialization into order, the existing order, into the experience that the world's educational knowledge is impermeable. Do we have here another version of alienation?

Now clearly any history of any form of educational knowledge shows precisely the power of such knowledge to create endlessly new realities. However, socialization into the specific framing of knowledge in its transmission may make such a history experientially meaningless. The key concept of the European collection code is discipline. This means learning to work *within* a received frame. It means, in particular, *learning* what questions can be put at any particular time. Because of the hierarchical ordering of the knowledge in *time,* certain questions raised may not enter into a particular frame.

This is soon learned by both teachers and pupils. Discipline then means accepting a given selection, organization, pacing and timing of knowledge realized in the pedagogical frame. With increases in the educational life, there is a progressive weakening of the frame for both teacher and taught. Only the few who have shown the signs of successful socialization have access to these relaxed frames. For the mass of the population the framing is tight. In a sense, the European form of the collection code makes knowledge safe through the process of socialization into its frames. There is a tendency, which varies with the strength of specific frames, for the young to be socialized into assigned principles and routine operations and derivations. The evaluative system places an emphasis upon attaining *states* of knowledge rather than *ways* of knowing. A study of the examination questions and format, the symbolic structure of assessment, would be, from this point of view, a rewarding empirical study. Knowledge thus tends to be transmitted, particularly to elite pupils at the secondary level, through strong frames which control the selection organization and pacing[4] of the knowledge. The receipt of the knowledge is not so much a right as something to be won or earned. The stronger the classification and the framing, the more the educational relationship tends to be hierarchical and ritualized, the educand seen as ignorant, with little status and few rights. These are things which one earns, rather like spurs, and are used for the purpose of encouraging and sustaining the motivation of pupils. Depending upon the strength of frames, knowledge is transmitted in a context where the teacher has maximal control or surveillance, as in hierarchical secondary school relationships.

We can look at the question of the framing of knowledge in the pedagogical relationship from another point of view. In a sense, educational knowledge is uncommonsense knowledge. It is knowledge freed from the particular, the local, through the various explicit languages of the sciences or implicit languages of the arts which make possible either the creation or the discovery of new realities. Now this immediately raises the question of the relationship between the uncommonsense knowledge of the school and the *commonsense* knowledge, everyday community knowledge, of the pupil, his family and his peer group. This formulation invites us to ask how strong are the frames of educational knowledge in relation to experiential, community-based non-school knowledge? I suggest that the frames of the collection code, very early in the child's life, socialize him into knowledge frames which discourage connections with everyday realities, or that there is a highly selective screening of the connection. Through such socialization, the pupil soon learns what of the outside may be brought into the pedagogical frame. Such framing also makes of educational knowledge something not ordinary or mundane, but something esoteric, which gives a special significance to those who possess it. I suggest that when this frame is relaxed to include everyday realities, it is often and sometimes validly done, not simply for the transmission of educational knowledge, but for purposes of social control of forms of deviancy. The weakening of this frame occurs usually with the less 'able' children whom we have given up educating.

In general then, and depending upon the specific strength of classification and frames, the European form of the collection code is rigid, differentiating and hierarchical in character; highly resistant to change particularly at the secondary level. With the English version, this resistance to change is assisted by the discretion which is available to headmasters and principals. In England, within the constraints of the public examination system, the heads of schools and colleges have a relatively wide range of discretion over the organization and transmission of knowledge. Central control over the educational code is relatively weak in England, although clearly the schools are subject to inspection from both central and local government levels. However, the relationship between the inspectorate and the schools in England is very ambiguous. To produce widespread change in England would require the co-operation of hundreds of individual schools. Thus, rigidity in educational knowledge codes may arise out of highly centralized *or* weak central control over the knowledge codes. Weak central control does permit a series of changes which have, initially, limited consequences for the system as a whole. On the other hand, there is much stronger central control over the organizational style of the school. This can lead to a situation where there can be a change in the organizational style *without* there being *any* marked change in the educational knowledge code, particularly where the educational code, itself, creates specific identities. This raises the question, which cannot be developed here, of the relationships between organizational change and change of educational knowledge code, i.e. change in the strength of classification and framing.

In general, then, the European and English form of the collection code may provide for those who go beyond the novitiate stage, order, identity and commitment. For those who do not pass beyond this stage, it can sometimes be wounding and seen as meaningless, what Bourdieu calls 'la violence symbolique'.

Integrated and collection codes

I shall now examine a form of the integrated code which is realized through very weak classification and frames. I shall, during this analysis, bring out further aspects of collection codes.

There are a number of attempts to institutionalize forms of the integrated code at different strengths above the level of the infant school child. Nuffield science is an attempt to do this with the physical sciences, and the Chelsea Centre for Science Education, Chelsea College of Technology University of London, is concerned almost wholly in training students in this approach. Mrs Charity James, at Goldsmiths College, University of London, is also producing training courses for forms of the integrated code. A number of comprehensive schools are experimenting with this approach at the middle school level. The SDS in Germany, and various radical student groups, are exploring this type of code in order to use the means of the university against the meaning. However, it is probably true to say that the code at the moment exists at the level of ideology and theory, with only a relatively small number of schools and educational agencies attempting to institutionalize it with any seriousness.

Now, as we said in the beginning of the paper, with the integrated code we have a shift from content closure to content openness, from strong to markedly reduced classification. Immediately, we can see that this disturbance in classification of knowledge will lead to a disturbance of existing authority structures, existing specific educational identities and concepts of property.

Where we have integration, the various contents are subordinate to some idea which reduces their isolation from each other. Thus integration reduces the authority of the separate contents, and this has implications for existing authority structures. Where we have collection, it does permit in principle considerable differences in pedagogy and evaluation because of the high insulation between the different contents. However, the autonomy of the content is the other side of an authority structure which exerts jealous and zealous supervision. I suggest that the integrated code will not permit the variations in pedagogy and evaluation which are possible within collection codes. On the contrary, I suggest there will be a pronounced movement towards a common pedagogy and tendency towards a common system of evaluation. In other words, integrated codes will, at the level of the teachers, probably create homogeneity in teaching practice. Thus, collection codes increase the discretion of teachers (within, always, the limits of the existing classification and frames) whilst integrated codes will reduce the discretion of the teacher in direct relation to the strength of the integrated code (number of teachers co-ordinated by the code). On the other hand, it is argued that the increased discretion of the teachers within collection codes is paralleled by *reduced* discretion of the pupils and that the reduced discretion of the teachers within integrated codes is paralleled by *increased* discretion of the pupils. In other words, there is a shift in the balance of power, in the pedagogical relationship between teacher and taught.

These points will now be developed. In order to accomplish any form of integration (as distinct from different subjects focusing upon a common problem, which gives rise to what could be called a *focused* curriculum) there must be some relational idea, a supracontent concept, which focuses upon general principles at a high level of abstraction. For example, if the relationships between sociology and biology are to be opened, then the relational idea (amongst many) might be the issue of problems of order and change examined through the concepts of genetic and cultural codes. Whatever the relational concepts are, they will act selectively upon the knowledge within each subject which is to be transmitted. The particulars of each subject are likely to have reduced significance. This will focus attention upon the *deep* structure of each subject, rather than upon its surface structure. I suggest this will lead to an emphasis upon, and the exploration of, *general* principles and the concepts through which these principles are obtained. In turn, this is likely to affect the orientation of the pedagogy, which will be less concerned to emphasize the need to acquire *states* of knowledge, but will be more concerned to emphasize *how* knowledge is created. In other words, the pedagogy of integrated codes is likely to emphasize various *ways* of knowing in the pedagogical relationships. With the collection code, the pedagogy tends to proceed from the surface structure of the knowledge to the deep structure; as we have seen, only the elite have access to the deep structure and therefore access to the realizing of new realities or access to the experiential knowledge that new realities are possible. *With integrated codes, the pedagogy is likely to proceed from the deep structure to the surface structure.* We can see this already at work in the new primary school mathematics. Thus, I suggest that integrated codes will make available from the beginning of the pupils educational career, clearly in a way appropriate to a given age level, the deep structure of the knowledge, i.e. the principles for the generating of new knowledge. Such emphasis upon various *ways* of knowing, rather than upon the attaining of *states* of knowledge, is likely to affect not only the emphasis of the pedagogy, but its underlying theory of learning. The underlying theory of learning of collection is likely to be didactic whilst the underlying theory of learning of integrated codes may well be more group- or self-regulated. This arises out of a different concept of what counts as having knowledge, which in turn leads to a different concept of how the knowledge, is to be acquired. These changes in emphasis and orientation of the pedagogy are initially responsible for the relaxed frames, which teacher and taught enter. Relaxed frames not only change the nature of the authority relationships by increasing the rights of the taught, they can also weaken or blur the boundary between what may or may not be taught, and so *more* of the private experience of teacher and taught is likely to enter this pedagogical frame. The inherent logic of the integrated code is likely to create a change in the structure of teaching groups which are likely to exhibit considerable flexibility. The concept of *relatively weak boundary maintenance* which is the core principle of integrated codes is realized both in the structuring of educational knowledge *and* in the organization of the social relationships.

I shall now introduce some organizational consequences of collection and integrated codes which will make explicit the difference in the distribution of power and the principles of control which inhere in these educational codes.

Where knowledge is regulated through a collection code, the knowledge is organized and distributed through a series of well insulated subject hierarchies. Such a structure points to oligarchic control of the institution, through formal and informal meetings of heads of departments with the head or principal of the institution. Thus, senior staff will have strong horizontal work relationships (that is, with their peers in other subject hierarchies) and strong vertical work relationships within their own department. However, junior staff are likely to have only vertical (within the subject hierarchy) allegiances and work relationships.

The allegiancies of junior staff are vertical rather than horizontal for the following reasons. Firstly, staff have been socialized into strong subject loyalty and through this into specific identities. These specific identities are continuously strengthened through social interactions *within* the department *and* through the insulation between departments. Secondly, the departments are often in a competitive relationship for strategic teaching resources. Thirdly, preferment within the subject hierarchy often rests with its expansion. Horizontal relationships of junior staff (particularly where there is no *effective* participatory administrative structure) are likely to be limited to *non-task-based* contacts. There may well be discussion of control problems ('X of 3b is a —— how do you deal with him?' or 'I can't get X to write a paper'). Thus the collection code within the framework of oligarchic control creates for *senior* staff strong horizontal- and vertical-based relationships, whereas the work relationships of junior staff are likely to be vertical and the horizontal relationships limited to non-task-based contacts. This is a type of organizational system which encourages gossip, intrigue and a conspiracy theory of the workings of the organization, for *both* the *administration* and the *acts of teaching* are *invisible* to the majority of staff. (See Figure 2.)

Now the integrated code will require teachers of different subjects to enter into social relationships with each other which will arise not simply out of non-task areas, but out of a shared, co-operative educational task. The centre of gravity of the relationships between teachers will undergo a radical shift. Thus, instead of teachers and lecturers being divided and insulated by allegiancies to subject hierarchies, the conditions for their unification exists through a common work situation. I suggest that this changed basis of the relationships, between teachers or between lecturers, may tend to weaken the separate hierarchies of collection. These new work-based horizontal relationships between teachers and between lecturers may alter both the structure and distribution of power regulated by the collection code. Further, the administration and specific acts of teaching are likely to shift from relative invisibility to *visibility*.

We might expect similar developments at the level of students and even senior pupils, for pupils and students with each increase in their educational life are equally sub-divided and educationally insulated from each other. They are equally bound to subject hierarchies and for similar reasons to staff; their identities and their future are shaped by the department. Their vertical allegiances and work-based relationships are strong, whilst their horizontal relationships will tend to be limited to non-task areas (student/pupil societies and sport) or peripheral non-task-based administration. Here again,

Ideal typical organizational structures

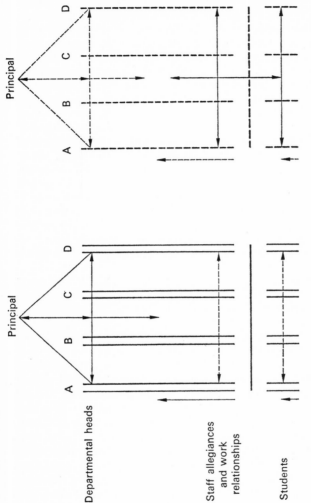

Key: Continuous lines represent strong boundaries, continuous arrows represent direction of strong relationships. Dotted lines represent weak boundaries Dotted line arrows represent direction of weak relationships

Collection code type = Strong classification: strong frames

Integrated code type = Weak classification: weak frames

Figure 2

we can see another example of the strength of boundary maintenance of collection codes; this time between task and non-task areas. Integrated codes may well provide the conditions for strong horizontal relationships and allegiancies in students and pupils, based upon a common work task (the receiving and offering of knowledge).[5] In this situation, we might expect a weakening of the boundary between staff, especially junior staff, and students/pupils.

Thus, a move from collection to integrated codes may well bring about a disturbance in the structure and distribution of power, in property relationships and in existing educational identities. This change of educational code involves a fundamental change in the nature and strength of boundaries. It involves a change in what counts as having knowledge, in what counts as a valid transmission of knowledge, in what counts as a valid realization of knowledge, *and* a change in the organizational context. At the cultural level, it involves a shift from the keeping of categories pure to the mixing of categories; whilst at the level of socialization the outcomes of integrated codes *could* be less predictable than the outcomes of collection codes. This change of code involves fundamental changes in the classification and framing of knowledge and so changes in the structure and distribution of power and in principles of control. It is no wonder that deep-felt resistances are called out by the issue of change in educational codes.

Collection, integrated codes and problems of order

I shall now turn to aspects of the problem of order. Where knowledge is regulated by collection codes, social order arises out of the hierarchical nature of the authority relationships, out of the systematic ordering of the differentiated knowledge in time and space, out of an explicit, usually predictable, examining procedure. Order internal to the individual is created through the formation of specific identities. The institutional expression of strong classification and framing creates predictability in time and space. Because of strong classification, collection does allow a range of variations between subjects in the organization, transmission and evaluation of knowledge. Because of strong classification, this code does permit *in principle* staff to hold (within limits) a range of ideologies because conflicts can be contained *within* its various insulated hierarchies. At levels below that of the university, the strong frames between educational knowledge and non-educationally relevant knowledge, *in* principle may facilitate diversity in ideology held by staff because it cannot be offered. At the same time, strong framing makes such intrusion highly visible. The range of personal freedoms at the *university* level is symbolized in the ethical system of some collection codes and so forms the basis for the cohesion of the differentiated whole.

Whilst it is usually the case that collection codes, relative to integrated codes, create strong frames between the uncommonsense knowledge of the school and the everyday community-based knowledge of teacher and taught, it is also the case that such insulation creates areas of privacy. For, inasmuch as community-based experience is irrelevant to the pedagogical frame, these aspects of the self informed by such experiences are also irrelevant. These areas of privacy reduce the penetration of the socializing process, for it is possible to distance oneself from it. This still means, however, that the socialization can be deeply wounding, either for those who wish for, but do not achieve, an identity, or for the majority for whom the pursuit of an identity is early made irrelevant.

Order created by integrated codes may well be problematic. I suggest that if four conditions are not satisfied, then the openness of learning under integration may produce a culture in which neither staff nor pupils have a sense of time, place or purpose. I shall comment briefly on these four conditions as I give them.

(1)   There must be consensus about the integrating idea and it must be very explicit. (It is ironic that the movement towards integration is going on in those countries where there is a low level of moral consensus.) It may be that integrated codes will work only[6] when there is a *high* level of ideological consensus among the staff. We have already seen that, in comparison with collection, integrated codes call for greater homogeneity in pedagogy and evaluation, and therefore reduce differences between teachers in the form of the transmission and assessment of knowledge. Whereas the teaching process under collection is likely to be *invisible* to other teachers, unless special conditions prevail, it is likely that the teaching process regulated through integrated codes may well become *visible* as a result of developments in the pedagogy in the direction of flexibility in the structure of teaching groups. It is also the case that the weak classification and relaxed frames of integrated codes permit greater expressions of differences between teachers, and possibly between pupils, in the selection of what is taught. The moral basis of educational choices is then likely to be explicit at the initial planning stage. Integrated codes also weaken specific identities. For the above reasons, integrated codes may require a high level of ideological consensus and this may affect the recruitment of staff. Integrated codes at the surface level create weak or blurred boundaries, but at bottom they may rest upon *closed, explicit ideologies*. Where such

ideologies are not shared, the consequences will become visible and threaten the whole at every point.

(2) The nature of the linkage between the integrating idea and the knowledge to be co-ordinated must also be coherently spelled out. It is this linkage which will be the basic element in bringing teachers *and* pupils into their working relationship. *The development of such a co-ordinating framework will be the process of socialization of teachers into the code. During this process, the teachers will internalize, as in all processes of socialization, the interpretative procedures of the code so that these become implicit guides which regulate and co-ordinate the behaviour of the individual teachers in the relaxed frames and weakened classification.* This brings us to a major distinction between collection and integrated codes. With a collection code, the period of socialization is facilitated by strong boundary maintenance both at the level of *role* and at the level of knowledge. Such socialization is likely to be continuous with the teacher's own educational socialization. With integrated codes both the role and the form of the knowledge have to be *achieved* in relation to a range of different others, and this may involve resocialization if the teacher's previous educational experience has been formed by the collection code. The collection code is capable of working when staffed by mediocre teachers, whereas integrated codes call for much greater powers of synthesis and analogy and for more ability to both tolerate and enjoy ambiguity at the level of knowledge *and* social relationships.

(3) A committee system of staff may have to be set up to create a sensitive feed-back system and which will also provide a further agency of socialization into the code. It is likely that evaluative criteria are likely to be relatively weak, in the sense that the criteria are less likely to be as explicit and measurable as in the case of collection. As a result, it may be necessary to develop committees for both teachers, students, and, where appropriate, pupils, which will perform monitoring functions.

(4) One of the major difficulties which inhere in integrated codes arises over what is to be assessed and the form of assessment; also the place of specific competencies in such assessment. It is likely that integrated codes will give rise to multiple criteria of assessment compared with collection codes. In the case of collection codes, because the knowledge moves from the surface to the deep structure, then this progression creates ordered principles of evaluation in time. The form of temporal cohesion of the knowledge regulated through the integrated code has yet to be determined and made explicit. Without clear criteria of evaluation, neither teacher nor taught have any means to consider the significance of what is

learned, nor any means to judge the pedagogy. In the case of collection codes, evaluation at the secondary level often consists of the fit between a narrow range of specific competeneies and states of knowledge, and previously established criteria (varying in explicitness) of what constitutes a right or appropriate or convincing answer. The previously established criteria together with the specific social context of assessment create a relatively objective procedure. I do not want to suggest that this necessarily gives rise to a form of assessment which entirely disregards distinctive and original features of the pupil's performance. In the case of the integrated code under discussion (weak frames for teacher and taught) then this form of assessment may well be inappropriate. The weak frames enable a greater range of the student's behaviour to be made public and they make possible considerable diversity (at least in principle) between students. It is possible that this might lead to a situation where assessment takes 'inner' attributes of the student more into account. Thus, if he has the 'right' attitudes, this will result later in the attainment of various specific competencies. The 'right' attitude may be assessed in terms of the fit between the pupil's attitudes and the current ideology. It is possible, then, that the evaluative criteria of integrated codes with weak frames may be weak, as these refer to specific cognitive attributes, but strong, as these refer to dispositional attributes. If this is so then a new range of pupil attributes become candidates for labels. It is also likely that the weakened classification and framing will encourage more of the pupil/student to be made public; more of his thoughts, feelings and values. In this way more of the pupil is available for control. As a result the socialization could be more intensive and perhaps more penetrating. In the same way as pupils/students defend themselves against the wounds of collection or distance themselves from its overt code, so they may produce new defences against the potential intrusiveness of the integrated code and its open learning contexts.

We can summarize this question of the problem of order as follows. Collection codes have explicit and strong boundary maintaining features and they rest upon a tacit ideological basis. Integrated codes have implicit and weak boundary maintaining features and they rest upon an explicit and closed ideological basis. The ideological basis of the collection code is a condensed symbolic system communicated through its explicit boundary maintaining features. Its covert structure is that of mechanical solidarity. The ideological basis of integrated codes is *not* a condensed symbolic system; it is verbally elaborated and explicit. It is an *overt* realization of organic solidarity made substantive through weak forms of boundary maintenance (low insulations). Yet the covert structure of mechanical solidarity of collection codes creates through its specialized outputs *organic* solidarity. On the other hand the overt structure of organic solidarity of integrated codes creates through its *less* specialized outputs *mechanical* solidarity. And it will do this to the extent to which its ideology is explicit, elaborated and closed *and* effectively and *implicitly* transmitted through its low insulations. Inasmuch as integrated codes do not accomplish this, then order is highly problematic at the level of social organization and at the level of the person. Inasmuch as integrated codes do accomplish such socialization, then we have the covert deep closure of mechanical solidarity. This is the fundamental paradox which has to be faced and explored.[7]

Change of educational code

I have tried to make explicit the relationships between educational codes and the structure of power and principles of social control. Attempts to change or modify educational codes will meet with resistance at a number of different levels irrespective of the intrinsic educational merit of a particular code. I shall now briefly discuss some reasons for a movement towards the institutionalizing of integrated codes *of the weak classification and weak framing (teacher and taught) type*[8] above the level of the primary school.[9]

(1) The growing differentiation of knowledge at the higher levels of thought, together with the integration of previously discrete areas, may set up requirements for a form of socialization appropriate to these changes in the structure of knowledge.

(2) Changes in the division of labour are creating a different concept of skill. The in-built obsolescence of whole varieties of skills reduces the significance of context-tied operations and increases the significance of general principles from which a range of diverse operations may be derived. In crude terms, it could be said that the nineteenth century required submissive and inflexible man, whereas the late twentieth century requires conforming but flexible man.

(3) The less rigid social structure of the integrated code makes it a potential code for egalitarian education.

(4) In advanced industrial societies which permit, within limits, a range of legitimizing beliefs and ideologies, there is a major problem of control. There is the problem of making sense of the differentiated, weakly co-ordinated and changing symbolic systems and the problem of inner regulation of the person. Integrated codes, with their stress on the underlying

unity of knowledge, through their emphasis upon analogy and synthesis, could be seen as a response to the first problem of 'making sense'. The *interpersonal* rather than *interpositional* control of the integrated code may set up a penetrating, intrusive form of socialization under conditions of ambiguity in the system of beliefs and the moral order.

If these reasons operate, we could consider the movement towards integrated codes as stemming from a technological source. However, it is possible that there is another and deeper source of the movement away from collection. I suggest that the movement away from collection to integrated codes symbolizes that there is a crisis in society's basic classifications and frames, and therefore a crisis in its structures of power and principles of control. The movement from this point of view represents an attempt to declassify and so alter power structures and principles of control; in so doing to unfreeze the structuring of knowledge and to change the boundaries of consciousness. From this point of view integrated codes are symptoms of a moral crisis rather than the terminal state of an educational system.

Conclusion

In this paper, I have tried to explore the concept of boundary in such a way that it is possible to see *both* the power and control components. The analysis focuses directly upon the structuring of transmitted educational knowledge.

Although the concept 'classification' appears to operate on a single dimension, i.e. differences in degrees of insulation between content (subjects/courses etc.) it explicitly points to power and control components. In the same way, the concept 'frame' appears to operate in a single dimension; what may or may not be taught in the pedagogical relationship. Yet the exploration of the concept again points to power and control components. Through defining educational codes in terms of the relationship between classification and framing, these two components are built into the analysis at all levels. It then becomes possible in one framework to derive a typology of educational codes, to show the inter-relationships between organizational and knowledge properties, to move from macro- to micro-levels of analysis, to relate the patterns internal to educational institutions to the external social antecedents of such patterns, and to consider questions of maintenance and change. At the same time, it is hoped that the analysis makes explicit tacit assumptions underlying various educational codes. It attempts to show, at a *theoretical* level, the relationships between a particular symbolic order and the structuring of experience. I believe that it offers an approach which is well capable of exploration by diverse methods at the empirical level.

It should be made quite clear that the application of the concepts requires at every point empirical evidence. I have not attempted to bolster the argument with references, because in many cases the evidence which is required does not exist in a *form* which bears directly upon the chain of inferences and therefore would offer perhaps spurious support. We have, for example, little *first*-hand knowledge which bears upon aspects of framing as this concept is used in the paper. We also have next to no *first*-hand knowledge of the day-by-day encounters realized by various types of integrated codes.

I hope that the kinds of questions raised by this approach will encourage sociologists of education to explore both theoretically, and empirically, the structure of educational knowledge which I take to be the distinctive feature of this field of enquiry.

Acknowledgments

I am most grateful to Professor Wolfgang Klafki, and particularly to Mr Hubertus Huppauf of the University of Marburg, for many valuable suggestions and constructive criticism. I should also like to acknowledge many hours of discussion with my colleague Mr Michael Young. I have also learned much from Mr David Adelstein, graduate student in the Department of the Sociology of Education, University of London Institute of Education. I am particularly grateful to Mr W. Brandis, research officer in the Department's Research Unit. I have also benefited from the stringent criticisms of Professor R. Peters and Mr Lionel Elvin, of the University of London Institute of Education. My greatest debt is to Professor Mary Douglas, University College, London.

I should like to thank the Director of the Chaucer Publishing Company, Mr L. G. Grossman, for a small but vital grant.

Notes

1 It follows that frame strength for teacher and taught can be assessed at the different levels of selection, organization and pacing of the knowledge.

2 Consider the recent acrimonious debate over the attempt to obtain

permission at Oxford to develop a degree in anthropology, sociology, psychology and biology—a relatively 'pure' combination.

3 The content of public examinations between the secondary and the tertiary level is controlled by the tertiary level, directly or indirectly, through the control over the various syllabi. Thus, if there is to be any major shift in secondary schools' syllabi and curricula, then this will require changes in the tertiary level's policy, as this affects the acceptance of students. Such a change in policy would involve changes in the selection, organization and pacing of knowledge at the tertiary level. Thus, the conditions for a major shift in the knowledge code at the secondary level is a major shift in the knowledge code at the tertiary level. Changes in the knowledge code at the secondary level are likely to be of a somewhat limited nature without similar changes at the tertiary level. There clearly are other interest groups (industry) which may affect a given curriculum and syllabus.

4 What is often overlooked is that the pacing of the knowledge (i.e. the rate of expected learning) is implicitly based upon the middle-class socialization of the child. Middle-class family socialization of the child is a hidden subsidy, in the sense that it provides both a physical and psychological environment which immensely facilitates, in diverse ways, school learning. The middle-class child is oriented to learning almost anything. Because of this hidden subsidy, there has been little incentive to change curriculum and pedagogy; for the middle-class child is geared to learn; he may not like, or indeed approve of, what he learns, but he learns. Where the school system is not subsidized by the home, the pupil often fails. In this way, even the *pacing* of educational knowledge is class-based. It may well be that frame strength, as this refers to pacing, is a critical variable in the study of educability. It is possible that the weak frame strength (as this refers to *pacing*) of integrated codes indicates that integrated codes presuppose a longer average educational life. Middle-class children may have been potential pupils for progressive schools because of their longer educational life.

5 It is possible that the weak boundary maintaining procedures of integrated codes at the level of the organizational structure, knowledge structure and identity structure may increase the pupils/ students informal age group affiliations as a source of identity, relation and organization.

6 In the sense of creating order.

7 An educational system is a cultural repeater. What is the social basis of a cultural repeater which is attempting to repeat the unrepeatable or the unlikely? E.g. a modern art school, anti-authoritarian pedagogy.

8 In the paper, I suggested that integrated codes rest upon a closed explicit ideology. It should then follow that this code would stand a better chance of successful institutionalization in societies where (1) there were strong and effective constraints upon the development of a range of ideologies and (2) where the educational system was a

major agency of political socialization. Further, the weak boundary maintaining procedures of the integrated code would (1) increase the penetration of the socialization as more of the self of the taught is made public through the relaxed frames and (2) deviancy would be more visible. On the other hand, integrated codes carry a potential for change in power structures and principles of control. I would therefore guess that in such societies integrated codes would possess weak classification, but the frames for teacher and taught would be strong.

9 It is a matter of interest that, in England, it is only in the infant school that there is relatively widespread introduction of this form of integrated code. This raises the general question of how this level of the educational system was open to such change. Historically, the primary school developed distinct concepts of infant and junior stages, and distinct heads for these two stages. Given the relative autonomy over the transmission of knowledge which characterizes the British system of education, it was in principle possible to have change. Although only a ceiling may separate infant from junior departments, two quite distinct and often incompatible educational codes can develop. We can regard this as a necessary, but not sufficient, condition for the emergence of integrated codes at the infant school level. It was also the case, until very recently, that the selection function started in the junior department, because that department was the gateway to the grammar school. This left the infant school relatively free of control by levels higher than itself. The form of integration in the infant school, again until recently, was *teacher* based, and therefore did not set up the problems which arise out of *teachers*-based integration. Finally, infant school teachers are not socialized into strong educational identities. Thus the English educational system, until recently, had two potential points of openness—the period between the ages of five to seven years, before selection began, and the period post-eighteen years of age, when selection is virtually completed. The major control on the structuring of knowledge at the secondary level is the structuring of knowledge at the tertiary level, specifically the university. Only if there is a major change in the structuring of knowledge at this level can there be effective code change at lower levels; although in any one school there may be a variety of knowledge codes.

References

BERNSTEIN, B. (1967), 'Open schools, open society?' *New Society*, 14 Sept.

BERNSTEIN, B., PETERS, R. and ELVIN, L. (1966), 'Ritual in education', *Philosophical Transactions of the Royal Society of London*, Series B, 251, No. 772.

DAVIES, D. I. (1970a), 'The management of knowledge: a critique of the use of typologies in educational sociology', *Sociology* 4, No. 1.

DAVIES, D. I. (1970b), 'Knowledge, education and power', paper presented to the British Sociological Association Annual Conference, Durham.

DOUGLAS, M. (1966), *Purity and Danger*, Routledge & Kegan Paul.

DOUGLAS, M. (1970), *Natural Symbols*, Barrie & Rockliff, The Cresset Press.

DURKHEIM, E. (1947), *On the Division of Labour in Society*, Chicago: Free Press.

DURKHEIM, E. (1956), *Education and Sociology*, Chicago: Free Press, (especially Chs. 2 and 3).

DURKHEIM, E. and MAUSS, M. (1963), *Primitive Classification* (translated by Needham, R.), Cohen & West.

HOYLE, E. (1969), 'How does the curriculum change? (1) A proposal for enquiries. (2) Systems and strategies', *J. Curriculum Studies* I, Nos 2 and 3.

JEFFERY, G. B. (1950), *The Unity of Knowledge: Reflections on the Universities of Cambridge and London*, Cambridge Univ. Press.

KEDDIE, N. G. (1970), 'The social basis of classroom knowledge', MA Dissertation, Inst. of Educ., London Univ.

MUSGROVE, F. (1968), 'The contribution of sociology to the study of the curriculum', in *Changing the Curriculum*, ed. Kerr, J. F., Univ. of London Press.

YOUNG, M. (1970), 'Curricula as socially organised knowledge', in *Knowledge and Control*, ed. Young, M., Collier-MacMillan.

Addendum: A note on the coding of objects and modalities of control

The coding of objects

The concepts of classification and frame can be used to interpret communication between objects. In other words, objects and their relationships to each other constitute a message system whose code can be stated in terms of the relationship between classification and frames of different strengths.

We can consider:

(1) The strength of the rules of exclusion which control the array of objects in a space. Thus the stronger the rules of exclusion the more distinctive the array of objects in the space; that is, the greater the difference between object arrays in different spaces.

(2) The extent to which objects in the array can enter into different relationships to each other.

Now the stronger rules of exclusion the stronger the *classification* of objects in that space and the greater the difference between object arrays in different spaces. In the same way in which we discussed relationships between subjects we can discuss the relationships between object arrays in different spaces. Thus the stronger the classification the more the object arrays resemble a collection code, the weaker the classification the more the object arrays resemble an integrated code. The greater the number of different relationships objects in the array can enter into with each other the weaker their framing. The fewer the number of different relationships objects in the array can enter into with each other the stronger their framing.*

We would expect that the social distribution of power and the

---

* If the objects in the array can be called lexical items, then the syntax is their relationships to each other. A restricted code is a syntax with few choices: an elaborated code a syntax which generates a large number of choices.

how?

principles of control be reflected in the coding of objects. This code may be made more delicate if we take into account:

(1)   The number of objects in the array
(2)   The rate of change of the array.

We can have strong classification with a large *or* a small number of objects. We can have strong classification of large or small arrays, where the array is fixed across time *or* where the array varies across time. Consider, for example, two arrays which are strongly classified; a late Victorian middle-class living-room and a middle twentieth-century trendy middle-class 'space' in Hampstead. The Victorian room is likely to contain a very large number of objects whereas the middle-class room is likely to contain a small number of objects. In one case the object array is foreground and the space background, whereas in the second case the space is a vital component of the array. The Victorian room represents both strong classification and strong framing. Further, whilst objects may be added to the array, its fundamental characteristics would remain constant over a relatively long time period. The Hampstead room is likely to contain a small array which would indicate strong classification (strong rules of exclusion) but the objects are likely to enter into a variety of relationships with each other; this would indicate weak framing. Further, it is possible that the array would be changed across time according to fashion.

We can now see that if we are to consider classification (C) we need to know:

(1)   Whether it is strong or weak
(2)   Whether the array is small or large (x)
(3)   Whether the array is fixed or variable (y)

At the level of frame (F) we need to know:

Whether it is strong or weak (p); that is, whether the coding is restricted or elaborated.

It is also important to indicate in the specification of the code the context (c) to which it applies. We should also indicate the nature of the array by adding the concept realisation (r.). Thus, the most abstract formulation of the object code would be as follows:

$$f\left(c, r, C(x,y), F(p)\right)$$

The code is some unspecified function of the variables enclosed in the brackets.

It is important to note that because the classification is weak it does not mean that there is less control. Indeed, from this point of view it is not possible to talk about amount of control only of its modality. This point we will now develop.

Classification, frames and modalities of control

Imagine four lavatories. The first is stark, bare, pristine, the walls are painted a sharp white; the washbowl is like the apparatus, a gleaming white. A square block of soap sits cleanly in an indentation in the sink. A white towel (or perhaps pink) is folded neatly on a chrome rail or hangs from a chrome ring. The lavatory paper is hidden in a cover and peeps through its slit. In the second lavatory there are books on a shelf and some relaxing of the rigours of the first. In the third lavatory there are books on the shelf, pictures on the wall and perhaps a scattering of tiny objects. In the fourth lavatory the rigour is *totally relaxed*. The walls are covered with a motley array of postcards, there is a various assortment of reading matter and curio. The lavatory roll is likely to be uncovered and the holder may well fall apart in use.

We can say that as we move from the first to the fourth lavatory we are moving from a strongly classified to a weakly classified space: from a space regulated by strong rules of exclusion to a space regulated by weak rules of exclusion. Now if the rules of exclusion are strong then the space is strongly marked off from other spaces in the house or flat. The *boundary* between the spaces or rooms is sharp. If the rules of exclusion are strong, the boundaries well marked, then it follows that there must be strong boundary maintainers (authority). If things are to be kept apart then there must be some strong hierarchy to ensure the apartness of things. Further, the first lavatory constructs a space where pollution is highly visible. In as much as a user leaves a personal mark (a failure to replace the towel in its original position, a messy bar of soap, scum in the washbowl, lavatory paper floating in the bowl, etc.) this constitutes pollution and such pollution is quickly perceived. Thus the criteria for competent usage of the space are both *explicit* and *specific*. So far we have been discussing aspects of classification; we shall now consider framing.

Whereas classification tells us about the structure of relationships in *space*, framing tells us about the structure of relationships in *time*. Framing refers us to interaction, to the power relationships of interaction; that is, framing refers us to communication. Now in the case of our lavatories, framing *here* would refer to the communication between the occupants of the space and those outside of the space. Such communication is normally strongly framed by a door usually equipped with a lock. We suggest that as we move from the strongly classified to the weakly classified lavatory, despite the potential insulation between inside and outside, there will occur a reduction in frame strength. In the case of the first lavatory we suggest that the door will always be closed and after entry will be locked. Ideally no effects on the inside should be heard on the outside. Indeed, a practised user of this lavatory will acquire certain competencies in order to meet this requirement. However, in the case of the most weakly classified lavatory, we suggest that the door will normally be open; it may even be that the lock will not function. It would not be considered untoward for a conversation to develop or even be continued either side of the door. A practised user of this most weakly classified and weakly framed lavatory will acquire certain communicative competencies rather different from those required for correct use of the strongly classified one.

We have already noted that lavatory one creates a space where pollution is highly visible, where criteria for behaviour are explicit and specific, where the social basis of the authority maintaining the strong classification and frames is hierarchical. Yet it is also the case that such classification and frames create a *private* although impersonal space. *For providing that the classification and framing is not violated the user of the space is beyond surveillance.*

However, when we consider lavatory four which has the weakest classification and weakest frames it seems at first sight that such a structure celebrates weak control. There appear to be few rules regulating what goes into a space and few rules regulating communication between spaces. Therefore it is difficult to consider what counts as a violation or pollution. Indeed, it would appear that such a classification and framing relationship facilitates the development of spontaneous behaviour. Let us consider this possibility.

Lavatory one is predicated on the rule 'things must be kept apart' be they persons, acts, objects, communication, and the stronger the classification and frames the greater the insulation, the stronger the boundaries between classes of persons, acts, objects, communications. Lavatory four is predicated on the rule that approximates to 'things must be put together'. As a consequence, we would find objects in the space that could be found in other spaces. Further, there is a more relaxed marking off of the space and communication is possible between inside and outside. We have as yet not discovered the fundamental principles of violation.

Imagine one user, who seeing the motley array and being sensitive to what he or she takes to be a potential of the space decides to add to the array and places an additional postcard on the wall. It is possible that a little later a significant adult might say 'Darling, that's beautiful but it doesn't quite fit' or 'How lovely but wouldn't it be better a little higher up?' In other words, we are suggesting that the array has a principle, that the apparently motley collection is ordered but that the principle is implicit and although it is not easily discoverable it is capable of being violated. Indeed, it might take our user a very long time to infer the *tacit* principle and generate choices in accordance with it. Without knowledge of the principle our user is unlikely to make appropriate choices and such choices may require a long period of socialization. In the case of lavatory one no principle is required; all that is needed is the following of the command 'Leave the space as you found it'.

Now let us examine the weak framing in more detail. We suggest that locking the door, avoiding or ignoring communication, would count as violation; indeed anything which would offend the principle of *things must be put together*. However, in as much as the framing between inside and outside is weak then it is also the case that the user is potentially or indirectly under continuous surveillance, in which case there is no privacy. Here we have a social context which at first sight appears to be very relaxed, which promotes and provokes the expression of the person, 'a do your own thing' space where highly personal choices may be offered, where hierarchy is not explicit yet on analysis we find that it is based upon a form of implicit control which carries the potential of total surveillance. Such a form of implicit control encourages more of the person to be made manifest yet such manifestations are subject to continuous screening and general rather than specific criteria. *At the level of classification the pollution is 'keeping things apart'; at the level of framing the violation is 'withholding'; that is, not offering, not making visible the self.*

If things are to be put together which were once set apart, then there must be some principle of the new relationships, but this principle cannot be mechanically applied and therefore cannot be mechanically learned. In the case of the rule 'things must be kept part', then the apartness of things is something which is clearly marked and taken for granted in the process of initial socialisation. The social basis of the categories of apartness is implicit but the social basis of the authority is explicit. In the process of such socialisation the insulation between things is a condensed message about the all-pervasiveness of the authority. It may require many years before the social basis of the principles underlying the category system is made fully explicit and by that time the mental structure is well-initiated into the classification and frames. Strong classification and frames celebrate the *reproduction* of the past.

When the rule is 'things must be put together' we have an *interruption* of a previous order, and what is of issue is the authority (power relationships) which underpin it. Therefore the rule 'things must be put together' celebrates the present over the past, the subjective over the objective, the personal over the positional. Indeed when everything is put together we have a total organic principle which covers all aspects of life *but* which admits of a vast range of combinations and re-combinations. This points to a very abstract or general principle from which a vast range of possibilities may be derived so that individuals can both register personal choices *and* have knowledge when a combination is not in accordance with the principle. What is taken for granted when the rule is 'things must be kept apart' is *relationships* which themselves are made explicit and problematic when the rule is 'things must be put together'. They are made explicit by the weak classification and frames. But the latter creates a form of implicit but potentially continuous surveillance and, at the same time, they promote the making public of the self in a variety of ways. We arrive, finally, at the conclusion that the conditions for the release of the person are the absence of explicit hierarchy but the presence of a more intensified form of social interaction which creates continuous but invisible screening. From the point of view of the socialised they would be offering novel, spontaneous combinations.

Empirical Note

It is possible to examine the coding of objects from two perspectives. We can analyse the coding of overt or visible arrays and we can compare the code with the codings of covert or invisible arrays (e.g. drawers, cupboards, refrigerators, basements, closets, handbags, etc.). We can also compare the coding of verbal messages with the coding of non-verbal messages. It would be interesting to carry out an empirical study of standardized spaces, e.g. LEA housing estate, middle-class suburban 'town' house estate, modern blocks of flats, formal educational spaces which vary in their architecture and in the pedagogy.

I am well aware that the lavatory may not be seen as a space to be *specially contrived* and so subject to *special regulation* in the sense discussed. Some lavatories are not subject to the principles I have outlined. Indeed some may be casually treated spaces where pieces of newspaper may be stuffed behind a convenient pipe, where the door does not close or lock, where apparatus has low efficiency and where sound effects are taken for granted events.

Postscript

Since the original publication, I have been aware of certain in-adequacies in the introduction. I shall try in this postscript firstly to show the inter-relationships between the work on socio-linguistic codes and 'educational knowledge' codes; secondly I shall fill out in rather more detail some of the conceptual problems entailed in the socio-linguistic thesis; and finally I shall comment upon a particular interpretation of the general thesis.

A major aim of the research has been to try and understand the basic social controls on the form and contents of symbolic orders transmitted initially in the family and in the process of education. Thus, there have been two major strands in the work I have been trying to do over the past decade: the research into socio-linguistic codes, and the research into education as an agency of social control. The underlying conceptual connection between these two strands was made explicit in the first draft of the classi-fication and frame paper, written in 1969 ('On the curriculum'). I shall give a brief account of this development.

The first paper, in the series of four on the school, was written in 1964 ('Sources of consensus and disaffection in education' 1966). This grew out of a paragraph in a paper entitled 'Some sociological determinants of perception' (chapter 1, page 43). The major idea was to create a simple conceptual framework capable of showing the inter-relationships between the family, peer group, school and work. In this analysis, the school was the basic variable and an attempt was made to show, theoretically, how the response of the pupil to the school was influenced by the form of the transmission of what I termed the instrumental and expressive orders of the school.

I distinguished between the organizational structure which controlled the curricula, pedagogy and assessment (the instrumental order) and the organizational structure which attempted to control the definitions of acceptable conduct, character and manner (the expressive order). I suggested a classification of types of relationships a pupil might develop (which had its basis in different forms of consensus and disaffection), according to the pupil's experience of the school's instrumental and expressive order. These pupil relationships can be summarized, with *great* over-simplification, as follows:

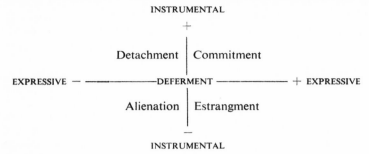

INSTRUMENTAL

$+$

	Detachment	Commitment
EXPRESSIVE — —————————DEFERMENT ————————— $+$ EXPRESSIVE
	Alienation	Estrangment

$-$

INSTRUMENTAL

LEGEND: $+$ high involvement/acceptance
$-$ low involvement/rejection

I argued that 'What the school does, its rituals, ceremonies, authority relationships, it incentives, rewards and punishments, its very image of conduct, character, and manner can modify or change the pupil's role as this has been initially shaped by the family. Thus the number of pupils initially involved in a particular role can be modified or changed by the school.'

In the 'Ritual in Education' paper (1966b), the analysis was taken a stage further. Here I distinguished between *two* different organizational structures for the transmission of the instrumental order and the expressive order. Each of these orders could be transmitted in such a way that each could give rise to social relationships which were highly stratified (strong and hierarchical definitions of roles, groups and subjects) or to social relationships which were more differentiated (weaker and less hierarchical definitions of roles, groups and subjects). In this paper, I explored changes in the forms of social control as expressive and instrumental orders moved away from 'stratified' towards more 'differentiated' social relationships. I suggested that non-examination children were more likely to experience the differentiated type. 'For the non-examination children, the school functions not so much as a delicate instrument of the division of labour, but much more as an instrument of social control regulating the behaviour of such pupils, their emotional sensivities, and their modes of social relationship to what is considered acceptable to a section of society to which the pupils often feel they do not belong.' At a higher level of abstraction, the shift from stratified to differentiated was derived from Durkheim's two forms of solidarity, mechanical and organic.'

In the 'Open schools – open society?' paper (1967), the distinction between 'stratified' and 'differentiated' was dropped, and was replaced by the distinction between 'open' and 'closed'. The diagram sets out the basic analysis of the paper, and also provides a scale for the degree of openness or closure. It is possible to see how changes in the distribution of power and the principles of social control affect the what, how, where, when and with whom, of school learning. *Thus the realizations of elaborated codes vary with the form of their institutionalization.*

At this point, the link with the socio-linguistic work begins to emerge. From one point of view, the concepts of restricted and elaborated codes took their starting point from Durkheim's two forms of solidarity. From another point of view, the socio-linguistic thesis attempted to demonstrate how the class structure affected the social distribution of privileged meanings and the interpretative procedures which generated them. It is also the case that as the organizational structure and 'knowledge' properties of the school change, so does the nature of the processes and the procedures of communication.

In the 'Open schools – open society?' paper (1967), I made use of Professor Douglas's exciting book *Purity and Danger* (1966). I analysed the curriculum in terms of its representing a structure which celebrated *purity* of categories (strongly bounded subjects) or in terms of a structure celebrating the *mixing* of categories (weakly bounded subjects). I linked the shift from one curriculum to another to changes in the form of authority and in the patterns of control. There was a conceptual error in this paper, for I had applied the concepts of mechanical and organic solidarity without making a sufficiently detailed analysis of the two types of 'knowledge' structures. The problem was more complex than I had anticipated (see Chapter 10). I developed the *New Society* paper in February 1969, but the draft was never published, although it existed in manuscript form (University of London Institute of Education Library 1969a). In this manuscript, I suggested 'Now we can begin to see that if we are to discuss curriculum we have also to consider pedagogy and evaluation ... The selective organization, transmission, and evaluation of knowledge is intimately bound up with patterns of authority and control.' I distinguished between two forms of the transmission of educational knowledge, 'collection' and 'integrated', and I speculated on their effect upon the formation of identities, concepts of property, the relationships between teachers and pupils, and upon the distribution of power and the principles of social control.

I was now in a stronger position to bring together the two strands.

Formal Controls

ORDERS

INSTRUMENTAL

Mixing of categories	Purity of categories
Teaching groups: Heterogeneous – size and composition varied	**Teaching groups:** Homogeneous – sizes and composition fixed
Pedagogy: Problem setting or creating / Emphasizes *ways of knowing*	**Pedagogy:** Solution giving / Emphasizes *contents* or states of *knowledge*
Teachers: Teaching roles cooperative/interdependent / Duties *achieved* / Fluid points of reference and relation	**Teachers:** Teaching roles insulated from each other / Duties *assigned* / Fixed points of reference and relation
Curriculum: Subject boundaries blurred (interrelated) / Progression: deep to surface structure of knowledge / Common curriculum	**Curriculum:** Subject boundaries sharp (less interrelation or integration) / Progression: surface to deep structure of knowledge / Curriculum graded for different ability groups
Pupils: Varied social groups reducing *group* similarity and difference – increased area of choice / Aspirations of the *many* raised / Fluid points of reference and relation	**Pupils:** Fixed and stable social groups emphasizing *group* similarity and difference – reduced area of choice / Aspirations of the *few* developed / Fixed points of reference and relation

TYPE – OPEN

(1) Ritual order celebrates participation/cooperation
(2) Boundary relationships with outside blurred
(3) Internal organization:
wide range of integrative sub-groups with active membership and success roles across ability ranges
If prefect system – wide area of independence from staff, but limited exercise of power
Range of opportunities for pupils to influence staff decisions, e.g. opportunities for self-government
(4) Teacher-pupil authority relationships:
Reward and punishment less public and ritualized
Teacher-pupil relationships of control – inter-personal

TYPE – CLOSED

(1) Ritual order celebrates hierarchy/dominance
(2) Boundary relationships with outside sharply drawn
(3) Internal organization:
narrower range of integrative sub-groups with active membership and success roles confined to high ability range
If prefect system – under staff control and influence, but extensive of exercise power
Limited opportunities for pupils to influence staff decisions, e.g. limited opportunities for self-government
(4) Teacher-pupil authority relationships:
Reward and punishment public and ritualized
Teach-pupil relationships of control – positional

EXPRESSIVE

Mixing of Categories — *Purity of categories*

It has always been very clear to me that the class structure affected access to elaborated codes through its influence upon initial socialization into the family *and* through its fundamental shaping of both the organizational structure and contents of education. I was also very sure that there were a variety of ways in which an elaborated code could be transmitted. (See later discussion of positional and personal family types which preceded 'stratified' and 'differentiated' schools.)

In the most recent paper in the series on the school 'On the classification and framing of educational knowledge', the lower order concepts of stratified/differentiated, open/closed finally disappeared as they could be derived from the concepts classification and frame. In this paper, the linkage with the work on socio-linguistic codes has been forged, to my mind, in a fundamental way. This can be seen if we raise the following question. If the social assumptions which give rise to restricted codes are those of intimacy, what are the social assumptions which shape the realizations of elaborated codes? Basically, all social assumptions must manifest themselves in the form taken by social relationships in the context of interaction, and in the structure of communication. I suggested that the realizations of elaborated codes vary according to the strength of classification and the strength of frames which regulate their transmission in schools or formal educational relationships. As the classification and frames of formal education change their strength, so does the system of meanings and the interpretative procedures, which are realized by code elaboration. The social assumptions which shape elaborated codes express themselves in classification and frames of various strengths.

It follows from this that elaborated codes are not necessarily middle-class communication procedures; they are not necessarily instruments for the alienation of the working class; neither does it follow that they function as repeaters of a particular class structure. Whether such codes perform the above functions depends more and [unpack] more in industrialized societies upon the classification and frames which control their transmission in formal education.

In this way, the work of socio-linguistic codes is vitally and inextricably interrelated with the work on so-called 'knowledge' codes made available through public education. I am not here concerned with the empirical truth of the thesis, only with the question of tracing the conceptual interrelationsip of its two strands. In one sentence, while the division of labour inevitably exerts an influence upon the contents of education, the class structure and its legitimizing ideology regulates the classification and framing of such contents. It is a travesty to relate the concepts of elaborated or restricted codes to superficial stylistics of middle-class and working-class forms of conversational behaviour, as implied by Labov (1970).

It is more than likely that the thesis, like any other in the field of social science, will be shown to be inadequate, empirically false, in some respects partial, and even misleading, but at least one has a right to expect recognition that one has attempted to treat a problem at the level it deserves. The exploration of the concepts developed to understand the form and contents of education inevitably influenced, and were influenced by, the concepts developed to understand forms of language-use, and *both* become further developed by empirical research.

I have difficulty in understanding, and I have very little sympathy with, complaints that the socio-linguistic thesis of 1958 is in some respects different from the thesis in 1972. Such a critique is based upon a complete misunderstanding of the nature of research. The single most important fact of research is where it *leads*, not where it starts. In one sense, of course, where it starts – i.e. the initial for-mulation of the basic problem – already predetermines the extent of the exploration. To have an idea is not difficult, but the attempt to clarify it, to rescue it from a local intuition, to make it explicit, yet always to be aware of the ambiguity upon which its growth depends, is quite another matter.

The basic thesis has been that forms of communication may be distinguished in terms of what is rendered implicit and what is rendered explicit. Thus the fundamental characteristic of a public language given in 1958 (see Chapter 1) was that a public language is a language of implicit meaning. This idea of implicitness and explicitness underwent a series of transformations:

1. Universalistic/particularistic (Chapter 5)
2. Context independent/context dependent (Chapter 9)

Now what was it that was rendered implicit or explicit? Clearly, any communication depends upon shared assumptions and rests upon inherent ambiguities, but the nature of the assumptions and the nature of the ambiguities may vary. Implicit/explicit represented for me the extent to which the *principles* underlying the social structuring of relevant meaning were made public and elaborated through the use of language *in the process of socialization*. The problem then became one of constructing defining criteria of *such forms* of implicitness and explicitness realized and transmitted in the use of language. It appeared to me (as to many others) that as the emphasis changed from implicitness to explicitness (*as previously defined*) then such a change in emphasis would act selectively on the grammatical and lexical choices. At no time did I ever consider that I was concerned with differences between social groups at the level of competency; that is, differences between social groups which had their origin in their basic tacit understanding of the linguistic rule system. I was fundamentally concerned with *performance*, that is; I was interested in the sociological controls on the use to which this common understanding was put. In the same way, I never believed that there was any difference between social groups in their *tacit* understanding of logical rules; of the rules of inference. The difference which concerned me was the usage to which this common tacit understanding was put. It was also made very clear in print that I was not essentially concerned with dialect or so-called non-standard speech (see Part I).

The identification of implicit usage with dialect or 'non-standard' speech probably arose out of the first characteristic given of public and formal language use, in which 'Short grammatical, simple, often unfinished sentences, a poor syntactic structure stressing the active mood' were contrasted with 'Accurate grammatical order and syntax regulating what is said'. None of the other characteristics in the list pointed towards 'standard' or 'non-standard' speech. Neither have I ever considered that these characteristics were in any sense the crucial determiners of the form of language-use. Indeed, even in the early papers it is clear that the primary paradigm of a public language is a context of intimacy. However, given the class structuring of speech, it was likely that formal language-use would be associated with so-called standard speech. Such speech, *in itself*, could not serve to indicate either public or formal language usage. In other words, I have never been concerned with what Labov and others call the superficial stylistics of middle-class speech. *Indeed, if I had been concerned with the relative presence or absence of such niceties of conversation, why did not Lawton or myself in the early research count such deviations from standard speech?* It would not have been difficult! I certainly would not wish to defend the indices created in those two lists, but I would resolutely oppose the view that the distinction between the two forms of communication rested upon, or necessarily pointed to, the difference between, 'standard' or 'non-standard' speech. Indeed, even the relationship between codes and social class was seen as contingent (Chapter 5).

The second formulation (Chapter 5) in terms of restricted and elaborated codes represented an attempt to formulate the regulative principles which I considered to underly implicit and explicit forms of communication. These terms pointed to the way the class structure acted upon the social distribution of privileged meanings and upon the interpretative procedures which generated them. The class structure distributes power unequally; it distributes access to, control over, and facility to exploit property, whether this property is physical or symbolic. It does this through its penetration into educational arrangements and processes and through its penetration into primary socialization within the family, in such a way that a vicious self-perpetuating circle is often set up between home, school and work. Any analysis of how class structures repeat themselves in the process of socialization must necessarily show the class realizations in the family *and* school *and* work.]

During this period of the re-formulation of public and formal language use into restricted and elaborated codes, I moved away from a descriptive correlational association between speech forms and certain demographic attributes of families, such as level of education and economic functions, to the formulation of two different types of families with differently focused communication structures. ('Family role systems, communication and socialization' (1962).) Different role options were made available in these hypothetical types of families and I connected causally the nature of these role options with the nature of the linguistic options; for the role options initially created and defined the social structuring of relevant meanings and established the interpretative procedures underlying their generation and reception. There were two aspects to the communication structure within the types of families:

1. The communications could focus upon either positional or personal attributes of family member (see connection between 'stratified' and 'differentiated' schools, 'collection'/'integrated' codes).
2. The realization of these attributes could be regulated by either restricted or elaborated codes.

We can express this formulation diagrammatically:

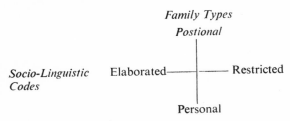

Family Types
Postional

Socio-Linguistic   Elaborated————————— Restricted
Codes

Personal

Thus, by about 1962, the crude correlation between forms of language use and social class had been made more sensitive, so that the basic unit had become a family type with a particular communication structure and focus. It was further possible to distinguish *both* within the middle class and the working class according to the type of family and to relate the incidence and change of the types to the more macro-institutional features of the society. The same model allowed for the distinction between object-focused codes (positional) and person-focused codes (personal).

While the sociological aspect of the analysis had now been more carefully specified, there were still major difficulties with the linguistic aspect. The code definitions in 1962 emphasized the relatively extensive range of alternatives in the case of an elaborated code and the relatively reduced range of alternatives in the case of a restricted code. These definitions brought the role options, at the sociological level, into a hypothesized causal relationship with the linguistic options. There were a number of conceptual problems in this formulation. To begin with, the concept of role option, or discretion, as it was then called, operated at a different logical level from the concept of code. Role options or discretion refer to sociologically controlled choices in specific interactional contexts, whereas the concept code referred to a regulative principle which shaped a general orientation. What was the relationship between these two concepts; essentially what was the relationship between code and context? If we turn now to the code definitions, it can be seen that I considered that the possibility of combination and recombination of syntactic alternatives was greater in the case of an elaborated code, therefore I considered that the possibility of predicting such alternatives was less than in the case of a restricted code. I associated complexity with a greater variety of choice.

The two parts of the thesis were now at odds with each other. The sociological aspect had its roots in roles and so it directed attention to interactional contexts or situations; whereas the linguistic aspect defined codes independently of context or situation. This was the conceptual position at the start of the major inquiries of the Sociological Research Unit, under my direction, in 1964. A descriptive account of these inquiries was given in the Introduction I wrote to the first SRU monograph (Brandis and Henderson, 1970).

Despite the inconsistency between the sociological and linguistic aspects of the thesis, the major research activity was directed towards examining code realizations in different contexts. In the first interview, for example, the mothers who took part in the research were asked how they *might* answer questions their child *might* put to them. Two and a half years later many of the same questions, together with a range of others, were put to the children of these mothers. This was the beginning of the exploration of the instructional context (Robinson and Rackstraw, 1972). In the same interview the mothers were asked what they *might* say *if* their child committed a series of misdemeanours. Two and a half years later the same questions (but with some modification) were were put to the children. This was the beginning of the analysis of the *regulative* context (Cook-Gumperz, 1970, 1972a; Turner, 1972a and b). We also obtained from the children at age five years and seven years, examples of speech elicited from contrived, imaginative and instructional contexts.

It was clear to me that we had to choose a linguistic theory to guide the analysis of the speech. The major linguistic theory at that time (1964) which was attaining supremacy, was transformation grammar. I deliberately decided for the following reasons not to use Chomsky's theory.

(1) The theory divorced linguistics from semantics. I could not see how such a theory could be appropriate to a study where the major area of inquiry was precisely the problem of the relationship between the social structuring of relevant meanings and the form of their linguistic expression.

(2) Chomsky's theory rested upon certain pyschological, even neurological assumptions which underpinned the concept of *competence*. The theory I was exploring rested upon clearly *social* assumptions about the nature of *performance*. I foresaw major difficulties in any attempt to bring together two theories which differed so markedly in their basic assumptions and focus.

(3) Chomsky's theory did not permit any linguistic descriptions above the level of the sentence. I considered that one of our major tasks was to carry out such a description which would entail an examination of the integrating devices between sentences. A major problem of the non-linguistic analyses carried out by Dr Lawton and myself arose out of the attempt to characterize the overall patterning of speech on the basis of counts of isolated frequencies of selected speech elements. While intuitively I believed that differences in such relative frequencies (sometimes even quite small differences) created a distinctly different overall patterning, there was no means (in the sense that I was not aware of the means) of making this intuition explicit and formal. It was also clear to me that the logical levels of the sociological and linguistic analysis must match. A necessary condition for this was the construction of a linguistic description above the level of the sentence from which could be *derived* a justification for any individual counts of speech elements. Such a linguistic description in turn would need to be directed by a primitive (in the sense of elementary or simple) specification of the semantic structure of codes. Interestingly enough, when such a specification was accomplished it was, and

indeed had to be, a context-free formulation (context dependent/ independent: high/low specificity).

(4) In 1964, Chomsky had not developed a phonological analysis. I considered (though in fact we never carried out such an analysis) that such an inquiry might at some point become necessary.

A year before the major research inquiry, we had used an early form of Professor Halliday's *Scale and Category Grammar* in an analysis of the written texts obtained from children aged eleven years. Geoffrey Turner, senior linguist of the SRU, carried out this application. As a result, we adopted Halliday's linguistic theory, for it satisfied all the requirements created by the sociological aspects of the thesis. The long association with Professor Halliday which followed provided for both of us a constant source of mutual stimulation and influence. Dr Hasan's development of Halliday's analysis of cohesion marked an especially critical step in the analyses of the speech. Perhaps the key to this analysis, and so to the relationship between the 'socio' and the linguistic features arose out of the exploration of the regulative context.

I had earlier (1962) developed a set of concepts which distinguished three basic modes of control: imperative, positional and personal. (Quite independently, Dr Hanson (1965) published a paper setting out a similar approach.) My own approach was never officially published until 1970, although the concepts were used in a paper given at an international meeting in 1964. The concepts of imperative, positional and personal modes of control were operationalized and applied to the social control data we had collected from the mothers and children. Dr Cook-Gumperz and I (in discussion with other members of the SRU, notably Dr Peter Robinson) created a coding grid for the analysis of the data. Briefly, we distinguished a number of sub-systems which could be applied to a range of parent-child regulative contexts. Each sub-system opened the way to a range of choices, all of which were derived from the thesis. We could then examine which of the sub-systems a mother or child entered *and* the nature of the choice within any sub-system. Further, each choice could be given a precise linguistic description. In other words, we had constructed a semantic network, derived from the thesis, which made possible an analysis of its contextual linguistic realization.

Thus:

Theory $\longrightarrow$ model of social control (regulative context) $\longrightarrow$ semantic specification of alternatives $\longrightarrow$ linguistic realization of the alternatives.

It was this formulation which allowed us to take over Professor Halliday's network theory, and theory of language functions.

We could also show the *different* linguistic realizations of different contexts *and* decide whether each context had evoked either a restricted or an elaborated variant. We now could examine both the emphasis and the range of choices (alternatives) an individual took up in the network. In this way, it was possible to return to the definition of codes in terms of the range of alternatives; *yet these alternatives would always be context specific.*

I certainly do not want to give the impression that the problem of the operationalizing of codes was solved, but at least a way had been found of approaching a possible solution. Geoffrey Turner, who was a graduate student of Halliday, played a vital role in the construction of networks used for the analysis of the regulative context. The way was now clear for the final definition of codes (Chapter 10).

I will now summarize the development of the final definition:

1. Public and Formal Language Use — list of apparently unrelated characteristics with no explicit conceptual backing

2. Elaborated and Restricted Codes (object- or person-focused) — context-free definition in terms of the predictability of syntactic alternatives. Implicit linkage with semantics

3. Elaborated and Restricted Codes (object- or person-focused) — context-independent definition in terms of semantics

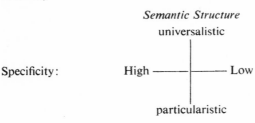

Semantic Structure
universalistic

Specificity: High ——————— Low

particularistic

but context-dependent linguistic analysis, on the basis of derivations from the above model appropriate to the contexts, crucial to the thesis.

I will now turn to the research on the family. The second interview with the mothers took place two and a half years after the first. It took the form of a set of closed questionnaires. I have commented on the methodological problems in such an approach in the Introduction to *Class, Codes and Control*, Volume II, 1972 (see also Cook-Gumperz, J., 1972b). The basic research aim was to test out the ideas of the positional and personal types of families as these might be realized in *both* the middle and working classes. To have a model is one thing, to explore it empirically takes a little time and normally it gives rise to more questions than answers. I considered that if we were to study communication in families in a way *relevant to the thesis*, we would need to see such communication as being shaped by the following variables:

(1) strong–weak linkage with family of origin
(2) strong–weak linkage with neighbourhood and local community
(3) strong–weak role definitions of family members
(4) strong–weak insulation between the meanings active in the family and the meanings active in agencies external to the family, to which members of the family were connected, e.g. work/family, school/family, trade union/family.

Clearly, the above variables would have to be examined against the economic, demographic and local characteristics of the family. The above formulation was very much influenced by *Family and Social Network* written by Elizabeth Bott (1957). One of the advantages of this approach was that we could distinguish between families within a particular social class category in terms of the strength or weakness of the various linkages and then examine the mothers' *reported* orientation to communication and control (see Bernstein and Henderson, 1969a; Henderson 1970). In principle, it would also be possible to examine the relationships between the language-use of the mothers and their children, and changes in the strength of the various linkages. In general, the stronger the linkages, the more likely that the family would resemble a positional type. At this point, one can begin to see that strong linkages (positional families) are families which create rather strong boundaries, whereas person-centred families tend to create weak or blurred boundaries. In this way, it should be possible to consider families rather like schools in terms of their *classifications* and *frames*.

There is a danger to such an analysis, because it appears to separate the communication structure from the power relationships of society, but this can be avoided if the same analysis can show the relationships between class structures and communication structures – which is where we began.

I have tried very briefly to give some idea of the relationships between the work on 'knowledge' codes and socio-linguistic codes, the development of the concept of code and some indication of the approach to communication within the family. In other papers I have tried to analyse, perhaps very inadequately, how macro-institutional features of the society affect the nature of primary and secondary socializing agencies.*

Finally, I should like to comment on a particular interpretation of the thesis offered by Labov ('The logic of non-standard English', 1970). I am not here concerned to examine Labov's analysis of the speech of Charles, M., and Larry, or the dialogue between Larry and John Lewis, for I have never asserted that differences between codes have any basis in a speaker's tacit understanding of the linguistic rule system, that non-standard forms of speech have, in themselves, any necessary conceptual consequences, or that reasoning is only possible in an elaborated code; nor have I ever suggested that differences between codes has anything to do with superficial niceties of speech. It has become very fashionable in the USA now to find the villain who was responsible for leading research astray. It is a matter of interest that over fifty per cent of the references (39) which I used in the first two papers (Chapters 1 and 2) came from American sources. Perhaps Americans have some difficulty in acknowledging the potential or actual influence on Americans by Americans. Indeed, it took me a little time to free myself of the standard USA work on socialization.

Labov, like Ginsburg (1972), confines his analysis to early work, presumably up to 1961, yet the work I am supposed to have influenced was not published until 1966–8 (Bereiter, G. and Englemann, S., *Teaching Disadvantaged Children in the Pre-School*, Prentice Hall, 1966; Deutsch, M. *et al.* (eds), *The Disadvantaged Child*, New York Basic Books, 1967; Deutsch, M., Katz, I., Jensen, A. R., *Social Class, Race and Psychological Development*, Holt, Rinehart & Winston, 1968). Between 1961 and 1966, I had written a number of papers which it seems much of the USA ignored, so busy were they confining their attention in an uncritical way to papers written up to 1961. The reader might care to contrast Ginsburg's or Labov's account with that of Lillian Weber, who compares the overall impact of the thesis in England and the USA in her book *The English Infant School and Informal Education* (Center for Urban Education Book, Prentice Hall, 1971).

While there is much I agree with in Labov's paper, I find the following puzzling, to say the least.

* It is possible for a code to be restricted in the verbal channel, but elaborated in others, e.g. music, painting. *See also* 'Class and pedagogies: visible and invisible', O.E.C.D. (C.E.R.I.), available from the SRU.

The most extreme view which proceeds from this orientation and one that is widely accepted is that lower-class Negro children have no language at all. This notion is first drawn from Basil Bernstein's writings that 'much of lower class language consists of a kind of incidental "emotional" accompaniment to action here and now' (Jensen 1968, p. 118). Bernstein's views are filtered through a strong bias against all forms of working-class behaviour so that middle-class language is seen as superior in every respect, as more abstract and necessarily somewhat more flexible, detailed and subtle' (Labov, p. 118).

Compare with

A public language contains its own aesthetic, a simplicity and directness of expression, emotionally virile, pithy and powerful and a metaphoric range of considerable force and appropriateness. Some examples taken from the schools of this country have a beauty which many writers might well envy*. . . . This is not to say that speakers of this language interact in a completely uniform manner, for the potential of a public language allows a vast range of possibilities. (Chapter 2.)

I must emphasize the point that in restricted code relationships, people are not non-verbal. There is no such thing as a non-verbal child; if a child is limited to a restricted code, it means not that this child is non-verbal, but simply that the kinds of roles he has learned have created in him a particular way in which he verbally transforms his world. *It is a whole lot of nonsense to speak of a non-verbal child, although he may be inarticulate in certain social contexts.* (Bernstein, 1966c, Public Lecture, New York, published 1967.)

Isn't it (the elaborated code) also turgid, redundant, bombastic and empty? Is it not simply an elaborated style rather than a *superior* code or system? (Labov, 1970, *my italics*.)

The preparation and delivery of relatively explicit meaning is the major function of this code. The meanings are not necessarily abstract, but abstraction inheres in the possibilities. Moreover, it cannot be assumed that because a person moves towards an elaborated code, the meanings he is signalling are of any great significance. A lot of nonsense can be signalled in this code. Regardless of the actual content, this code promotes the transmission of certain kinds of meanings rather than others. (Bernstein 1966, *op. cit.*)

I am well aware that the issues raised by Labov and others cannot be settled by exchange of quotations; it is always possible for a sentence, paragraph or a paper to be abstracted from the spirit of the total work.

---

* All children, irrespective of code, explore the creative potential of language. Indeed, where the initially received code is restricted, such exploration may be less trammelled than in the case of an elaborated code, for in its transmission, children may well be constrained by too early socialization into explicit criteria.

The verbal-deficit thesis has one of its roots in an American theory of learning (stimulus-response) which, when applied to language, becomes a particular type of theory of verbal mediation. In turn, the theory tends to give rise to an approach to change by means of 'behaviour modification' (various forms of conditioning responses by rigourous control over the stimuli). The verbal-deficit thesis also draws upon American child development studies which place an overwhelming emphasis upon the significance of the early years of the child's life. Both of these two groups of theories, for different reasons, are likely to view problems of educability as arising out of interactions which are considered to be deficient, inadequate or even pathological. These theories offer little purchase upon the wider institutional and cultural contexts which define the form, content and evaluation of what is to be learned, how it is to be learned and the organizational context. It is also the case that, certainly up to the middle sixties, much of the research into the problem of 'who is able to learn what' was carried out by psychologists whose intellectual training and whose own socialization led them to define the problem in a limited way.

It was only with the radicalizing of American academics through Vietnam, the rise of Black Power, through the exposure of the failure of the American urban school, that fundamental questions were raised about the political implications of forms of education during the late sixties.*

I believe that the following extract was among one of the first public critiques of the deficit thesis:

Mario Fantini: I am wondering if you can offer us some clarification on how we can actually use your model in terms of the problems that we face: for example, the problem of deprivation.

Basil Bernstein: I think what underlies this particular problem (in my thesis) is a notion of the formation of social experience somewhat different from the notions of social experience that inhere in some intervention approaches. Let me make this very concrete. It follows from my view that the notion of deficit is inadequate and perhaps misleading. Deficit is not a theory, it is simply a statement of certain lacks or deficiencies. This notion of treating children as exhibiting various kinds of deficits turns the social scientist into a plumber whose task is to plug, or rather fill, the deficits. It may lead to a partial relation with the child. You see a child as

* 'Like many Americans, I belatedly discovered the "crisis" in urban education in the late 1960s.' (Ginsburg, 1972, Preface, p. ix.)

a cognitive or perceptual deficit, and so lose track of the vital nature of the communal experience of the child, and the many cultural and psychological processes at work in him, when he is to be 'enriched'.

It is of critical importance to draw into our work researchers in sociology and anthropology, in order that the various socializing agencies can be seen in relation to each other, and that the dynamics which flow from the political and economic nature of the society can inform our thinking and our actions. We must have more work of a sociological nature on both the school and the college of education as socio-cultural systems. (Bernstein, 1966, *op. cit.*)

[In a fundamental sense, a restricted code is the basic code. It is the code of intimacy which shapes and changes the very nature of subjective experience, initially in the family and in our close personal relationships. The intensifications and condensations of such communication carry us beyond speech, and new forms of awareness often become possible. An elaborated code is the basic code by means of which our experience of persons and things is objectified and a different exploration of consciousness made possible. The social controls on the distribution, institutionalization and realization of elaborated codes may, under certain conditions, create alienation; this is not necessarily in the order of things.]

Appendix to the Postscript

When we obtained the speech from the children we constructed a number of different situations which the children were invited to talk about. Although the researcher spent one day in the classroom with the children, the interview situation was an unusual situation for a child for at least the following reasons:

(1) The child is removed from both his normal school *and* non-school setting.
(2) The child enters a situation (the experimental setting) which is unlike any other setting he has met.
(3) He is presented with tasks which are unfamiliar and he is asked to create meanings often far removed from those he offers and receives in his day-by-day experience or even perhaps in his infant class.
(4) He interacts with a relatively strange adult, who provides only minimal guidance in a setting where he is given minimal clues as to what is or is not an appropriate response.

The question immediately arises as to what inferences can be made from the child's behaviour in this context compared with other contexts. Further, why should any measures of the mother's behaviour or social setting (e.g. social class position of the family) bear any relation to the child's behaviour? We could say that the experimental setting abstracts the child from his normal settings, abstracts the child from his normal tasks, abstracts the child from his normal social relationships with other adults, and, finally, abstracts the child from the meanings he normally creates and receives. The setting, tasks, social relationships and meanings are independent of the child's normal settings, tasks, relationships and meanings. In this sense, the experimental setting is a *context-independent* setting for the child. Now some children in this setting produce speech or responses which differ markedly from the speech or meanings of other children. Why do the children differ in their interpretation of the context? It certainly has nothing to do with differences in the children's tacit understanding of grammar and little to do with differences in the children's vocabulary. I suggest that what we are witnessing are differences in the *ground rules* the children are using to generate their meanings and so their speech.* One group of children are applying rules for the creation of context-independent speech, whereas another group of children are doing this to a lesser extent. In the language of the thesis, one group of children are realizing elaborated speech variants, whereas the other group are realizing more restricted speech variants. The children are following different ground rules. Thus the experimental setting itself, in its *totality*, that is, in terms of the setting, social relationships, tasks and meanings, acts *selectively* upon the ground rules the children are using. One group of children, through their intitial socialization, are applying one set of ground rules, and another group of children are applying a different set. What is being measured at a fundamental level is the process of socialization which underlies the children's selection of ground rules. Let me give an example. When the children were seven years of age, they were asked (after two earlier attempts) to explain how the game 'Hide and Seek' was played, to a child who did not know the game. Analysis of their speech carried out by Miss Lesley Lineker (a research assistant in the Sociological Research Unit) indicates that there is a tendency for lower-working-class children to explain the game very much in terms of their family/ neighbourhood setting, whereas there is a tendency for the middle-class children to refer much less to a local setting; their explanations

* Ground rules lie behind manifest behaviour in ways similar to those in which grammatical rules lie behind speech. Elaborated and restricted codes from this perspective have their basis in different ground rules.

are relatively context *independent*, whereas the lower-working-class children's explanations are rather more context *dependent*. Now it may well be the case that the lower-working-class children's form of explanation, as a teaching device, is more efficient than that of the middle-class children, but from the point of view of the thesis, the orientation to *different* forms of explanation is the crucial interest.

Thus, the inference from the experimental setting to other settings is based less upon differences in the spoken grammar and lexes, and more upon what *ground* rule the children will select in what context. Similarly, when we find a relationship between the speech and meanings of the mother and those of the children, it is because what has been taken over by the children is less the particulars of a grammar and lexes (although these are of some importance) but more a ground rule for developing meanings and speech. The child is not explicitly taught these ground rules by his parents. These ground rules are implicit in the meanings, speech and social relationships realized in the process and contexts of socialization.

It is also a matter of some interest that the means we often (but not always) use for testing children in schools involve:

(1) The removal of the child from his normal non-school environment.

(2) An unusual setting where the child is isolated from other children.

(3) Interaction with an adult who provides minimal guidance and support, and where the child is often given, at the time, minimum clues at to what is or is not an appropriate response.

(4) Tasks which are very different from the ones the child is concerned with outside the school.

Thus, there is a broad analogy between the experimental setting and the test situation in the school. They are both relatively context independent, although it is true that the child is given opportunities to learn the requirements of the school test situation. Basically, I am suggesting that there are certain social assumptions underlying the experimental setting and test situations, and that the middle-class child, at least from the age of five years, has an understanding of the ground rules of these assumptions and so he is differently oriented to context-independent settings. If we see the problem from this point of view, we can go on to ask how it is that some lower-working-class children do select the ground rules for context-independent meanings, and how it is that some middle-class children do not. Why, for example, in a similar experimental setting, do middle-class children at five years of age score much higher on verbal tests than working-class children, and why, on non-verbal tests, is this advantage very much reduced? This opens up, of course, questions of how it is that context-independent meanings are both assessed and acquired in a particular way, a way which is more favourable to middle-class children than to working-class children. The basic argument applies equally to the mother's responses to the interview situation.

References

BEREITER, G. and ENGLEMAN, S. (1966), *Teaching Disadvantaged Children in the Pre-School*, Prentice Hall.

BERNSTEIN, B. (1962), 'Family role systems, socialization and communication', unpublished manuscript, S.R.U., University of London Institute of Education.

BERNSTEIN, B. (1964), 'Social class, speech systems and psychotherapy', *British Journal of Sociology*, 15.

BERNSTEIN, B. (1966a), 'Sources of consensus and disaffection in education', *Journal of Assistant Mistresses*; expanded version appeared in Open University Course Unit 5 (Educational Studies, E283).

BERNSTEIN, B. with ELVIN, H. L. and PETERS, R. S. (1966b), 'Ritual in education', *Philosophical Transactions of the Royal Society of London, Series B.*, Biological Sciences No. 772 C.I. 251; also reprinted in Open University Reader, *School and Society*, Routledge & Kegan Paul, 1971.

BERNSTEIN, B. (1966c), 'The role of speech in the development and transmission of culture', Public Lecture to the Bank Street Fiftieth Anniversary Symposium; published in *Perspectives on Learning*, Klopf, G. L. and Hohman, W. A. (eds), Mental Material Center Inc., 1967.

BERNSTEIN, B. (1967), 'Open schools, open society?' *New Society*, 14 September 1967.

BERNSTEIN, B. (1969a), 'On the curriculum', University of London Institute of Education Library.

BERNSTEIN, B. with HENDERSON, D. (1969b), 'Social class differences in the relevance of language to socialization', *Sociology*, 3.

BERNSTEIN, B. (ed.) (1972), *Class, Codes and Control*, vol. II, Routledge & Kegan Paul.

BOTT, E. (1957), *Family and Social Network*, Tavistock.

BRANDIS, W. and HENDERSON, D. (1970), *Social Class, Language and Communication*, Routledge & Kegan Paul.

COOK, J. (1970), 'An Enquiry into Patterns of Communication and Control between Mothers and their Children in Different Social Classes', University of London Library (Ph.D. thesis).

COOK-GUMPERZ, J. (1972a), *Socialization and Social Control*, Routledge & Kegan Paul.

COOK-GUMPERZ, J. (1972b), *Class, Codes and Control*, vol. II, Bernstein, B. (ed.), Routledge & Kegan Paul, ch. II.

DEUTSCH, M. *et. al.* (eds) (1967), *The Disadvantaged Child*, New York: Basic Books; 1968, *Social Class, Race and Psychological Development*, Holt, Rinehart & Winston.

DOUGLAS, M. (1966), *Purity and Danger*, Routledge & Kegan Paul.

GINSBERG, H. (1972), *The Myth of the Deprived Child*, Prentice Hall.

HANSEN, D. (1965), 'Personal and positional influences in informal groups', *Social Forces*, 44.

HENDERSON, D. (1970), 'Contextual specificity, discretion and cognitive socialization', *Sociology*, 3.

LABOV, W. (1970), 'The logic of non-standard English', *Language and Poverty*, Williams, F. (ed.), Markham Press, reprinted in *Open University Course Unit*.

ROBINSON, W. P. and RACKSTRAW, S. J. (1972), *A Question of Answers*, vols, I & II, Routledge and Kegan Paul; *see also* Robinson, W. P., *Class, Codes and Control*, vol. II. Bernstein, B. (ed.), Routledge & Kegan Paul, ch. 8.

TURNER, G. (1972a), *Class, Codes and Control*, vol. II, Bernstein, B. (ed.), ch. 7.

TURNER, G. (1972b), 'A socio-linguistic analysis of the regulative context' (forthcoming monograph).

WEBER, L. (1971), *The English Infant School and Infant Education*, Center for Urban Education Book, Prentice Hall.

Index

Adjectives, use by social class, 102, 115
Adverbs, use by social class, 101–2, 115
Algebra, 35

Behaviour:
  antisocial, 51
  language related to, 53–4, 71–5
  public language and, 51
  social class influence on, 23, 32
  subordinated to linguistic code, 125
Bernhard Baron settlement, 2–3
Bernstein, Basil, 2–11 *passim*;
D. G. MacRae on, xii–xiv
Birmingham University, 191
Boas, F., 121
Bruner, J. S., 27
Burt, Sir Cyril, 190

Capital, cultural, 172
Cassirer, Ernest, xiv, 6, 171
Categoric statements, 45–6
Cazden, Courtney, 18
Chelsea Centre for Science Education, 216
Chelsea College of Technology, 216
Child (*see also* Family; Middle-class child; School; Working-class child):
  backward, 151, 190
  deprived, education for, 190
  limited to restricted code, 134–5, 151
  linguistic codes and social orientation, 145
  non-verbal, 194, 197
  parents' aid in learning, 192
  role system and, 149
  sex related to language, 161

socialization, 174
  by social control, 156–60
  by speech, 196–7
Chomsky, N., 173
City Day College, 4–6
Civil Rights Movement (U.S.), 162
Code, *see* Educational code; Linguistic code
Communication systems, family:
  closed, 154–5, 160
  open, 153–4, 160
Conjunctions, use by social class, 103, 115
Conservatism, speech and, 48, 50
Cook, J., 9, 16–17, 182
Corporal punishment, 58
Coulthard, Malcolm, 18
Creativity:
  scientific, xi–xii
  sociological, xii
  speech and, 172
Culture:
  mass, 74
  transmission of, by linguistic code, 121–2, 145, 163–4
Cultural capital, 172
Cultural deprivation, 190, 192, 199
Cultural identity, 174
Cultural system, linguistic rule system and, 173
Curiosity:
  limited by public language, 46, 48, 50
  working-class level, 36
Curriculum:
  boundary maintenance, 205–6, 212, 224
  collection, 204
  definition, 203
  integrated, 205
  types, 203–5

Davis, Allison, 27
Department of Education and Science, 191
Deprivation, 190, 192, 194, 197, 199
Dialect, 199
Douglas, Mary, 2, 17
Durkheim, E., xiv, 3, 17, 119–20, 171–2, 202–3

Economics:
  educational code changes and, 225
  linguistic code switching and, 150, 162–3, 186–7
Educability:
  definition, 200
  linguistic code and, 150–2, 183–4
  social determinants, 136
  universalistic and particularistic meanings, 196
Education (see also Curriculum; Pedagogy; School):
  compensatory:
    criticism of concept, 191–3, 199
    definition, 190
    diploma, 191
    research, 191
  definition, 199
  deprived children, 190
  discipline, 214
  egalitarian, 225
  environment inadequate, 191–3
  innovation in, 4, 5
  linguistic codes and, 136
  primary, as unity, 193
  public language effects on, 34, 58
  resistance to, 24, 34
  secondary, 208, 214, 224
  social class related to, 23–39, 136
  social context, 199–200
  socializing agency, 145, 150, 186

sociology of, 202, 211–12, 214–15, 219, 221, 223, 225–6
staff-pupil relations, 219–21, 223
Educational code:
  central control of, 215
  change in, 216, 225–6
    resistance to, 212, 221, 225
  collection, 207–16
    characteristics, 213, 215–17, 221–4
    definition, 207
    English, 208, 211–13, 215–16
    European, 208, 210–16
    non-specialized, 207–8
    organizational consequences, 218–21
    Scotland, 209
    specialized, 208, 211–12
    U.S., 208–9, 211
  integrated, 207, 209–11
    characteristics, 217, 222–4
    classification and framing weak, 216–25
    cultural consequences, 222–4
    definition, 209
    infant schools, 229
    institutionalization, 225
    organizational consequences, 219–21
    teacher-based and teachers-based, 209
  types, 207, 211
Educational identity, change in, 212
Educational knowledge:
  classification, 202, 205, 208, 210, 213, 221–2, 226
    change in, 216
  differentiation, 225
  evaluation, 203, 217
  framing, 202, 205–6, 208–10, 213, 216, 218, 221–2, 226
  private property, 213
  transmission, 202, 205–7, 210, 213
Eells, K., 27
Egocentric sequences, 114–15

England, educational codes in, 208, 211–13, 215–16
English, innovation in teaching, 5
Europe, educational codes in, 208, 210–16
Expressive symbolism, 33, 37, 44, 47

Family:
    boundary maintenance, 184–7
    linguistic codes and, 12, 16–17
    person-oriented, 153–4, 160–1, 185, 187
    positional, 152–3, 160–1, 184–7
    public language in, 32–3
    social control in, 155–60
    socializing agency, 145, 150, 174–5
    working-class, 32
        positional, 161, 187
Family-role system, linguistic codes and, 136, 152–3
Family structure, communication variants, 16–17, 184–7
Firth, R., 122, 176
Floud, Jean, 9, 23
France, Baccalauréat, 207
Freud, S., 120
Fry, D., 7–8

General Certificate of Education, 207
Germany:
    Abitur, 207
    SDS, 216
Goldman-Eisler, Frieda, 7–8, 72, 85, 89, 91, 99
Grammatical analysis:
    public language, 44–5
    social class comparison, 95–117
Grimshaw, Alan, 18
Guilt, minimized by public language, 49–50, 73–4
Gumperz, John, 8

Halliday, Michael, 15, 17
Hasan, R., 12

Hawkins, Peter, 16, 178, 194
Hegel, G. W. F., 171
Henderson, Dorothy, 16, 183
Henriques, Sir Basil and Lionel, 3
Hesitation phenomena:
    research into, 8
    social class comparison, 82, 85, 87, 91–2, 113, 117, 146
Hess, R., 9
Himmelweit, H., 23
Hoggart, R., 36
Hoijer, H., 122
Humboldt, W. von, 121, 171
Hymes, Dell, 8, 119, 146, 173

Individualized failure, 38
Individuation, 27–8, 113
Innovation:
    educational, 4, 5; see also Educational code, change in
    science and, xi
Intelligence tests,
    public-school, 62–7, 82–4
    social class comparison, 62–7, 82–4
    working-class, 30–2, 62–7, 82–4

James, Charity, 216
Jargon, 145
Judaism, 3

Kant, I., 171
Kingsway Day College, 4
Knowledge (see also Educational knowledge):
    universalistic, 197

Language (see also Linguistic codes; Speech):
    behaviour related to, 53–4, 71–5
    formal,
        characteristics, 55–6
        contrasted with public language, 45–8, 56
        definition, 28
        middle-class use of, 37

Language *(continued)*
functions, 15–17
public, *see* Public language
schoolchildren's, 71–5
sex related to, 161
social class related to, 61–7,
82–92, 151, 175
social structure related to, 53–4
sociological factors in, 175
sociology and, 118–21
speech distinguished from, 123
Lawton, D., 8
Learning:
environment,
inadequate, 191–2
optimum, 152
mechanical, 35
parents' aid in, 192
programmed, 206
Linguistic code (*see also* Socio-
linguistic code):
access to, 79, 176
behaviour controlled by, 125
best indicator of, 114
concept of, 8, 12, 15–16, 145–6,
170, 198
criticism, 18–19
culture transmitted by, 121–2,
145, 163–4, 198
definition, 80–2, 125
elaborated:
characteristics, 176
context-independent, 197
definition, 76–7, 145–6
disadvantages, 186
effects, 81, 109–13, 132,
middle-class use of, 81,
112–13, 135, 151, 161, 187
object-oriented, 133, 151,
165–6, 185, 187 (monolithic
society) 150
organic solidarity by, 147
person-oriented, 133, 148, 151,
165–6, 185, 187 (pluralistic
society) 150
role system open, 148
schools based on, 136

social class limits access to,
176
sociological conditions for,
78–80, 147
syntactic prediction low,
128–30
two modes, 133, 166
universalistic meanings, 176,
178–9, 181–2, 197–8
family-role system and, 136,
148–50
independent of measured intelligence, 109, 115
orientation to, 135
restricted:
characteristics, 134–5, 176
child limited to, 134–5, 151
context-dependent, 181, 197–8
criticism, 19
definition, 76–8, 145
educability problem, 183–4
effects, 81, 109–13, 132,
146–8
groups using, 77
lexical prediction, 126–7, 130
linguistic deprivation and,
194
particularistic meanings, 176–
7, 181, 183, 197
positional family, 185–7
role switching limited by, 147
role system closed, 148
social control by, 156, 165
social solidarity by, 147
sociological conditions for,
77–80, 146–7
syntactic prediction, 127–8,
130
value, 136, 152, 186
working-class use, 81, 91,
135–6, 161, 187
role systems related to, 148–50,
152–5
social control and, 156–60
social factors affecting, 12,
15–16
social origins, 78–9, 144–8

Linguistic code *(continued)*
  social relations related to, 123–9,
  131–2, 135–6, 146
  sociological conditions for,
  77–80, 129–30, 146–7
  speech patterns and, 12–15
  switching, 129, 135–6, 161–6, 186
    causes, 150–1, 162–3, 186–7
  types, 9, 76–7
    contrasted, 132, 147–8, 150–1
    verbal planning related to, 80–2,
    89–92, 124, 127–8, 131–2
Linguistic deprivation, 190, 192,
194, 197, 199
Linguistic rule system, cultural
system and, 173
Linguistics, psychology and, 122
London School of Economics, 3–4,
6
London University:
  Chelsea College of Technology,
  216
  Goldsmiths College, 216
  Institute of Education, 10–11
  University College, 7
Luria, A. R., 6, 8, 123, 176
Lynd, R., 200

MacRae, D. G., 3, 6, 8; on Basil
Bernstein, xii–xiv
Malinowski, B., 122, 176
Marx, Karl, 171–2, 202–3
Mathematics, new primary, 218
Mead, George, 119, 121–2, 172,
202
Meaning:
  particularistic, 129–30, 175–7,
  195
  universalistic, 129–30, 175–6,
  178–9, 182, 195–7, 199
Metaphor, 176–7
Middle class:
  definition, 24–5
  linguistic codes used by:
    both, 163
    elaborated, 81, 112–13, 135,
    161

speech:
  grammatical analysis, 95–117
  mode, 61
  tests, 84–92, 178–81, 194
Middle-class child:
  factors affecting speech, 25–6,
  178–81
  formal language used by, 37
  individuation, 27–8
  intelligence tests, 62–7, 82–4
  sensitivity to structure, 29
Monolithic societies, 150, 163
Murray, W., 27

Newsom Report, 191
Nuffield science, 216
Number, working-class difficulties with, 35
Nursery schools,
  needed, 193
  social class and, 38

Parents, aiding child's learning,
192
Parsons, Talcott, 2
Pedagogy *(see also* Education;
School; Teachers):
  change in, 217–24
  definition, 203
  frame concept, 205–6, 214
Peer group as socializing agency,
145, 150, 186
Plowden Report, 191
Pluralistic societies, 150, 163
Poetry, 5–6
Prepositions, use by social class,
103, 111
Programmed learning, 206
Pronouns, use:
  impersonal, 44–5
  personal, 98–9, 104–11, 115–16
Psychology, linguistics and, 122
Psycho-therapy, public language
problem in, 51–3

Public language:
  antisocial behaviour and, 51, 74
  change in, 54
  characteristics, 38–9, 42–50
  definition, 28
  educational effects, 34, 58
  family use, 32–3
  guilt minimized by, 49–51, 73–4
  immediacy, 48; see also Time-span of anticipation
  implications, 50–1
  persons limited to, 32–4, 43–4
  psychiatry and, 51–3
  resistance to formal education, 34
  schoolchildren's use of, 73
  social solidarity maximized by, 46–8, 50, 73
  social structure and, 43
  tender feelings and, 48, 50, 52–3
  working-class use of, 37
Public school:
  intelligence tests, 62–7, 82–4
  speech tests, 84–92

Rackstraw, Susan, 16
Religion, social class and, 3
Replication, xii
Robinson, Peter, 16
Role systems, related to linguistic codes, 148–50, 152–5
Rosenthal, R. and Jacobson, L., 190
ROSPA House, 4–5
Rule systems, 173

Sapir, E., 6, 26, 53, 121–2, 171, 176
S.C., see Sympathetic circularity
Schatzman, L., 6
School (see also Curriculum; Education; Pedagogy):
  comprehensive, 216
  contexts, 199
  discipline, 214
  distant goals, 29, 36
  heads, 215
  inadequate, 191–3
  infant, 193
    integrated educational code at, 229
    use of speech, 10
  junior, 193
  language in, 34–5, 54
    punishment and, 58
  linguistic codes at, 12, 143
    elaborated, 81–2, 136, 186
    restricted, 81, 183–4
  mechanical learning, 35
  middle-class child at, 36–7
  middle-class contexts, 199
  organization, 215–16, 218–21
  public language problem in, 34–5
  social basis of teaching in, 19
  socializing agency, 145, 150, 186, 223–4
  staff-pupil relations, 219–21, 223
  universalistic meanings in, 196–7, 199
  working-class child at, 27, 34–8, 136, 143–4, 191, 196
Schoolchildren's lore and language, 71–5
Schools Council, 191
Science, innovation in, xi
Scotland, educational codes, 209
Serendipity, xii
Sex, language related to, 161
Shame, minimized by public language, 49, 73–4
Snow, C. P., 133
Social change, linguistic code change related to, 160–3
Social class (see also Middle class; Working class):
  access to elaborated code limited by, 176
  behaviour influenced by, 23, 32
  education related to, 23–39
  grammatical analysis by, 95–117
  intelligence tests by, 62–7, 82–92

Social class *(continued)*
  knowledge distribution and, 175
  language related to, 61–7, 175
  linguistic codes and, 81, 126–9, 135–6, 145, 176
  religion and, 3
  resistance to education and, 24
  sensitivity to content and structure and, 24–5, 29, 33, 37
  speech and, 11–13, 76–8; *see also* Public language
  speech tests by, 84–92
  time-span of anticipation related to, 25, 29–30, 32–3, 36
  transmitted by communication, 143
Social control:
  change in, 164–5
  education related to, 202, 208
  family, 155–6, 185
  modes, 156–60
Social deprivation, 190
Social identity:
  change in, 144, 164–5
  role of speech in, 119, 121
Social inequality legitimized, 38
Social roles, critical, 145; *see also* Role systems
Social Science Research Council, 191
Social solidarity:
  maximized by public language, 46–8, 50, 73
  restricted code reinforcement, 78, 81, 147
Social structure:
  language related to, 53–4, 118–21, 124–5
  linguistic codes and, 12, 15–16, 122–5, 131–2, 144–8
  speech related to, 174
  symbolic systems linked with, 172
  theory, xii–xiv
Socialization, 119–21
  by linguistic code, 144, 196–7
  contexts, 181–2, 198

definition, 174
educational, 211–12, 214–15, 219, 221, 223, 225–6
family role systems and, 154
Socializing agencies, 145, 150, 174, 223
  boundary maintenance, 186–7
  personalization, 163
  positional, 163
Sociocentric sequences, 114, 116
Socio-linguistic codes, 12, 170–1
Sociological creation, xii
Sociology,
  educational, 202, 211–12
  language and, 118–21
Solidarity,
  mechanical, 224–5
  organic, 147, 225
  social:
    public language and, 46–8, 50, 73
    restricted code reinforcement of, 78, 81, 147
Speech *(see also* Hesitation phenomena; Language; Public language; Verbal planning):
  codes, 173–4; *see also* Linguistic code
  context-dependent, 13–14, 176–7, 179, 194–5, 197–8
  context-independent, 14, 176, 178–9, 194–5, 197
  creativity made possible by, 172–3
  exophoric, 13–14
  Freudian theory of, 120
  grammatical analysis by social class, 95–117
  individuated, 113
  infant schoolchildren's use, 10
  language distinguished from, 123
  linguistic codes and, 12–15, 109–13, 144–6
  social class and, 11–13, 76–8, 84–92, 95–117, 178–81, 194–6
  social control by, 185

Speech *(continued)*
  social identity role, 119, 121
  social structure related to, 174
  tests, by social class, 84–92, 178–81
  variants, 176–8, 197–9
Strauss, A., 6
Subordination, grammatical, 99–100, 109, 114–15
Sweden, Studente Exam, 207
Symbolic systems, 172
  changing, 225
Symbolism, expressive, *see* Expressive symbolism
Sympathetic circularity (S.C.), 97–100, 104, 106, 111–14

Teachers *(see also* Pedagogy):
  discretion, 217
  integrated educational code and, 209, 211, 217–24
  socialization, 223
  unstable, 191
Teaching:
  homogeneous, 217
  social basis, 19
Tender feelings, speech and, 48, 50, 52–3, 74
Time-span of anticipation, by social class, 25, 29–30, 32–3, 36
Turner, Geoffrey, 16–17, 179, 183

United States of America:
  Civil Rights Movement, 162
  deprived children in, 190
  educational codes in, 208–9
  linguistic code change in, 162
  socializing agencies in, 163
University *(see also* Birmingham; London):
  degrees, 207–8
  personal freedom at, 222
University College, London, 7

Verbal planning:
  linguistic codes related to, 80–2, 89–92, 124, 127–8, 131–2, 146

social class comparison, 82, 88–92
Verbs, use by social class, 100–1, 115
Vernon, P. E., 23
Vocabulary, working-class attainments related to, 32
Vygotsky, L. S., 6, 123, 176

Wales, educational research in, 191
Weber, M., 119–20
Westminster College of Education, 4
Whorf, B. L., 6, 121–3, 171
Williams, Frederick, 18
Work, as socializing agency, 145, 150
Working class:
  changes in, 161–2
  definition, 25
  family structure, 32
    positional, 161
  intelligence tests, 30–2, 82–4
  linguistic codes and, 143–4
    restricted, 81, 91, 135–6, 163
  speech:
    grammatical analysis, 95–117
    mode, 61–2
    tests, 84–92, 194
Working-class child:
  attainments:
    potential and actual, 23, 31, 37
    related to vocabulary, 32
  backwardness related to language, 151
  curiosity level low, 36
  educational orientation, 165
  educational results, factors in, 23–4, 33–8
  public language used by, 34, 37
  school problems, 34–8, 136, 191, 196
  sensitive to content, 33, 35
  speech, factors affecting, 26–7, 178–81

Class, Codes and Control, Volume 2, contains the following papers:

Bernstein, B. and Young, D.   Social class differences in conceptions of the uses of toys. *Sociology*, 1, 2, 1967.

Bernstein, B. and Henderson, D.   Social class differences in the relevance of language to socialization. *Sociology*, 3, 1, 1969.

Henderson, D.   Contextual specificity, discretion and cognitive socialization: with special reference to language. *Sociology*, 4, 3, 1971.

Hawkins, P. R.   Social class, the nominal group and reference. *Language and Speech*, 12, 2, 1969.

Turner, G. J. and Pickvance, R. E.   Social class differences in the expression of uncertainty in five-year-old children. *Language and Speech*, 14, 4, 1971.

Robinson, W. P. and Creed, C. D.   Perceptual and verbal discriminations of 'elaborated' and 'restricted' code users. *Language and Speech*, 11, 3, 1968.

Turner, G. J.   Social class and children's language of control at age five and age seven.

Robinson, W. P.   Where do children's answers come from?

Hawkins, P. R.   The influence of sex, social class and pause-location in the hesitation phenomena of seven-year-old children.

Hasan, R.   Code, register and social dialect.

Cook, J. A.   Language and socialization: a critical review.

Halliday, M. A. K.   The functional basis of language.